1978

TOLSTOY

TOLSTOY

THE INNER DRAMA

by

HUGH I'ANSON FAUSSET

NEW YORK

Russell & Russell

FIRST PUBLISHED IN 1927
REISSUED, 1968, BY RUSSELL & RUSSELL
A DIVISION OF ATHENEUM HOUSE, INC.
BY ARRANGEMENT WITH THE ESTATE OF HUGH I'ANSON FAUSSET
L. C. CATALOG CARD NO: 68-11327
PRINTED IN THE UNITED STATES OF AMERICA

CONTENTS

PORTRAITS

These portraits are reproduced by kind permission of Mr. Aymer Maude from his *Life of Tolstoy*.

FOREWORD

THIS is not, in the narrow sense, a literary study. For although Tolstoy was a great artist and a great critic of art, he is equally significant to us to-day as the baffled searcher after an art of life. It is as such that I have studied him here, exploring his personality in relation to his art and his life, and examining his doctrine in the light of his personality.

Such an aim has necessitated what may seem to be a somewhat arbitrary use of the material whether literary or biographical at my disposal.

In my treatment, for example, of *War and Peace* and *Anna Karenina* I have concentrated exclusively on those elements that express and clarify the inner drama which I have tried to trace to the neglect of any specific literary criticism of these great novels. Similarly in Parts IV and V I have devoted myself primarily to Tolstoy's interpretation of Christianity and his criticism of art, to the neglect of much of his creative writing, notably his Plays and his Tales and Parables of Simple Life. The unity of conception and execution at which I have aimed has inevitably dictated such exclusions, since the material at a critic's disposal is in Tolstoy's case so considerable and in some ways so identical in its import.

Admirers of Tolstoy may complain too that by the severity of my criticism I have played into the hands of those who dismiss his teaching, after citing a few of its extravagances, as valueless, because it conflicts with their self-interest.

But blind enthusiasm is of as little service to a great

man as destructive prejudice, and it is because Tolstoy has been as ill-served by uncritical devotees as by those who have condemned him, with worldly superiority, as a savage or a fanatic, that I have tried here, a hundred years after his birth, to disentangle what was true in his vision of life from what was dictated by the violence of self-disgust.

Certainly the negative side of his nature was conditioned by an intense positive zest for physical experience, as his moral violence was interwoven with moral fineness, his egotism with a profound humility and a love of simple men and things. But apart from his greatness as a creative artist, he served humanity more notably as an indicter of a false civilization than as the prophet of a true one, as the champion of a moral conception of human life than as the discoverer of a really creative morality.

And yet in his very failure to achieve a new moral relation to life he revealed, more tragically perhaps than any other great writer, not only how necessary to personal and social happiness such a relation is, when once man has outgrown the primitive, but also the forces which must be harmonized, if it is to be achieved.

In this book I have tried to reconstruct his moral problem upon a psychological basis, believing that a moral view of art and life has not ceased to be relevant, as an extreme scientific school of criticism would seem to suggest, but that Tolstoy erred in his moral judgment only in so far as he was unable to realize that identity of moral and æsthetic values in which art and life may ultimately become one.

H. I'A. F.

'Poor soul, here for so little, cast among so many hardships, filled with desires so incommensurate and so inconsistent, savagely surrounded, savagely descended, irremediably condemned to prey upon his fellow lives: who should have blamed him had he been of a piece with his destiny and a being merely barbarous? And we look and behold him instead filled with imperfect virtues . . . sitting down, amidst his momentary life, to debate of Right and Wrong and the attributes of the Deity.'

R. L. S.

To

C. H. W.

TOLSTOY

PROLOGUE

Tolstoy wrote so much and lived so distractedly that he excites more intensely perhaps than any other modern writer conflicting emotions. Admiration for his superb artistic powers and his relentless pursuit of self-perfection predominates. Seldom indeed has there been an artist so naturally endowed or so morally obsessed, and one consequently who projected into his characters so much of moral questioning or elaborated a personal creed with such relentless sincerity. His writings are 'one vast diary of fifty years, one endless and minute "confession."' They justify therefore in a greater degree possibly than any others that personal interpretation which is the aim and method of this book.

And yet he is not among those writers who are most intimately loved. No one perhaps has expressed love as a passion, lyrical or malign, more vividly: no one has preached it as an ideal more urgently. But he preaches love with too fearful an intensity to inspire it. Homeless, he seeks for human fellowship and cannot find it. With Nature and animals he is at home; with men and women, as spiritual and intelligent beings, he is remote and ill at ease. He moves through his life in a self-tormented isolation.

He is alone as a force of Nature and in his hatred of Nature; alone as he aspires to the far sky that taunts him with its peace, alone in the careless world that would not heed his doctrine, and even at last in his own family circle, where he sits, as Gorki described him in old age, 'in a corner tired and grey, as though the dust of another earth were on him, and he looks attentively at everything with the look of a foreigner or of a dumb man.'

Often the look is bitter and inquisitorial as that of a captive peering through bars, and out of that terrible inner solitude his voice issues, the voice of Nature and of a soul struggling to transcend Nature. From year to year the struggle grows more intense, the possibility of easy relationship more difficult. He enthralls and overpowers, demoralizes and disintegrates, spinning about us the web of his life-long moral dilemma. We feel with him the beauty and the cruelty of the world, and we feel it physically, since his words have the quality of sensations. And with him through more than sixty years of dynamic experience we seek a salvation beyond recurrent ecstasy and despair.

He tells us that he has found it in a renunciation of desire and responsibility. Yet no assured serenity succeeds. His face is still harrowed and distraught; preaching humility he betrays his pride; he hates the senses as fanatically as he loved and loves them; he is an egotist in the excesses of his altruism. Always we feel the clutch of his tenacious hands that are pitiful as the peasant's and pitiless as the autocrat's. His keen small eyes pierce us with their defiant appeal; they demand uncompromised acceptance. But the very intensity of his demands impedes our response. His suffering disproves his claims, his solution is too simple and self-interested.

Yet only when we have realized the forces with which he struggled so continuously and frenziedly, have weighed the burden of intense pleasure and pain which he was fated to carry, can we do justice to the truth which he wrung amid error from his own ordeal and the falseness which he exposed so scathingly because he knew how seductive it was.

In the study of these forces and Tolstoy's response to them something more than the history of a great but tormented individual is involved. Tolstoy's final rejection of the modern Western idea of civilization was dictated by his inner needs and must be judged in relation to these needs. That he did not discover happiness in this rejection, despite all his protestations, is indeed itself a strong argument against its validity. But the problem of his individual consciousness is so intimately related to the conditions governing the growth of human consciousness and involves as a primary consideration the use of such general terms as 'civilization' and 'Nature,' 'the conscious' and 'the instinctive,' that it will be well at once to define briefly the conception of human consciousness, in which the present study is grounded, and of which Tolstoy's experience is so convulsive an expression.

We may observe in the growth of individuals and to a less degree in that of peoples three stages of Consciousness; the first primitive or animal, in which the self is still undifferentiated; the second self-conscious, in which the critical intelligence has separated itself from instinct; the third ideally human, in which intelligence is again reconciled with instinct as in the first stage but without a sacrifice of the individual consciousness achieved at the cost of dislocation in the second.

The first stage has been rather arbitrarily described as

the 'Natural,' and for convenience the meaning of purely instinctive life will be attached in the following pages to such phrases as 'natural life' or a 'state of Nature.' In such life a perfect identity exists between the individual and physical Nature, the part and the whole. Knowledge, so far as it exists, is still implicit in being, the subject and the object are one. Experience may be profound and elemental, but whether as animal insight or animal lust, it is momentary and without afterthought.

With the emergence of self-consciousness this unity is disturbed. The subject, in becoming more aware of itself, separates itself from the object which it contemplates. What religion has described as a 'fall,' and associated with a sense of sin or division, occurs. And inevitably the gulf tends to widen both between the instinctive and rational faculties of the individual and between the individual and everything external to himself.

He now exploits, now criticizes the impulses and appetites which before he implicitly obeyed as expressions of natural law, and he comes to regard all objects as means of self-gratification. Thus the more he increases his conscious individuality, the more does he become alienated from or even antagonistic to life outside himself, which he perceives only externally. The instincts and emotions that previously bound him intimately to life are either paralysed or enslaved by the self-regarding intellect. This disintegrating process may be gradual, and in many individuals may amount to no more than a warping of generous sentiments, a desire to acquire or enslave, or a contentious and narrow egotism. Any organism however so divided is diseased, and unless it can reintegrate its elements, is doomed to increasing discomfort, pain and deterioration. Self-consciousness, when it ceases to be a stimulus, becomes a prison-cell. The egotist glutting himself upon life derives no real nourishment. He becomes aware at last of his morbid isolation. Self-love is succeeded by self-hate and the jaded or feverish intellect is tormented by the instincts which it has exploited and strives to recover the balance and wholeness of being which it has selfishly destroyed.

This condition of aggravated individuality is typical of modern Western Civilization. The antagonism between the intellect and instincts of the individual corresponds to that between the predatory and exploited elements of society, and if it has reached an extreme point, so violent a conflict ensues that the disease proves fatal.

But the individual may realize the peril of his disharmony soon enough to recover, with a difference, the unity of being which he has lost. It is difficult to demonstrate how this reconciliation is effected. The great artists and the great mystics have revealed it, and the process by which they have done so may perhaps be suggested by the analogy of society.

A society which has become divided into exploiters and exploited through the acquisitiveness of a small minority of individuals who have accumulated wealth and power in their hands, can only regain its harmony when these individuals either voluntarily or by compulsion put their power and intelligence to the service of the whole community. In so doing they need not sacrifice their individuality; skilled organizers, for example, need not become manual workers; but they will direct it more and more disinterestedly. They will recognize a real identity of interest and well-being as existing between themselves and every other member of the society to which they belong and this recognition may and must finally extend to the whole of humanity, making it impossible for any man to exploit or enslave another out of self-interest, since to injure another will be known and felt to be to injure oneself.

A similar recognition characterizes the third stage of Consciousness. Here again the self-consciousness, gained at such cost in the second stage, is not sacrificed. The knower does not cast away his knowledge, mean and insignificant though it be as a mere acquisition and analysis of fact, or the subject deny himself. Rather he extends himself until nothing is alien to him. The sympathetic faculties of instinct and emotion are no longer at war with intelligence. They fuse together, and in fusing constitute a new intuitive faculty, a faculty by which the object is at once felt and known, felt in its ideal essence, known in its formal manifestation. Reality cannot be perfectly apprehended save by this combination of active, critical thought and passive, sympathetic feeling, by virtue of which a man absorbs the world intelligently and recreates it imaginatively. The individual therefore does not submerge his identity, as in the primitive stage of Consciousness, in a life of undifferentiated and unvalued sensation. Instead he realizes it completely by harmonizing his instinctive and rational faculties and in so doing achieves a perfect relation of intimate understanding with every object outside himself.

In this intelligent but disinterested affirmation of self lies the only hope of salvation from the malady of exasperated egotism. And it needs most carefully distinguishing alike from despairing attempts to relapse into primitive life and from violent or sentimental renunciations of individuality. The man who has passed into the third stage of Consciousness has become again as a little child but with all the conscious wisdom too of maturity. He has recovered his identity with the fertilizing life-force and his sense of innocence, but he has recovered them by extending and deepening the sources of his knowledge. His innocence is immensely enriched and certified by this knowledge, and no fears, no false illusions, such as may haunt the child or the primitive, who are still at the mercy of the subconscious, can threaten his freedom. He has, in Keats' words, learnt how to school an Intelligence and make it a Soul, and he not only instinctively reflects the life-purpose or the race-consciousness, as the child does, but he knows the meaning of life and can define its reality through all the varied forms and degrees of its expression.

To emphasize this distinction is an essential preliminary to a study of Tolstoy, since the drama of his personality, his art, and his teaching, turns upon it.

Tolstoy's rejection of Civilization was primarily a rejection of the Conscious Mind, of the faculty which has increasingly dominated Western Civilization since the Renaissance. He knew it in his own person and in the

Russia of his time as a principle of discord and disease, of separation and torture. And he thought by denying it to recover the harmony for which he longed.

But the Conscious Mind cannot be denied. Its conflict with the subconscious is indeed an essential stage in the individual's advance to pure Consciousness, to his liberation from the dark lusts of the brute body and the dark fears and fetiches of the Ancestral Mind. Tolstoy himself admitted this when he wrote as a young man in his Diary — 'If I meditate as I contemplate nature, I perceive everything in nature to be in constant process of development, and each of nature's constituent portions to be unconsciously contributing towards the development of others. But man is, though a like portion of nature, a portion gifted with consciousness, and therefore bound, like the other portions, to make conscious use of his spiritual faculties in striving for the development of everything existent.'

The growth of self-consciousness may have cleft human nature in two, but the resultant sense of sin has proved as great a dynamic to moral growth as that of rational responsibility to material progress. To sanctify the instinctive is as great an error as to sanctify the rational. The savage may be more natural, may be more virtuous than the pseudo-civilized man, but he is further removed from the possibilities of a completely realized humanity.

The Mind, if later in development than the instincts and capable of morbid activity, is equally rooted in nature, and is indeed the faculty through which Nature would seem to seek her purest expression. In a perfect humanity the Mind is not at war with the Body, marring its grace and dimming its physical brightness. It is rather the lens which gives perfect definition to the passionate impulses of the Body, and the channel through which they may be purified and their range extended. Through it the flame of physical life is transformed into the radiance of spiritual insight; the body is beautiful in the eyes of the mind and the mind derives its wisdom from the counsel of the body.

Only thus can the self-conscious individual recover the organic consciousness which he has lost, and transform the passions which he has inherited from his animal past and distorted by conscious misuse into purer modes of expression.

But Tolstoy felt with too much anguish the abuse and exploitation of the senses by the individual and of the manual worker by society, to see in modern Civilization any issue but death. And from this death he sought escape now in physical life and now in its violent denial.

It is the purpose of this book to show how inevitably he was driven to this imperfect solution of the problem by the forces, both primitive and moral, of his nature, and to trace the steps which led him to a false and final renunciation. To do so involves the whole question of modern civilization, its relation to Christianity, and whether it can or should be preserved. And our answer to this question too must in the last resort depend upon our conception of the growth and value of human consciousness.

Tolstoy has been dismissed by some as a savage and reverenced by others as a saint. In fact he was neither, but he strove in turn for the integrity of both. The savage preserves his integrity instinctively, the saint fulfils his spiritually; the one is below good and evil, the other is above it. The one co-operates with Nature as a creature, the other as a creator. But between these two are a multitude of men, in whom a creature submission and creative aspirations are at war, men who neither reflect a unity of physical forces nor have reconciled these forces with really human values. They are divided within themselves and alone in the Universe. The Creature in them loves Nature, the Creator in them intensifies this love and turns it into hate. They are at once voluptuaries and ascetics, but self-contempt no less than self-indulgence alienates them from life, preventing that positive fusion of all the faculties by which the natural is made human and the human natural.

Such a man was Tolstoy. Champion of so many humane causes, he was never completely human himself. For the perfect humanity to which the individual and civilization must aspire is a condition of positive harmony free from repressions and negations. Moral violence is but inverted physical servitude and Tolstoy's life and writings are charged with both. He was a great artist endowed alike with extraordinary physical insight and elemental power, because he could live the life of the senses without reserve. He was a distorted moralist, because he hated such a life in retrospect. He hated it because he loved it, would have perpetuated it eternally, and yet found in it no permanence or peace.

How to live the life of Nature without its transience and want of purpose, was what he sought. For a time he sought it in a vague mysticism, by losing himself in 'the distant sky, not clear, yet immeasurably lofty,' compared to which everything seemed insignificant. But an infinite sensation is as transient as a finite. His instincts were too strong and earthy to allow him to escape by way of a vague transcendentalism. He was also too honest. For if a perpetual need of self-confession (itself a symptom of self-confinement) was typical of Tolstoy, so also was a hatred of self-deception.

In *Childhood* he describes how he suffered for the insincerity of two lines in some verses he wrote to present to his grandmother on her name day, and later in *Boyhood* he tells how the fact that he had suppressed at Confession what seemed to him a particularly shameful sin compelled him to drive early the next morning to the priest to ease his conscience.

The quality illustrated in these two early incidents persisted, and it was because of his inherent honesty that he was so painfully haunted in his later years by a sense of discrepancy between his professions and his practice.

And that is why, despite his bias against modern civilization, he is nearer to our needs than Emersonian mystics or Victorian moralists. An evasive mysticism may provide gracious retreats for world-weary initiates, but like a conventional morality it fails to further, if it does not actually retard, the true march of man.

Tolstoy could not view modern science or the ideal of disinterested reason, of which it was the tentative expression, in a right perspective, because he could not, in his own experience, harmonize his conscious mind with his

other faculties. But at least he admitted the discord and
refused to accept or to preach any facile solution of it.
Late in his life he wrote in *Resurrection*:

'The animalism of the brute nature in man is disgusting . . . but as long as it remains in its naked form we
observe it from the height of our spiritual life and despise
it; and, whether one has fallen or resisted, one remains
what one was before. But when that same animalism hides
under a cloak of poetry and æsthetic feeling, and demands
our worship – then we are swallowed up by it completely,
and worship animalism, no longer distinguishing good
from evil. Then it is awful!'

The emancipated man does not look down on his brute
nature and despise it. He is not disgusted by a nude body,
for example, as Tolstoy was, because he is not sensually
enslaved by it. He can contemplate and appraise its
beauty as he does the tracery of a tree or the lines of a
landscape, all of which indeed he feels sensuously (for
the senses are the necessary channels to perfect intimacy)
but without that desire to possess, to exploit physically,
which is the characteristic of the sensualist.

Tolstoy could not experience thus disinterestedly, and
in the art and life and religion of his class and country he
found proof enough of that possessive animalism, that
inhuman, yet calculated pursuit of self-gratification which
is typical of pseudo-civilization.

But although he erred in trying to divorce the spiritual
from the physical, he thereby did a better service to mankind than by sentimentalizing animalism and calling it
love, and sentimentalizing naturalism and calling it mysti-

cism. Far better is it to face the antagonisms, typical of the second stage of human consciousness, between brute instinct and conscience, reason and faith, than to pretend to reconcile them emotionally.

Tolstoy faced them ruthlessly. All his life he refused to conclude a sentimental peace between the two forces of his nature. His life was a battle to the end, and so far as his conscience triumphed, it triumphed by attack and could only preserve its precarious victory by renewed attack. Perfect illumination is not to be achieved in the stress of such battle. It is impossible to be impartial in a fight for life. But at least the two forces are thrown into stern relief, and since they are also the two forces which strive for the mastery of modern civilization, and upon the true reconciliation of which depends its very survival, it is essential to estimate their nature. In Tolstoy their nature and interaction are violently revealed, and it is therefore in relation to this violent temperamental conflict that we think his life, his art, and his ideas may be most fruitfully examined.

¶ PART ONE

THE ELEMENTS OF CONFLICT

THE ELEMENTS OF CONFLICT

§ I

THE popular conception of Tolstoy's life as abruptly divided in middle-age into two halves is misleading. There was, in fact, no period in his life when either the artist or the natural man can be said to have been definitely superseded by the moralist. In a sense indeed *A Confession* is as inevitable a work of art as *War and Peace*. And there is equally no period after early childhood when the moralist in him was not astir. All the fluctuations and convulsions of his early life were but premonitions of the crisis which occurred at the age of fifty. They were the preliminary skirmishes which led inevitably to the fierce engagement.

Certainly among all these skirmishes two stand out as particularly defining the position of the antagonists and conditioning the later battle. Both inflicted shocks more profound than the occasions of sentimental disillusionment which had preceded them. Both struck down to the roots of that Nature in the joyous energy of which Tolstoy had sought forgetfulness of moral values.

The first of these shocks, as will be shown, occurred at Sebastopol, when he was twenty-seven; the second, five years later, at the death-bed of his brother Nicholas. Marriage might delay for some sixteen years the stark grappling with the problem which war as a horrible, and death as a meaningless, physical event had set him, but the animal delight which he never ceased to take in Nature and the expression of Nature in art seemed to him from

1860 a lie, an alluring lie, which he continued spasmodically to live and to tell, but with a deepening sense of shame and wretchedness, and a deepening conviction that there must be some truth which would raise the life he loved above the death he hated, and that in seeking for that truth lay his only hope of salvation.

Subconsciously, however, this was always his conviction. The first and strongest impression of his life, he confessed, was that of lying bound and wishing to stretch out his arms as an infant. 'I scream and cry, and my screams are disagreeable to myself, but I cannot stop. Some one – I do not remember who – bends over me. . . . To them it seems necessary that I should be bound, but I know it is unnecessary and I wish to prove this to them, and I again burst into cries which are unpleasant to myself but are yet unrestrainable.'

This may seem rather to be an example of that symbolism of which the man was so great a master than an authentic record of a child's experience. How kindred it is, for example, to the desolate cry in *A Confession* – 'I, a fallen fledgling, am lying on my back and crying in the high grass. I cry because I know that my mother bore me within her, covered me, warmed, fed, loved me. Where is she, that Mother?'

Yet we know from his own record how early in his life he began to feel this sense of desertion by Mother Nature, this resentment of the wild creature against the fetters imposed by domesticated humans upon the primal instincts. Even the small child was conscious of the shadow of the prison-house closing upon him, and when he was moved downstairs at the age of five from his nursery to the elder boys experienced a sense of irreparably losing his innocence and happiness, and 'for the first time and therefore more strongly than ever since . . . the consciousness of the cross every man is called upon to bear.'

And although this feeling might be dimmed in adolescence, it never left him, and in middle and later life it gained an enhanced poignancy as he saw the gulf inevitably widening between himself and ecstatic natural life and was harrowed by the terrible paradox that only in death, which he dreaded, could he mix again with the earth that he loved.

In many passages of his later writings he has expressed the joy and torture with which he recollected the pure physical delight of living which once was his. In *Resurrection*, for example, he described how above all there came back to Nekhlyudov's mind 'the joyous sense of health, strength, and freedom from care: the lungs breathing in the frosty air so deeply that the fur coat is drawn tightly on his chest; the fine snow dropping from the low branches on to his face; his body warm, his face fresh, and his soul free from care, self-reproach, fear or desire. . . . How beautiful it was. And now, O God! what torment, what trouble!'

But in this, above all, the child was father to the man, and in particular to the old man. The pathos and perplexity of his later married life – that perplexity which drove him out at last into the night, a fugitive, to meet his death at the railway-station of Astapovo – was conditioned by the same morbid longing to recover an innocence which every human relationship seemed to contaminate and a liberty which every human attachment restricted. What began as a sense of divorce from Nature became later a sense of sin, of 'this burden of death;' but behind the twisted Christian ethic which the self-conscious sinner of later days preached and tried to practise lay always the remembrance of those moments in early childhood, when Mother Nature and her offspring were one, moments of rapture of which the first ecstasy of love was to be a later manifestation, and which brought a sudden sense of ease in his soul, a passing forgetfulness of the sick moral nerve which made him suffer.

'Do in after life,' he wrote in *Childhood*, 'the freshness and light-heartedness, the craving for love and for strength of faith, ever return which we experience in our childhood's years? What better time is there in our lives than when the two best virtues – innocent gaiety and a boundless yearning for affection – are our sole objects of pursuit? Where now are our ardent prayers? Where now are our best gifts – the pure tears of emotion which a guardian angel dries with a smile as he sheds upon us lovely dreams of ineffable childish joy? Can it be that life has left such heavy traces upon one's heart that those tears and ecstasies are for ever vanished? Can it be that there remains to us only the recollection of them?'

The passage is typical of a young man who at the age of fifteen wore a medallion of Rousseau next his body instead of the orthodox cross and who still longed sentimentally to recover a state of Nature long after it had proved, when put to the test, something other than the 'immediate expression of beauty and goodness . . . of boundless, disinterested love,' which he liked to think it. Until the actual crisis occurred in middle-age he made attempt after attempt to re-establish his integrity by simple self-abandonment, and even after he realized that for the self-conscious egotist there was no such facile way of escape and that a purely physical life had no issue but death, he continued to exaggerate its virtues and to claim for it a moral significance which it did not possess.

That as a child, however, he should already carry the burden of divided consciousness, which has haunted the maturity of so many of the most sensitive spirits of the modern world, explains perhaps why he never succeeded in unifying his consciousness. The cleft in his nature was too deep and inherent to be closed.

A sense of isolation preyed constantly upon the boy. It made him shy, and dissatisfied and morbidly aghast at what he considered his ugliness. 'I thought,' he wrote, 'that no human being with such a large nose, such thick lips, and such small grey eyes as mine could ever hope to attain happiness on this earth.' And already he sought compensation for physical shame in moral and intellectual pride. Despairing of his outward being, he set all his hopes upon his inward being, examining it for signs of distinction, applauding its nobler impulses and chastising its grosser.

But his primary need was to forget himself. And he forgot himself in the intoxication of listening to music, in admiring a peasant's 'strongly-marked, bearded face, and the veins and muscles as they stood out upon his great powerful hands whenever he made an extra effort,' in the tense excitement of a hunt, in the elementalism of a thunderstorm and the cool earthy exhalation that followed it.

'From above us, from every side, came the happy songs of little birds calling to one another among the dripping brushwood, while clear from the inmost depths of the wood sounded the voice of the cuckoo. So delicious was the wondrous scent of the wood – the scent which follows a thunderstorm in spring, the scent of birch-trees, violets, mushrooms, and thyme – that I could no longer remain in the *britchka*. Jumping out, I ran to some bushes, and, regardless of the showers of drops discharged upon me, tore off a few sprigs of thyme, and buried my face in them to smell their glorious scent.'

Or again he forgot himself, dancing with a little girl, Sonetchka, with whom he fell extravagantly in love. 'I could not imagine that the feeling of love which was filling my soul so pleasantly could require any happiness still greater, or wish for more than that this happiness should never cease. I felt perfectly contented. My heart beat like that of a dove, with the blood constantly flowing back to it, and I almost wept for joy.'

To lose himself in music and Nature and love, to float in a stream of sensation, was in boyhood as intense a source of delight as in manhood it was of increasing terror. But even in boyhood self-surrender was succeeded by self-reproach. In reaction from these moments of physical ecstasy he became more conscious of himself and fretted at his limitations.

And yet there were those about him who possessed a secret which raised them above the ebb and flow of sensations, who drew upon an inner serenity in which every desire was centred and by which disgust was annulled. It was the secret which his brother Nicholas announced that he possessed and had written on a green stick and which, when disclosed, would ensure the happiness of all men. 'There would be no more disease, no trouble, no one would be angry with anybody, all would love one another, all would become Ant-Brothers. . . . The Ant-Brotherhood was revealed to us, but not the chief secret.'

Tolstoy was only five when this announcement was made, and since he spent his life searching for that secret, it was fitting that he should be buried at the spot where the green stick was supposed to lie. But there were people, he knew, who had no need to hunt for green sticks. His Aunt Tatiana, in particular, was in the secret. She was never troubled or self-satisfied, but 'peaceful, sweet, submissive and loving.' She communicated 'the spiritual delight of love,' and not by words, but by her whole being. 'I saw, I felt, how she enjoyed loving, and I understood the joy of love.' There were the half-crazy saints too, who travelled from house to house, innocents who apparently devoted their life to a vision, oblivious of poverty and contempt, and in whose faces he read 'something restful, thoughtful, and even grand.' They too had climbed above the backwash of egotism, possessed a faith so strong that they felt the actual presence of God and a love so great that it dictated the words which fell from their lips.

And lastly there was the old domestic who had been his

mother's nurse, one of those Russian peasants who had never had any worldly goods, education, or independence, but who in consequence had developed to an extreme degree the unworldliness to which Christ referred when he said 'Blessed are the poor,' – a being utterly devoid of pretence, whose life 'had been one of pure, disinterested love, of utter self-negation,' and who, therefore, when she came to die, 'accomplished the highest and best achievement in the world: she died without fear and without repining.'

To the boy who had lost his father at the age of eight and experienced an unforgettable horror when he was admitted shortly afterwards to kiss his grandmother's swollen white hand as she lay dying of dropsy, the problem of life was already dimly involved with that of death. Seventy years later Tolstoy was to describe in *Resurrection* how Nekhlyudov hated himself for desiring his mother's death, so that he might be relieved of the physical repulsion that her long, discoloured fingers aroused in him, a repulsion which a youthful portrait of her in a low-necked, black-velvet dress intensified.

The boy of course could not realize how fundamental in his experience the awful identity of physical life and death was to prove, but already he felt that there could be no greater proof of the value of the secret which his aunt and the 'holy fools' and this old domestic cherished than that it should deliver them at the same time from the flux of life and the terror of death.

Clearly too the secret consisted in self-forgetfulness through submission to some higher power. But what the nature of this power was or to what extent those who accepted its ruling did so blindly and because their natures demanded nothing more, or in the assurance of a real spiritual perception, were questions which he was still too young to ask, but which had first to be answered before their secret could be effectively applied to himself. It was indeed because he never did succeed in answering these questions clearly, although commanding conformity with the self-negation of the poor and the simple, that he never wholly comprehended the secret by relating it justly to his own needs.

§ 2

Meanwhile in the conviction that the destiny of man was 'a process of incessant self-perfection,' he began to devote himself to self-analysis and self-chastisement. In this as in all else he went from extreme to extreme, now holding heavy dictionaries in outstretched hand for five minutes or flogging his back, now lapsing at the thought of death into luxurious indolence, lying in bed for two or three days novel-reading and eating gingerbread and honey. For a time he cherished a furtive passion for the 'extraordinarily handsome, magnificently developed' maid-servant Masha and an intense hatred towards his tutor. But his chief solace lay in solitary reflection and observation, and particularly in 'abstract thoughts on man's destiny, on a future life, and on the immortality of the soul,' subjects which at first seemed to offer wide vistas of escape from the uneasy privacies of the self.

Because, however, his mind could achieve no certainty

in these things but could only flounder from one con-
jecture to another, in turn dizzied by infinite speculations
and arrested by hateful recollections of the scientific
scepticism which he had imbibed at school, he soon became convinced that the intellect was the foe to moral
health. 'From all this weary mental struggle I derived
only a certain pliancy of mind, a weakening of the will, a
habit of perpetual moral analysis and a diminution both of
freshness of sentiment and of clearness of thought.'

Once again it was the instinctive revolt of the creature
against the disintegration of consciousness. And indeed
to develop thought as a self-sufficient faculty, 'to think of
what I am thinking concerning my own thoughts,' as
Tolstoy described the condition at its worst, must disturb
the harmony of the inner being and also its relation to the
outer world. Late in life he expressed the same view when
he wrote that 'the longer I live, the more convinced I am
that our excessive mental development is a hindrance to
us.' And a hindrance it is so far as it imprisons men in a
mental vacuum, divorced at once from a natural and an
imaginative life.

But to deny the intellect is as impossible to the man
in whom it has once asserted its rights as to deny the
instincts is to the savage. To attempt to do so, as Tolstoy
did all his life, is merely to confirm its despotism, until
finally it asserts its power over the very instincts which
seek to flout it, forcing them to a denial of themselves.
The self-analysis and abstract speculation against which
he revolted so early, he still contrived to practise. Nor
could he do otherwise. For such weary mental struggle is

a necessity to man's true development from the natural to the spiritual life, and for that very reason is resented by all the animal forces in his nature.

At the root of Tolstoy's life-long hatred of the intellect lay this animal resentment. His moral revolt against science for example, justified so far as science claimed to be more than a critical instrument which might eventually conduce to a higher order of consciousness and a more efficiently equipped humanity, was essentially an instinctive revolt. And by denying intellect instead of reconciling it with the instincts which it both rightly and wrongly opposed, he merely perpetuated the conflict which he condemned.

But through adolescence as later, and notably in the first years of his marriage, romantic speculation provided an agreeable escape from moral analysis. To him, as to Wordsworth, mighty was the charm

> Of those abstractions to a mind beset
> With images, and haunted by itself.

From the feverish pursuit of self-perfection he would seek and find relief in the realm of abstract thought, and the more unsubstantial the thought was, the more was he delivered from the crude opposition of his material self to the ideal of virtue for which he professed an ecstatic worship.

In dreams he found the same relief. 'Let no man blame me,' he wrote with prophetic insight in *Youth*, 'because the dreams of my youth were as foolish as those of my childhood and boyhood. I am sure that, even if it be my fate to live to extreme old age and to continue my story with the years, I, an old man of seventy, shall be found dreaming dreams just as impossible and childish as those I am dreaming now. . . . Four leading sentiments formed the basis of my dreams. The first of these sentiments was love for *her* – for an imaginary woman whom I always pictured the same in my dreams. . . . My second sentiment was a craving for love. I wanted every one to know me and to love me. . . . My third sentiment was the expectation of some extraordinary, glorious happiness that was impending – some happiness so strong and assured as to verge upon ecstasy. . . . Lastly, my fourth and principal sentiment of all was abhorrence of myself, mingled with regret – yet a regret so blended with the certain expectation of happiness to which I have referred that it had in it nothing of sorrow. It seemed to me that it would be so easy and natural for me to tear myself away from my past and to remake it – to forget all that had been, and to begin my life with all its relations, anew – that the past never troubled me, never clung to me at all. I even found a certain pleasure in detesting the past, and in seeing it in a darker light than the true one.'

Such were the sentiments in which the boy and the youth indulged in the intervals of writing down 'Rules of Life,' which he could not keep, in regard to himself, his neighbour and his God. To enjoy the expansive sentiment and yet satisfy the teasing conscience was the problem of adjustment which he was to spend his life in trying to solve. Always he was thus to dramatize his experience,

now shedding tears of tenderness to himself, like
Nekhlyudov in *Resurrection*, at his own conceptions of
infinite goodness and happiness, now tears of remorse
over the apparent contrast of his actual depravity. The
exaggerated conception dictated the exaggerated fact and
he was caught in the vicious circle of false romanticism
and false realism from which the sentimentalist can never
find an exit.

But the important thing to note at this point is that
all the constituents of the problem existed, in the forms
too which they were always to preserve, at a precocious
age. Even when full allowance is made for the maturer
interpretation which Tolstoy, writing at the age of twenty-
three, wove into his account of his childhood and youth,
proof enough of an astonishing precocity remains. And
it was surely this precocious experience of antagonism in
his nature which prevented that gradual growth in which
they might eventually have been resolved. 'The cause of
my sorrow,' he was to write in his Diary at the age of
twenty-three, 'must be that I applied myself too early to
the serious things of life – I applied myself to them before
I was yet ripe, but when able to feel and understand.'
Development of course there was to be, but it was less
organic growth than variations, ever more violent and
explicit as his hopes of self-release diminished, in the
expression of a divided personality which essentially
remained the same.

And not only the personality remained the same with
its hunger for a moral harmony which would preserve the
joy but deliver from the servitude of instinctive life, but

also the circle of desires and revulsions, within which the personality rotated in search of an issue.

The horror which filled the child at the spectacle of physical death was the same which terrified the man. The author of *The Death of Ivan Ilyich* was only more conscious of what the sensation implied and could visualize death as an abyss yawning between the natural and the spiritual life. But his reaction to it was still that of physical nausea. Similarly the boy who romanticized love when he danced with Sonetchka and felt it as a grosser force when he cast furtive glances at the chambermaid Masha was all his life to be allured and disgusted by the passion which women excited in him, and never to achieve a really humane conception of love because he had learnt as a youth to deny that women 'could think or feel like human beings.'

Certainly his dread of passion and contempt for women as exciting it were morbidly aggravated by the dissipations in which he was to indulge as a young man, encouraged by the depraved tone of the 'high' society in which he moved. But the 'horror, loathing and heartache' which haunted his old age when he thought of these years and drove him to a false asceticism, could not have so affected him had not these dissipations expressed a basic carnal enslavement.

Again the youth who was affected even to tears by music (of all arts the most sensational in its appeal) and who was enraptured and driven to the verge of distraction by the 'Sonate Pathétique' was, half a century later, to express this identical conflict of emotions in perhaps the most tortured story which he ever wrote, and to betray, as he listened to music, 'a slight pallor and a scarcely perceptible grimace, suggestive of something like terror.'

And the paths too along which he sought escape from his inner conflict were always to remain virtually the same, although gradually as age sapped his physical energies, the tendency to deny his instincts more and more triumphed over the need of indulging them. Increasingly too he came to associate the release from possessive egotism for which he strove with the hour when men accepted the lordship of death.

There is a sense in which such an acceptance is vital to a complete perception of and submission to reality. But the characters in whom Tolstoy depicted this release accepted death passively. They found in death not so much the final affirmation of life as the cessation of individual desire and the reassertion of the natural order in which the creature is valueless save as an element in a physical process. And because this was an imperfect and negative conception of death, Tolstoy, as we shall show, was never freed from the dread of it, and could only achieve some measure of relief from this dread by continuing to deny ever more fanatically the worth of physical and intellectual life.

The same negative tendency conditioned his view of a right acceptance of the lordship of life and explains his life-long idealization of those working peasants in whose presence, as a youth, he experienced at first 'an involuntary, overpowering sensation of awkwardness,' so that he always tried to avoid their seeing him.

In this feeling admiration for their physical integrity was blended with self-reproach and a poignant regret for his own loss of it, and it worked so powerfully in him that it compelled him later to make the peasant, quite un-critically, the final criterion of moral, æsthetic and spiritual value and blinded him to the fact that the struggle for social justice must be in the last resort 'a war of all the good of all the classes against all the evil of all the classes,' and that 'in no one class is either all the good or all the evil.'

Later, indeed, he did admit on more than one occasion that the peasants were only prevented by want of oppor-tunity from indulging the same vices as their exploiters. But he attributed this to infection by the diseased minority of society rather than to the selfish instincts inherent in all human nature and particularly active at a certain point in its development.

Tolstoy's exclusive admiration of the peasant was of course to a considerable extent caused by the corruption, insincerity and inhumanity which characterized privileged Russian society. But essentially it was rooted in the demands of his own temperament. For him the way back to physical integrity was so much more compelling, so much nearer, than the way forward to a higher order of consciousness. One so dominated by the senses as he was, who, like Maupassant, felt vibrating in him something common to every kind of animal, some of all the instincts, of all the dim desires of the lower creation, as inevitably abandoned himself to Nature, with a fine sensuous aware-ness, as later in self-defence he moralized the Natural.

The virtues of the peasant were essentially those of the acquiescent creature. He was as Adam before the Fall. He accepted the ruling of physical life and his common kinship with everything that shared this life. And to Tolstoy, whose instincts continued throughout his life to assert their rights against conscience and eventually conditioned the terms which his conscience despairingly imposed upon them, this natural morality seemed the highest harmony within man's reach.

It corresponded in the realm of conduct with the perfect natural insight which he revealed as an artist. It expressed the element of mutual help in Nature as distinct from the conflict of her forces, and the peasant's loyalty to life as a social animal blinded him to the animal limitations, which must go with such a loyalty.

His own intense animal response to Nature was at once his consolation and his curse. In the periods of his greatest despair, when he was crying out in torment that life had no meaning for him, he would feel suddenly and even for months at a time, as he did in youth, 'joyously conscious of having within me the same young, fresh force of life as nature was everywhere exuding around me.' He would luxuriate in all the 'welter of life,' in the wet ground, the reddish twigs of lilac with their swelling buds, the raw odorous air and radiant sunlight, and the overpowering sensation which possessed him would extend through all the scale of natural life, from the rank to the ethereal.

The experience was fugitive, the season changed, his own vitality ebbed, and unlike the peasant, whose laborious life allowed of no superfluous energy and who

lived in the moment, he could not accept the change and
wait unconsciously for the revival. What later he described as 'all those cessations and reanimations that
recurred within me hundreds of times' were cause of deep
mental anguish. Between the ebb and the flow, he was
isolated. The egotism latent in however generous a sensational surrender to life became conscious of itself, of its
pride, its vanity and its ugliness. Nature was

> Enjoy'd no sooner but despised straight;
> Past reason hunted, and no sooner had
> Past reason hated . . .
> A bliss in proof, and proved, a very woe;
> Before, a joy proposed; behind, a dream.

It may be that Tolstoy's later attack upon Shakespeare
originated in a secret resentment against a poet who by
his own intrepid and individual imagination had learnt
how 'to shun the heaven that leads men to this hell.'
Certainly his gross insensitiveness to Shakespeare's creative resolution of the conflict of appetite and remorse in a
higher order of consciousness proves how fundamental
was his own incapacity to do the same.

Yet even in his youth he suffered acutely in the passive
intervals between active, physical enjoyment. But Nature
then never deserted him for long and it seemed still
possible to find perfection in her and a final happiness in
the self-abandonment which she invited. 'At such times
everything would take on for me a different meaning.
The look of the old birch trees, with the one side of their
curling branches showing bright against the moonlit sky

and the other darkening the bushes and carriage-drive
with their black shadows; the calm, rich glitter of the
pond, ever swelling like a sound; the moonlit sparkle of
the dewdrops on the flowers in front of the veranda; the
graceful shadows of those flowers where they lay thrown
upon the grey stonework; the cry of a quail on the far
side of the pond; the voice of some one walking on the
high road; the quiet, scarcely audible scrunching of two
old birch trees against one another; the humming of a
mosquito at my ear under the coverlet; the fall of an
apple as it caught against a branch and rustled among the
dry leaves; the leapings of frogs as they approached
almost to the veranda steps and sat with the moon shining
mysteriously on their green backs – all these things took
on for me a strange significance – a significance of exceed-
ing beauty and of infinite love. Before me would rise *she*,
with long black tresses and a high bust, but always
mournful in her fairness, with bare hands and voluptuous
arms. She loved me, and for one moment of her love I
would sacrifice my whole life! But the moon would go
on rising higher and higher, and shining brighter and
brighter, in the heavens; the rich sparkle of the pond
would swell like a sound, and become ever more and more
brilliant, while the shadows would grow blacker and
blacker, and the sheen of the moon more and more transparent; until, as I looked at and listened to all this, something would say to me that *she* with the bare hands and
voluptuous arms did not represent *all* happiness, that love
for her did not represent *all* good; so that, the more I
gazed at the full, high-riding moon, the higher would true

beauty and goodness appear to me to lie, and the purer and purer they would seem – the nearer and nearer to Him who is the source of all beauty and all goodness. And tears of unsatisfied, yet tumultuous, joy would fill my eyes.

'Always, too, I was alone; yet always, too, it seemed to me that, although great, mysterious Nature could draw the shining disc of the moon to herself, and somehow hold in some high, indefinite place the pale-blue sky, and be everywhere around me, and fill of herself the infinity of space, while I was but a lowly worm, already defiled with the poor, petty passions of humanity – always it seemed to me that, nevertheless, both Nature and the moon and I were one.'

In this single passage the essential characteristics of the young Tolstoy are to be found, and also the explanation of the fatal introversion of instinct which tortured the mature man. It reveals first a wonderful absorption in the sights and sounds of Nature. He has the senses of the savage, alive to every physical vibration. But he cannot for long keep his senses in simple contact with earth. They dissolve in vague dreams of infinite beauty and love, seek satisfaction in an image of voluptuous womanhood, and then crave some purer pleasure, remote and intangible as the moon riding the far reaches of the sky.

And the impulse behind all these fluctuations was always the same. He was as sensational when he tried to project himself into some high, indefinite place as when he hungered for a mistress with a high bust and voluptuous arms. And because the impulse was at once sensational and abstract, it was doomed to frustration. Tolstoy might refuse to admit the frustration, might delude himself that 'nevertheless both Nature and the moon and I were one,' but his very words deny his claim. Even when he aspired towards the heaven, 'nearer and nearer to Him who is the source of all beauty and all goodness,' he remained alone, conscious of defilement by 'the poor, petty passions of humanity.'

The voluptuary in the midst of his raptures, longing to lose his identity in an infinite sensation, hates his humanity which localizes his sensations and reveals them for what they are.

This conflict is inherent in romantic naturalism. But unlike Wordsworth who in fullness of content could write of his boyhood that he

> held unconscious intercourse
> With the eternal Beauty, drinking in
> A pure organic pleasure from the lines
> Of curling mist, or from the level plain
> Of waters colour'd by the steady cloud,

Tolstoy could never so completely subdue his consciousness to a purely instinctive apprehension of the natural world as to suffer no dissatisfaction in the process. He was, even in youth, both too aspiring and too conscience-stricken to gather obliviously

> New pleasure, like a bee among the flowers,

to possess securely

A consciousness of animal delight,
A self-possession felt in every pause
And every gentle movement of my frame.

He longed to tear from Nature by purely sensational means a final satisfaction which is not to be won in this way by a self-conscious being.

It was by deepening his distinctively human faculties of sympathy and thought and grafting them on to the instinctive paganism of his boyhood that Wordsworth ceased to be baffled by a sensationalism which could only entail disillusionment when the period of self-sufficient animal delight was outgrown.

But Tolstoy never crossed that isthmus which Wordsworth described as dividing 'our native continent' from 'earth and human life,' never learnt to spiritualize his instincts by making them intelligently human. He tried, as we shall see, first to silence the accusing voice of his humanity in purely physical activities and experiences and to extend his instincts infinitely, and then to deny their finite rights.

And inevitably he found no final harmony in either attempt, because in both he did violence to one element in his nature and provoked an inevitable reaction.

§ 3

The first two conscious attempts which Tolstoy made as a young man to achieve disinterestedness were on the family estate at Yasnaya Polyana and with the Army in the Caucasus. And both experiments failed. Nature rejected him equally in the persons of the peasants whom he wished to help and the Cossack girl whom he wished to love.

In *A Russian Proprietor*, which like *The Cossacks*, is closely autobiographical, he has told how, disgusted by the ideal of *comme il faut*, which had once appealed to his youthful vanity, and with the world of fashion in which he could not shine, he left the University and retired to Yasnaya Polyana, full of benevolent intentions. His aunt to whom he confided these intentions told him that he had always wished to appear original, and that his originality was nothing else but morbidly developed egotism.

This imputation is always made by resigned elders against the altruistic strivings of the young, and there is enough truth in it to hurt. Few men have ever done any great or original work in the world whose motives were not, in the beginning at least, egotistic. Altruism has very often grown out of a desire for fame, distinction, and self-applause (by all of which the young Tolstoy was strongly affected), and a man is to be judged by the extent to which he transforms these impulses into purer modes of expression.

Admittedly Tolstoy did succeed in purifying his motives very considerably, and even this first experiment in practical philanthropy was an advance upon the conventional distinctions to which he had aspired and as an army officer was still indeed to aspire. Nevertheless it may be said with some truth that throughout his life his activities were essentially dictated less by a desire to help others than to help himself by exchanging a sense of self-esteem for one of self-disgust. His preferences were for those beings and those activities which served best his own needs and he assumed too readily that these needs were typical and that a true life depended wholly on their satisfaction.

He could not indeed be fair to any individual or any class which did not further his own requirements or whose capacities were different from his own. And conversely he unduly idealized those with whom he felt direct affinities. It is this element of selfishness which explains his refusal to admit the essential defects which were the conditions of the peasants' qualities. Certainly their terrible poverty pained him, but try as he would to forget himself in ministering to them, his paramount impulse was to ease his own pain rather than theirs.

Consequently neither at this time among the down-trodden peasants nor later in the slums of Moscow did he succeed in establishing relations of real intimacy with those he sought to help. Eventually indeed he was to interpret this failure as an inevitable judgment upon himself and all the exploiting class to which he belonged who gave away pence in charity with one hand and seized pounds in robbery with the other.

But the exploitation was not merely economic. It was personal too. Tolstoy's attitude to the peasants was an interested one. He was using them to increase his own self-esteem or silence his self-disgust. And the poor, when they have not been corrupted by patronage, have, as Tolstoy later realized, an instinctive suspicion of such philanthropy. They feel that their would-be benefactor is moved by other motives than that of pure and intelligent humanity. And although they may cringe and pretend to gratitude, out of a dim resentment they obstinately prefer even a sordid life which is their own to a dictated life of cleanliness.

This, perhaps, even more than the animal conservatism which can only be cured by the rational education and scientific methods which Tolstoy descried, is the root cause of such resistance to philanthropic effort as he has described in *A Russian Proprietor*. But the objection to the reforming efforts of rational but patronizing Liberals, to which he became more and more averse as he grew older, lay in the fact that they were patronizing and not that they were rational. Tolstoy, however, did not make this distinction. He dismissed the rational effort as worthless because it was associated with patronage. No one, he claimed, had the right or indeed the power to dictate to the poor how they should live, and since truly human relations in his view could only exist between individuals, the systematic application of science to the problem of poverty was necessarily inhuman and so unjustifiable.

Admittedly such an attitude arose out of a real sense of unworthiness, but it also explains, as it provided a convenient excuse for, his own failure to find any practical solution of the problem. For that solution can only be found in the disinterested application of science to the injustices of human life. Science may indeed, as Tolstoy was to assert, merely increase the power of exploiters. But the power which it represents is as essential to the removal of social injustice as to individual self-mastery, while the accumulation of knowledge tends eventually at least to modify the inherited savagery and stupidity, which allows the poor to be the prey of the rich and the rich to prey upon the poor.

Tolstoy, however, would have been more justified in considering science merely as the instrument of self-interest, which in the past it has generally been, if his own relations with the peasants had been quite disinterested. That they were not so, explains alike his inability to bring rational methods patiently to bear on the problem, and his consequent disillusionment.

At this time he wanted to preserve 'the fullness of the morally pleasant feeling' which he experienced, when he first conceived of himself as a beneficent proprietor. He wanted the peasant to fit into his scheme of philanthropy and to justify his belief in the inherent virtues of a state of Nature.

And the peasants refused to satisfy his wants. 'We are very grateful for your kindness,' they would answer, '*but* . . .' There was always a '*but.*' Habituated to sordid poverty and demoralized by it, they had lost the power of initiative. They were like men who have served a long term of imprisonment, to whom the free world has become a cold, forbidding place. 'Here is our place in the world,' they said, 'we are happy in it. . . . Let us stay here and say our prayers; do not take us from our nest.'

And Tolstoy who would not admit that such an attitude was typical of the grimmer side of that state of nature which he idealized, that to the brutes and the brutalized even filth is homely, could only cry out of his own suffer-

ing sense of shame, 'Why are you so poor?' The very
hopelessness of his task lay in the imperviousness of the
peasant to rational appeals, to the animal piety, at once
true and false, which argued – 'it ain't the manure that
makes the corn grow, but God,' and which led him to
excuse himself from human effort on the plea of divine
supervision.

Tolstoy sympathized too much himself with this attitude to learn from it the defects of a natural but unintelli-
gent fidelity to life. The disenchantment which he experienced did not compel him to modify his views of the
natural man and his religion or to realize that the primitive consciousness of the peasant was as much a barrier to
the truly human relations which he desired as the patronage of Liberal economists and educationists, while they
were, at least theoretically, anxious to remove the barrier
in the only way in which it can be removed.

Instead he attributed his failure to the external methods
which he had adopted and still believed that the peasant,
if he were not economically enslaved, would prove so
ideally equipped by instinct as to have no need of science
and that his passive trust in God was enough to ensure
efficient farming.

But Tolstoy's real disenchantment in this first social
experiment as in all others was with himself. His failure
intensified his self-consciousness, and although he said
over and over again, smiling and waving his hands –
'Love is self-denying. That is the only true happiness
independent of chance,' although he even consoled himself with dreams of a rural existence with a sympathetic

wife and children, or released his imagination from all mundane constraint at the piano, happiness eluded him.

The call of a pagan life was too strong, the life which Ilyushka, the team-driver, led with his handsome, robust form, bright curls, shining, narrow blue eyes and fresh complexion, a life of action and gaiety and thoughtlessness in the open air at all seasons. 'Splendid!' he whispered to himself. 'Why am I not Ilyushka?' Defeated by the animal obstinacy of the peasants, robbed of the delight which he had hoped to derive from their appreciation, he longed to cast his moral sensibility away, and capture their physical wholeness.

But in the Caucasus he was to find that this too was not allowed to him.

§ 4

Tolstoy's experience in the Caucasus, where he joined the Army at the age of twenty-three, proved an interesting descent from abstract to concrete naturalism. Of the night of his arrival he wrote – 'Last night I hardly slept. I began to pray to God. I cannot possibly express the sweetness of the feeling that came to me when I prayed. . . . I felt the desire of something very great, very beautiful. . . . What? I cannot say what. I wanted to be one with the Infinite Being: to be dissolved, comprehended, in Him.'

This hunger to grasp something which eludes definition but in which all reality is felt to reside is of course the foundation alike of æsthetical and mystical perception. It may remain, as it did with Tolstoy on this night, a vague expansive impulse, or it may, by an implicit effort of will and intelligence, be focused upon the phenomenal world and transformed into intuition.

In the one case it begets a sort of vertigo, if it does not actually plunge the individual who indulges it into that bottomless abyss of the unconscious, into which Tolstoy confessed that he often wished to throw himself headlong 'without knowing why or wherefore.' In the other it begets an illumination by which the individual at once conceives and perceives the phenomenal world from its creative centre, a centre from which everything, including the individual himself, falls inevitably into its correct relation.

This creative vision, in which knowing and being, inner and outer experience, combine, has its roots in the ecstatic naturalism which Tolstoy experienced on his first night in the Caucasus. But it has also passed through the discriminating focus of an individual intelligence. The intelligence alone, in seeking to impose order on life, is given to arbitrary exclusions; the senses alone, in their craving for physical satisfaction, blot out all distinctions. In true vision the two faculties are perfectly harmonized, the body of life with its informing spirit, the finite many with the infinite one. And the conditions of true vision correspond exactly with those of harmonious being.

The discord therefore in Tolstoy's life and the distortion in his vision were due to the same causes. When he aspired towards reality and freedom, as here, his senses and feelings submerged his intelligence in a diffused ecstasy, which he was to attempt more successfully to define and spiritualize in *War and Peace*, where he made it create a crisis in the inner life of the two characters into which he projected himself. In it, as in his surrender to grosser instincts, he abandoned himself to physical life and found only death. His egotism was momentarily dissipated, but it was not liberated, so that he had to confess that 'a man is never such an egotist as at moments of spiritual ecstasy.' 'I want to understand,' he wrote, 'but I dare not. I abandon myself to Thy will.' And consequently, within an hour he abandoned himself as readily to what he called 'the voice of vice. . . . I struggled, but succumbed to it. I fell asleep and dreamt of fame and women. Yet it was not my fault. I could not help it.'

The overmastering will was in both cases essentially the same. It was the energy of life, flowing like a torrent through the individual, equally unconcerned with sin or virtue, but inevitably carrying one who had become conscious of such concerns into a gulf of pessimism and self-disgust.

How consciously concerned Tolstoy was, may be judged from *The Story of a Yesterday*, the fragment of 'a daily register of the spiritual side of my life,' which he wrote shortly after his arrival in the Caucasus and which is actually his first literary production. The detailed self-analysis of which this fragment consists is remarkable. He examines his feelings, his remarks and embarrassments as relentlessly as a modern psycho-analyst, and he applies the same treatment to the speech, actions and facial expressions of others, inquiring minutely for example whether a woman of his acquaintance is a coquette, and, if so, whether her coquetry is charming or vicious according to its degree of calculation and innocence.

He considers the causes of his awkwardness in the presence of people whom he dislikes or likes excessively, and concludes that it is due in both cases to a desire to display his feelings and himself and a consequent abashment, and he even arranges under three heads the vices underlying a lie told in declining an invitation to dinner.

This probing, however, into character and motive was rooted, as always with Tolstoy, in direct physical insight. When, for example, he describes a face, he identifies himself with the life that dictates its lines – 'She leant back with her face in full relief, so that I could contemplate the delicate, rounded contours, its dark, half-closed, energetic eyes, its slender, pointed nose, and the mouth that was always one with the eyes, yet always expressing something different.'

The insight of the last phrase is typical of the power of physical evocation which he was to wield so notably as an artist.

But perhaps the chief interest of this fragment lies in the following passages –

'How can one of one's own accord become "fully human," and lead a purposeful life? For it is impossible to propound one's own purpose in life. Many times I have tried that, and always I have failed. Rather, instead of inventing one's purpose, one needs to discover it. . . . Such a purpose I believe myself at length to have discovered. It is, in every way to educate and develop my faculties.' And again – 'Spirit is a homogeneous entity, consciousness is made up of the same number (three) of parts as the human being. Which three parts are the intellect, the sensibility, and the body. . . . Of these the intellect is the highest.'

If Tolstoy could have acted upon this conception he might have discovered a meaning in life without denying it. But it remained an abstract conception because his body was too wilful to assimilate it, that body which dictated this apostrophe upon sleep – 'O Morpheus, take me into thine arms! . . . How I love that phrase *dans les bras*. Vividly, delicately, I began to picture myself *dans les bras* – then to picture the *bras* themselves – bare to the shoulder, curved and dimpled, framed in a white, indiscreetly open nightgown. For arms can indeed be beautiful, and especially one fold in them.'

No, as he wrote, 'I am only deceiving myself.' What use to educate the intelligence as the highest faculty when 'our every bodily pleasure is annulled by realization of it, and therefore bodily pleasures never ought to be realized. . . . Why had God given us realization, if realization was to make life more difficult?'

The only escape from this dilemma seemed to lie in the pursuit of moral pleasure divorced from the body. But there was one other possibility – to annul the realizing faculty by a complete abandonment to bodily experience. And it was this possibility which he next explored in the Caucasus.

§ 5

Inspired by this aim Tolstoy felt, as he was to feel so often again, that he was beginning a new life in which there were, as yet, no mistakes. What that new life was and how nearly he possessed himself of it is told enchantingly in *The Cossacks*. Although this was written ten years later and allowance must be made for a certain imaginative rehandling of the actual experience, the facts are known to correspond so closely with actuality that they may be drawn upon as confidently as Tolstoy's private Diary.

In Daddy Eroshka, the old hunter, Maryanka the untamed girl, beautiful in her spontaneity 'as the first woman must have come from her creator's hands,' and in the incidents of primitive Caucasian life Tolstoy not only drew a picture of what a state of Nature really is, but lived it in imagination himself.

Yet in the person of Olenin, the young cadet, whose experiences we may accept as Tolstoy's own, he confessed that however kindred to the life of Eden he was and however intimately he could project himself into it, the Cherubim with flaming sword still stood at its threshold and refused him entrance.

Daddy Eroshka, however, is perhaps the most truly conceived primitive, whom Tolstoy ever drew. His reality, unlike that of the peasant Saint, Platon, in *War and Peace*, or his fellow Nabotov in *Resurrection*, is untainted by any element of imported idealism. He stands before us, a giant with red-brown face all furrowed by deep lines. 'For an old man, the muscles of his legs, arms, and shoulders were quite exceptionally large and prominent. There were deep scars on his head, under the short-cropped hair. His thick sinewy neck was covered with deep intersecting folds like a bull's. His horny hands were bruised and scratched. He stepped lightly and easily over the threshold, unslung his gun and placed it in a corner, and casting a rapid glance round the room noted the value of the goods and chattels deposited in the hut, and with out-turned toes stepped softly, in his sandals of raw hide, into the middle of the room. He brought with him a penetrating but not unpleasant smell of *chikkir* wine, vodka, gunpowder, and congealed blood.'

Tolstoy's habit of defining his characters in terms of animal psychology was never happier or more justified than here. Daddy Eroshka is typically primitive in his coarse innocence of sin, in his conviction that 'God has made everything for the joy of man,' a conviction which justifies, because it preserves on the level of pure instinct, all predatory passion. 'A sin to look at a nice girl? A sin to have some fun with her? Or is it a sin to love her? Is that so in your parts? . . . No, my dear fellow, it's not a sin, it's salvation! God made you, and God made the girl too. He made it all; so it is no sin to look at a nice girl. That's what she was made for; to be loved and to give joy. That's how I judge it, my good fellow.'

And Tolstoy, in whom the Old Testament already strove with the New, a patriarchal paganism with the conviction that he who looks at a woman to lust after her has already committed adultery in his heart, would fain have believed him. It was tempting to agree with Daddy Eroshka when he said that he had 'grown too clever.' To cease to be clever might take, for example, the sting out of death.

For the old hunter death presented no difficulties.

'When you die the grass will grow on your grave, and that's all,' he quoted laughing, and it followed that to kill was an equally trivial matter. Such are the ethics or rather want of ethics of the animal world which lives in the moment, and because Daddy Eroshka shared them, he drew too, like any wild creature of the woods, upon the deep-flowing forces of Nature and her secret wisdom. To him the beast was not a fool. 'No, he is wiser than a man, though you do call him a pig! He knows everything.'

And Tolstoy, weary of the drawing-rooms of Moscow, with their luxurious elegance, grimacing conventions, and 'futile, useless life devoid of occupation or aim,' conscious of that 'continual *ennui* in the blood' typical of the falsely civilized, longed to immerse himself in this life of instinct.

And almost he succeeded. He plunged for days into the untrampled forest and gradually its swarming life ceased to repel him. 'These myriads of insects were so well suited to that monstrously lavish wild vegetation, these multitudes of birds and beasts which filled the forest, this dark foliage, this hot scented air, these runlets filled with turbid water which everywhere soaked through the Terek and gurgled here and there under the overhanging leaves, that the very thing which had at first seemed to him dreadful and intolerable, now seemed pleasant. . . . And it was clear to him that he was not a Russian nobleman, a member of Moscow Society, the friend and relative of So-and-so and So-and-so, but just such a mosquito, or pheasant, or deer, as those that were now living all round him. "Just as they, just as Daddy Eroshka, I shall live awhile and die, and as he says truly: grass will grow and nothing more." '

He tried hard to preserve this illusion, so physically refreshing while it lasted. But it never lasted long. One moment he felt 'cool and comfortable and did not think of or wish for anything'; his blood beat to a sub-human measure. And the next his thoughts raced away and questions swarmed like the mosquitoes. Once again he was 'a being quite distinct from every other being, now lying all alone,' and the old problem presented itself. 'How then must I live to be happy, and why was I not happy before?'

And suddenly that new light, which was so often to tantalize with its elusiveness, seemed to break in upon him, a light which was, in some mysterious way, one with the shimmering foliage about him. 'Happiness is this!' he said to himself, 'Happiness lies in living for others. . . . When trying to satisfy it selfishly – that is, by seeking for oneself riches, fame, comforts, or love – it may happen that circumstances arise which make it impossible to satisfy these desires. It follows that it is these desires that are illegitimate, but not the need for happiness. But what desires can always be satisfied, despite external circumstances? What are they? Love, self-sacrifice.'

But Daddy Eroshka was too happy in obeying the laws of his primitive nature to ask what happiness was. It was not in him to argue, 'since one wants nothing for oneself, why not live for others?' He wanted many things for himself and he took them without scruple by force or cunning.

Again it was true that the Cossacks showed a heroic

carelessness of self as soldiers, and at the end of his life, when 'civilization' had become even more repugnant to Tolstoy, he was to contrast in *Hadji Murad* as vividly as in any of his writings the dignity and selflessness of a barbarous mountaineer with the petty conceit and profligacy of the Emperor and his officers. But the selflessness to which he aspired was of a different order from this. And already he felt that between its realization and the primitive life which allured him lay a gulf which he could not bridge.

The Cossacks who lived as Nature lives appeared to him 'beautiful, strong and free'; and the sight of them made him feel ashamed and sorry for himself. But even in his most primitive moments he was dimly conscious that he could not live as they, because he was differently constituted. The idea of a higher freedom than the natural, of a loyalty to a moral ideal instead of to physical forces divided him from primitive life, and yet these forces ruled his body too powerfully for him to realize it in practice and compelled him to denounce the consciousness which was his human birthright. 'I tried to throw myself into that kind of life,' he wrote, 'but was still more conscious of my own weakness and artificiality. I cannot forget myself and my complex, distorted past; and my future appears to me still more hopeless.'

The tragedy of a divided impulse was crystallized in his relations (for Olenin's history is his own) with a Cossack girl. The sex-haunted and sex-accusing moralist of later years was already foreshadowed in the baffled lover of this story. The physical conception too of womanhood which always prevented Tolstoy from portraying a really human relationship between the sexes was grounded in his feverish admiration for such splendid animals as Maryanka.

Not only the Stepanida of his short story *The Devil*, the characterless magnet of a middle-aged sensuality (again drawn from his own experience) or the animal Princess Hélène of *War and Peace*, but even the adorable Natasha of the same novel, derived from Maryanka. The realistic detail which Tolstoy employed in describing how the firm stately build of this young beauty, who was 'quite savage, just like a wild filly,' allured him, is itself proof of the intensity of his appetites.

'He kept lifting his eyes . . . and looking at the powerful young woman who was moving about. Whether she stepped into the moist morning shadow thrown by the house, or went out into the middle of the yard lit up by the joyous young light so that the whole of her stately figure in its bright coloured garment gleamed in the sunshine and cast a black shadow – always he feared to lose any one of her movements. It delighted him to see how freely and gracefully her figure bent: into what folds her only garment, a pink smock, draped itself on her bosom and down her shapely legs; how she drew herself up and her tight-drawn smock showed the outline of her breathing bosom; how the soles of her narrow feet in her worn red slippers stood on the ground without altering their shape; how her strong arms with the sleeves rolled up, exerting the muscles, used the spade almost as if in anger, and how her deep dark eyes sometimes glanced at him.'

Physical awareness, short of actual touch, could scarcely go further. He devoured her with his eyes. But, as in his relations with Daddy Eroshka, the physical life of which she was the personification allured only to frustrate. And for long he kept at a distance. In his heart he knew that she was inaccessible to him, and he tried to console himself and stifle his desires by acts of apparent disinterestedness, by a generous gift to her Cossack lover, Lukashka, and by pretending to favour his suit.

But it was of no avail. His passions were too strong for him. 'Self-sacrifice,' he confided to his Diary, 'is a very ordinary form of egotism.' It seemed to ensure at best only an abstract happiness, to be at worst but sublimated self-esteem. 'It is even difficult for me to believe,' he wrote, 'that I could prize such a one-sided, cold, and abstract state of mind. Beauty came and scattered to the winds all that laborious inward toil; and no regret remains for what has vanished! Self-renunciation is all nonsense and absurdity! . . . "Live for others and do good!" – Why? when in my soul there is only love for myself, and the desire to love her, and to live her life with her. Not for others, not for Lukashka I now desire happiness. I do not now love those others. Formerly I should have told myself that this is wrong. . . . Now I don't care. I do not live my own life, there is something stronger than me which directs me.'

Once again Tolstoy sought to recover a physical wholeness. Maryanka was happy; she was like Nature, 'consistent, calm, and self-contained; and I, a weak distorted being, want her to understand my deformity and my torments. . . . I tried to escape from my love, by self-renunciation . . . but thereby only stirred up my own love and jealousy. . . . I love her not with my mind, or my imagination, but with my whole being. Loving her, I feel myself to be an integral part of all God's joyous world.'

The fatality of such love lay in the fact that his mind, and hence his moral sense, was forcibly denied the share which it had come to demand in all his experience, and by asserting its rights destroyed the wholeness of being, that he claimed.

In the flood of primal instinct he might forget the difficulty which he experienced in achieving straight and simple relations with Maryanka, might believe that he loved with the unconsciousness that he desired. But Maryanka knew better; she understood his deformity with the insight which is neither of mind nor of imagination, but of unperverted sense. And like the peasants of Yasnaya Polyana she refused to serve his needs. 'Now then, what are you drivelling about?' was her answer to his protestations of passion. She did not try to conceal animalism in high phrases or expect to be loved as a 'personification of all that is beautiful in nature.' She was ready to mate as the creatures mate, carnally and yet without conscious carnality, to serve the forces of life without questioning what they were.

But Tolstoy knew too well what they were to accord them this oblivious loyalty. And his knowledge outraged Maryanka. Out of the depths of her primitive health she scented his disease. 'Get away. I'm sick of you!' shouted the girl, stamping her foot, and moved threateningly towards him. And her face expressed such abhorrence, such contempt, and such anger, that Olenin suddenly understood that there was no hope for him, and that his first impression of this woman's inaccessibility had been perfectly correct.'

Even so, if in a somewhat different sense, did Katusha reject the Nekhlyudov of *Resurrection* – 'You want to save yourself through me. You've got pleasure out of me in this life, and want to save yourself through me in the life to come.'

To regain the status of the natural world, it was necessary to forget all acquired consciousness, to live the life of the body without thought or scruple, and that, save for moments for which he paid later in remorse, Tolstoy could not do. Nor was salvation in anyone's power but his own.

Certainly Daddy Eroshka was kinder than Maryanka. 'Why, I love you,' he said in parting, 'and how I pity you! You are so forlorn, always alone, always alone.'

And so Tolstoy left the Caucasus the same distracted egotist as when he came to it. His experience there had intensified his appetites without appeasing them. 'He loved Maryanka more than ever and knew that he could never be loved by her.' But this knowledge was of no real avail to him.

There are natures which can be tempered by experience, which adapt themselves gradually to their environment and balance in the process their elements. But Tolstoy's nature was not one of these. It is unfair to chide him, as some critics have done, for aspiring to be a saint and remaining a sinner. His reality as an artist and a man is rooted in this contradiction. The force of his instincts was such that no disillusionment could tame them; the force of his conscience was such that no purely instinctive life could satisfy him. There could be no peace between such uncompromising forces.

And *The Cossacks* stands to his youth, as *A Confession* to his middle-age. In the one he reveals how his instincts overran his conscience without gaining the victory. In the other he shows how his conscience fought his instincts to a standstill; but here too the final victory was never won nor the combatants reconciled.

¶ PART TWO

THE ANTAGONISMS DEFINED

THE ANTAGONISMS DEFINED

§ I

WHEN Nature in the person of Maryanka had rejected Tolstoy, he turned with renewed hatred upon his animal self. That repentance for the abuse of the best years of his life in acts of carnal indulgence, which was to grow more and more intense as the tide of youth ceased to flow, began to torment him. That he had lived sensually is proved by the confessions of his Diary. In entry after entry he accuses himself of violent voluptuousness or describes such incidents as the following: 'Yesterday could not forbear signalling to some one in a pink dress who looked comely from a distance. Opened the back door, and she entered. Could not even see her; all seemed foul and repellent, and I actually hated her for having caused me to break my rule.'

As an old man two offences in particular tortured his memory, and, in his own words, poisoned his existence, the seduction of a parlour-maid in his aunt's house, upon which the terrible study in *Resurrection* of animal desire triumphing over the gentler instincts and violating innocence, was based, and a liaison with a peasant woman from which the incidents of *The Devil* probably derived.

We have quoted these unpleasant details, because it has often been suggested that Tolstoy's hatred of his lower nature had little basis in fact. That it was morbidly exaggerated is doubtless true, but the reality of such dissipations depends less on their actual extent than on the reaction of the individual concerned to them. The intensity and persistence of Tolstoy's passions may be judged by the intensity of his revulsions, and by the fact that he could never cease to 'feel the torments of hell' when he recollected 'the whole abomination' of his past life.

And if his reiterated confessions in his Diary of gluttony, sloth, vanity, mendacity and diffidence were conditioned by the ideal of self-perfection to which he constantly aspired and for which allowance must be made, they were none the less based on fact. And it was a fact which distorted not only his life but his opinions, giving him indeed a searching insight into the brutal impulses which masqueraded behind the sentimentalities of society, its love-making and war-making and religious and civic ceremony, but an insight so terrible in its personal reminders that he could only find relief in flagellations whether of himself or of the elements in life which seemed to conspire with his lower nature.

It was, for example, because his senses were enslaved by women that he could write in his Diary at the age of twenty – 'Regard feminine society as an inevitable evil of social life, and, in so far as you can, avoid it. From whom, indeed, do we learn voluptuousness, effeminacy, frivolity in everything, and many another vice, if not from women? Who is responsible for the fact that we lose such feelings inherent in us as courage, fortitude, prudence, equity, and so forth, if not woman?'

From whom, it might equally be said, do we learn selflessness, purity, grace, wonder and lyrical insight, if not from women? But Tolstoy could not learn these qualities because women, like music, like Nature herself, appeal through the senses to the higher faculties. We receive from them according as we give. And his sensual response to them was so engrossing that it excluded all else.

That a licentious social atmosphere might aggravate such sensuality was of course perfectly true, and Tolstoy was right both as an artist and a moralist to stress the fact. He did so for the first time in a short story which he conceived at this time and later entitled *How Love Dies*.

In this story, as in his repeated treatment of the same circumstances throughout his work, the nature which is corrupted by a vicious society is 'a young soul upon which a consciousness of wrong had not yet cast its shadow.' He falls romantically in love, as Vronsky was to fall in love with Anna Karenina, at a ball. The vividness of Tolstoy's description of this ball, the sense of intoxication which he communicates, explains the particular bitterness which he cherished against a society which could provide such occasions of sense-enslavement.

'Who can have forgotten the striking impression produced by the brilliance of the thousands of lights, by the eyes and diamonds and flowers and velvet and silk and bare shoulders and muslin and hair and black combs and white waistcoats and satin shoes and multi-coloured uniforms and liveries; the fragrance of flowers, and the scent of women; the thousands of voices and footsteps under the gay, enticing melodies of waltz and polka; the unceasing movement; the bizarre effect of all these elements combined?'

It is in this atmosphere that Sereja falls in love with the

Countess Shofing, who like Anna Karenina has contracted a loveless marriage, and in whom Sereja's purity excites beautiful dreams. Dancing with her, 'all his powers become centred in listening to the strains of music . . . and in a consciousness of the Countess's form as it so harmonized with his every movement as to make him and her seem one.'

For the first time in his life he experienced the feeling of love, the dim, unintelligible yearning which rises in the heart of youth as from the very sources of his being and which Tolstoy was to describe so wonderfully again and again as an ineffable joy which could not centre itself upon one object, but extended itself to all and sundry. 'To him a life holding aught save moments of love and rapture now seemed impossible.'

And then in grim contrast with this dreamy intoxication Tolstoy sketched the sequel. From the ball Sereja goes with a worldly Prince and a depraved old General to the gipsy girls and from there, wholly ignorant of the nature of the place and fuddled with drink, to a brothel, where he loses his innocence. 'The fault,' Tolstoy concluded, 'was Society's, yours, for tolerating such men – and not only tolerating them, but choosing them as social leaders.'

But the victim was at fault too. Tolstoy idealized the fact that he 'loved and worshipped as only innocent youth can.' And he was always to idealize it with a sick longing to recover the delirious freshness of that first surrender to passion. But this very innocence was Sereja's undoing. The intoxication in the ballroom only differed in degree from that in the brothel. The one involved the sentiments as well as the senses, but both were valueless; both sprang from ignorance and led to self-abandonment. To enlighten ignorance, to educate the senses rationally is of more avail against such potential tragedies than to idealize the instinctive innocence which falls a prey to any sexual stimulus. A sentimental enslavement by the senses, such as Sereja's, leads inevitably through disillusionment to a moral hatred of them, to that false opposition too of fact to fancy which Tolstoy made when he wrote – 'Always, originally, are impulses of the heart pure and elevated. It is actuality that destroys their innocence and charm.'

And it was because Tolstoy was so enslaved and could not free himself by rational self-mastery that he transferred the vileness which he felt in himself to every bare shoulder, and invested the transports of sensuous adolescence with a sanctity and a moral significance which they did not, save by analogy with something higher, possess.

This is not to say that his attacks upon the luxurious, aimless and indolent life of society were not justified. But in his hatred of its elegant brutalities he came to attribute corruption to every physical expression of life which did not serve some practical end. For the same reason, as we shall see, he could only justify beauty in women if it was associated with motherhood, and beauty in art, if it served explicitly a moral purpose. For his sensual susceptibility was such that all physical grace enslaved him, blinding him to the possibility that it was spiritually expressive. The unending struggle that was in process within him distorted his vision no less than his life.

§ 2

One valuable result however of his disillusionment in the Caucasus was to open his eyes to the futility of the life which he led there as a cadet among 'stupid officers, stupid conversation, and nothing else.' His reaction against this life was still primarily personal. The Service, he felt, hindered vocations of which he had become conscious and, disappointed of the 'glittering prizes' of war (more than once he had merited the St. George's Cross for bravery but had not received it), he sought other roads to distinction.

He did not yet interpret the stupidity against which he reacted in the terms, for example, of *Resurrection* in which he wrote that 'military life in general depraves men. It places them in conditions of complete idleness, that is, absence of all rational and useful work; frees them from their common human duties, which it replaces by merely conventional duties, to the honour of the regiment, the uniform, the flag.' But in a deeper sense his change of view was another aspect of his revulsion from naturalism, a revulsion which was to express itself in perhaps the fiercest and also the most practical conviction of his life, that of the folly and futility of war.

On many occasions Tolstoy exhibited remarkable bravery. When death was contingent upon violent physical effort, it had no terrors for him. He went to meet it like a lover, all that was primitive in him exulting in the forcible suppression of thought, in the release from the meanness and responsibilities of self-consciousness. But the primitive man in Tolstoy had been rebuffed; he was less ready to fling himself into war's brutal tide and began to see the savagery inherent in its elementalism. Soon he was to ask whether it was impossible for men to live in peace, in this world so full of beauty, under this immeasurable starry sky, although still clinging to the delusion that 'all there is of evil in the human heart ought to disappear at the touch of Nature.'

Events, however, were now to strike at the roots of this delusion. Owing to the war with Turkey his resignation as a soldier was not accepted for some years and at the age of twenty-five he was drafted to the Crimea. Stimulated by a new environment he once more embraced the military life enthusiastically. 'Thank God,' he wrote, 'that I have seen these people and live in this glorious time.' And in this spirit the first of the three narratives entitled *Sebastopol* was written. Once again he could delight in the simplicity of the natural man, in the unpretentious individual who contrasted so favourably with strutting staff-officers and drew on depths of physical resource for his heroism. War, itself a denial of the higher morality, invests the natural virtues with a moral grandeur, and Tolstoy in their presence forgot for a time his disillusionment with a natural life, perfect only in its limitations.

But the Homeric phase soon passed, and the more he became a detached observer, the more odious and unforgivable did it seem to prostitute heroic impulses to such inhuman ends. The mangled and tortured bodies which strewed the Fourth Bastion at Sebastopol compelled him to realize in all its frightful consequences the predatory reality of war. Any vague religious mysticism excited by the imminent idea of death was refuted by its fact. And his second narrative contained a bitter attack on war and the Christianity which tolerated it, the first direct utterance of that splendid protest which he was to make again and again in his later years, notably in *The Kingdom of God is Within You* and never more trenchantly than in *Christianity and Patriotism*, when he wrote of the victim of patriotism — 'That victim is the everlastingly deceived, foolish working people – the people who with their blistered hands have built all those ships, and fortresses, and arsenals, and barracks, and cannons, and steamers, and harbours, and bridges, and all those palaces, halls, and platforms, and triumphal arches, and have printed all the newspapers and pamphlets, and procured and brought all the pheasants and ortolans, and oysters, and wines eaten and drunk by all those men who are fed, educated, and kept by them, and who, deceiving them, are preparing the most fearful calamities for them; it is always the same good-natured foolish people who, showing their healthy white teeth as they smile, gape like children, naïvely delighted at the dressed-up admirals and presidents, at the flags waving above them, and at the fireworks, and the playing bands; though before they have time to look about them, there will be neither admirals, nor presidents, not flags, not bands, but only the desolate wet plain, cold, hunger, misery – in front of them the slaughtering enemy, behind them the relentless government, blood, wounds, agonies, rotting corpses, and a senseless, useless death.'

Tolstoy never fairly allotted the responsibility for war,

and so never discovered the best means of transforming the dull resentment of the masses against it into an effective force. For once again, as with Sereja, the deceived share in it as well as the deceivers. A 'good-natured foolish people,' though they be such through no fault of their own, are the victims of their own ignorance no less than those who 'after a good dinner with a cigar between their teeth and unfinished glasses of good wine beside them . . . mark with pins on the map the spots at which so much cannon flesh . . . must be left.'

At Sebastopol, however, horror overcame even his delight in the healthy white teeth of the common soldier. For a time he succeeded in preserving a poetic conception of war. Danger excited him and he avoided looking attentively at the dead and wounded, regarding them almost as a sportsman does a slaughtered animal.

But when death ceased to excite, it horrified, and he knew himself to be participating in a ghastly frivolity. As he was to write later, it was not suffering and death which were terrible in themselves, but that which allowed people to inflict suffering and death; and the pagan spirit, so lovely in some of its manifestations, allowed them to do this.

Tolstoy never wholly disentangled his love of this spirit from his hatred of it, but already he began to realize the kindred vanity of a sensational mysticism and of pagan heroics. He wrote in his Diary that he had conceived 'a stupendous idea, to the realization of which I feel myself capable of devoting my life. This idea is the founding of a new religion *corresponding to the present state of mankind*:

the religion of Christianity, but purged of dogmas and mysticism: a practical religion, not promising future bliss, but giving bliss on earth. . . . *Deliberately* to promote the union of mankind by religion – that is the basic thought which, I hope, will dominate me.'

To concentrate upon man, whose humanity the elemental forces may enrich or submerge – that indeed was to be the direction of all Tolstoy's later effort. And in seeking to promote the union of mankind, he did but project his own problem and his own bias into the world at large. For in man frenziedly snatching at some elemental bliss and enslaved by an elemental strife he saw himself, 'ugly, awkward, uncleanly . . . not modest, intolerant, and as shame-faced as a child.'

§ 3

Sebastopol inflicted the first profound shock upon Tolstoy's naturalism. If it did not cure him of sentimentalism, it made it impossible for him to find any easy refuge from realism in 'that vague, feminine, whimpering passion.' As with so many of our own generation war not only shattered any belief which he had had in the men who controlled and directed society but also went far to destroy the illusion of the kindness of life.

And so, when he returned to Petersburg, the literary hero of the hour, he saw everywhere the deception for which thousands of corpses lay rotting in the Crimea. Those who gave dinners with toasts to the heroes of Sebastopol were not troubled by such visions. For them war was a pleasant excitement; they considered it in terms

of human pain as little as they considered hunting in terms
of animal pain. And Tolstoy, listening to them, pressed
his lips closely together and only opened them to brief
envenomed observations.

But at least in the men of letters who welcomed him he
hoped to discover the conscience of the age. He pictured
them as priests of a gospel of pure sincerity and invested
them with all the abstract perfection to which his vehement
nature aspired. And then gradually, as the pleasure which
he derived from their flattery diminished, he became convinced that almost all his fellow-writers were priests of no
religion but that of self-importance, and that many of
them were of 'bad, worthless character,' and even inferior
to those whom he had met in his former dissipated and
military life. 'These people,' he wrote later, 'revolted me,
I became revolting to myself, and I realized that that faith
was a fraud.'

His failure to find a conscience in men of education
pained him even more than his failure to lose his own conscience in primitive living. For the natural man, whom he
had tried to emulate, attracted him physically, but the
Petersburg writers satisfied him neither physically nor
spiritually. They merely reminded him of himself; but,
to his amazement and chagrin, they did not suffer as he
did. Like himself they were men of mixed motive and
uncertain impulse, ordinary men with, it might be, extraordinary or unusual talents which they exploited in their
art. But these talents did not make their lives more moral
and often they made them less moral than those without
their gifts. However liberal their public sentiments might

be, their private lives were often dissolute. And however dissipated Tolstoy's own life might be, he never pretended that such dissipation was the justifiable license of a superior being.

His persistent distrust, therefore, of Liberalism was based on a curious blend of pride and humility in himself and culminated in his detestation of those who were vain and morally insensitive enough to expound the way of public virtue to others while carelessly indulging in private vice themselves.

Ideally of course Tolstoy's view of what the great writer or the great reformer should be was a true one. Perfect disinterestedness of vision demands a perfect, a dedicated personality, one which, if it has not risen above good and evil, is for ever testing in action the distinction between them and striving after selflessness as the absolute good. The artist's knowledge, unlike the scientist's, is the expression of his whole being and its truth is conditioned by his personal integrity.

But art, like life, has many levels, and although each of these levels may and, we think, must be measured morally in any final estimate of their value, art may on each achieve a relative perfection, exploring and harmonizing in its expression a limited province of truth. But Tolstoy demanded that the writer should strive after nothing less than an absolute harmony and the final truth of life. He demanded that he should combine in his activity the saint's, the priest's and also the teacher's functions, because he himself wished to discover in writing that perfect moral activity which he was always seeking.

In fact few of the Petersburg writers who so disappointed him were consciously preoccupied either with
the good of humanity or their own self-perfection.
Primarily they were engaged in self-expression. They
accepted their natures as they accepted life instead of trying to better them, and by this very acceptance they
achieved a poise, however limited, which Tolstoy lacked.
It was a consciousness of this which explains the strange
mixture of violent attraction and repulsion which characterized Tolstoy's relations with Turgenev.

Tolstoy began by passionately admiring and reverenc-
ing him. He followed him about 'like a woman in love.'
He was convinced that the author of *Fathers and Sons*
must be a man of exquisite moral purity. But he found
instead a being ironical, compassionate, deprecatory, now
witty, now indifferent, a being good-natured indeed, but
only so because he lacked either convictions or prejudices
and could discuss with complete unconcern the qualities
of his latest mistress. And yet this man, who claimed to be
no more than a writer of the transition, had exquisitely
delineated life and possessed a spiritual repose which
Tolstoy lacked.

The fact not only seemed to contradict his theory of the
necessary relation between art and a good life, but also to
depreciate the ideal of moral self-perfection upon which
that theory was based. Tolstoy could not accept his
nature as Turgenev did, because it was in perpetual conflict with itself. And so he at once envied and despised
Turgenev for his refusal to endanger a comparative
serenity and an unexacting but wonderfully sensitive

insight by striving after absolute values. It was hateful to be wished 'good health, activity – and freedom, spiritual freedom' by one who achieved a far greater measure of this freedom than he himself did and yet lived, apparently, without principle. Tolstoy as an artist would admit the possibility of this, but as a moralist, battling desperately against carnal temptation, he denied it with all the vehemence of his nature.

Stepan, for example, in *Anna Karenina* is a perfect example of a man who enjoyed life because he was untouched by moral scruple. His whole person which 'seemed to shine with suppressed joy' is drawn in sharp contrast to that of Levin, who, like Tolstoy himself, is melancholy and ill at ease because he is trying without success to perfect himself and others. Stepan is an agreeable animal, generous as he is self-indulgent, and quite oblivious of the pain which his license may inflict on others. Tolstoy in creating him as such admitted his happiness, and yet as a moralist he would argue that no one could achieve happiness who was not a Christian in the extreme sense in which he interpreted the word. For as a moralist he was compelled, in his struggle to counterbalance the force of his appetites, to do violence to human life as to himself.

Nevertheless it is plain that no exhortation could have made Stepan a Christian because he was perfectly satisfied to be a pagan. It is well to emphasize this point here, because Tolstoy's refusal as a moralist to admit that humanity reveals different levels of development underlay all his intolerance towards others and himself, all his hatred of 'Culture' as a relative measure of refinement in man's advance from the animal to the ideally humane, and his unwarrantable assumption, upon which the main argument of *The Kingdom of God is Within You* depends, that mankind was only prevented by a few corrupt authorities from accepting the creed of self-denial which he preached.

It was natural, however, that at this time he should regard even a relative culture which aspired towards something more humane with cynical bitterness. For he had seen in the Crimea, beneath the veneer of popular heroism, the crudity of life at close quarters, and to the very passions which war had so ruthlessly exposed, 'ambition, love of power, covetousness, lasciviousness, pride, anger and revenge,' cultivated Russian society paid a devout respect.

And so towards those who accepted the relative, whether as writers or theoretical reformers, he felt an instinctive hostility. They were aiding the conspiracy by which the ignorant were slaughtered in war or the young corrupted. They were tolerant because they were weak and insincere, and their self-satisfaction added insult to injury.

Doubtless his irritability at this time was in part mere nervous egotism. He opposed others violently because he was far from certain of himself. There were elements in it also of the aristocrat's and the officer's contempt for the trade of letters. Writing appealed to him as a means of salvation, but he had conveniently no need to practise it as a means of livelihood.

Yet beneath these superficial antagonisms lay the revolt of a distracted sincerity against men who were happier because less ruthless than himself and who were to that extent in a better moral relation with life. Even in Turgenev he felt a moral indifference, a whimsical frivolity which constantly irritated. Certainly Turgenev had studied man, his own heart and the really great writers, as he advised Tolstoy to do, and had thereby evolved an art which exquisitely reflected the irony and pathos of life. But Tolstoy, who was too engrossed in his own heart to make a passive study of men or of great writers, despised, even while he envied, such detachment and literary refinement. A writer who expressed charmingly the pathos of life seemed to him to put a sort of gloss upon its tragedy, and so to administer a narcotic which would prevent men from facing the stark reality of wrong living.

He himself could not live rightly, but at least he strove to do so and knew how intensely hard it was. And this knowledge made him sceptical of all facile moral pretensions or all merely artistic talent. It was because he suspected every one of not telling and living the truth, that he fixed them with that extraordinarily piercing and discomforting glance, which Turgenev has described.

§ 4

Additional proof of the intenser moral seriousness which Tolstoy acquired in the Crimea is to be found in the letters which he wrote during the two years following his return to a young girl, Valeria Arsenev, with whom he fell in love and became informally engaged. As a child he had loved sentimentally, in the Caucasus he had tried to love primitively, but now, conceiving himself to be at the age of twenty-eight 'a man morally old, who in his youth committed many follies for which he paid with the happiness of the best years of his life, and who has now found his aim and vocation – literature,' he sought a stable relationship in harmony with this vocation.

His requirements therefore in the woman whom he hoped to marry were as exacting as in the writers whose vocation he had embraced, and his letters to Valeria Arsenev foreshadow the demands which he was to make of Sophie Behrs and the distress which eventually came of her failure to satisfy them in their most exacting form.

Already indeed he doubted whether he was born for family life, although he felt strongly its attraction, and he knew that marriage for him would succeed or fail in the degree that it assisted his moral development. 'There are people,' he wrote, 'who think when they marry: "Well, I have failed to find happiness; I have my life ahead of me . . ." This idea never occurs to me. I stake everything on one throw.'

No young girl, fond of society, flattery and pleasure, could possibly appreciate the worried seriousness of such a lover, particularly as it took so didactic a form. Tolstoy himself apologized for the tone of his letters. 'I am again *teaching*,' he wrote, 'but what's to be done? I can't understand relations with some one I love without that.'

It was a pathetic but illuminating confession. He could not put himself on an equality, could not cease to be an egotist, even with a woman whom he loved. The 'certain degree of mental development,' to which he attributed his habit of doubting everything, made it impossible for him to accept his fellow-beings uninquiringly as the simple or magnanimously as the wise, and the very qualities which attracted him in this girl separated him from her. 'Certain people,' he wrote to her, 'don't know all through their lives either joy or suffering – moral of course. It often seems to me that you have such a nature, and I am dreadfully pained by it.'

The easy acceptance of life which had attracted him in the Cossack girl and which he still admitted to be 'extraordinarily lovable,' offended him in Valeria Arsenev as, in a different degree, it did in Turgenev. Again it was wrong that she should be happy when he suffered. For his own moral perception brought him more pain than joy, and although he was compelled to assert its importance, he was continually rebelling against the burden which it imposed. 'I could be happy, if I were different from what I am,' he wrote, and unhappy in his efforts to be perfectly moral, he condemned those who accepted the happiness of the moment, instead of indulging, as he did, in vain expectation of a great happiness and lamenting their incapacity to realize it.

This resentment was the basis of that depreciation of women, which became ultimately a conviction of their innate inferiority to men, as attested, for example, by his statement to M. Jules Huret – 'You ask me whether I consider woman man's equal. I reply that I *know* she is, in all respects, morally inferior'; or again by the following reference to his wife, written in 1892: 'I wish most earnestly that I had the power to transmit to my wife a portion of that religious conscience which gives me the possibility of sometimes raising myself above the sorrows of life . . . although this conscience is hardly accessible to women.'

To Tolstoy there were two types of women and both tantalized him by avoiding the affliction of his own moral dilemma. There were those, like the Princess Mary of *War and Peace*, or his Aunt Tatiana from whom she derived, who realized in their lives the poetry of Christian self-sacrifice at the cost of little, if any, apparent effort, thus transforming their weakness into strength. Her father, for example, 'continually and painfully offended Princess Mary, but it cost her no effort to forgive him.'

And there were those like Maryanka, Natasha or Katusha, who were children of Nature, submissive alike in their virtues and vices to the life-force which they served instinctively. In these too no moral problem could arise. They had not eaten enough of the tree of knowledge for its fruit to poison them.

And although such instinctive integrity is of a lower order than a spiritual integrity achieved after a conscious struggle, it is preferable to moral disintegration. It was because Tolstoy knew this that he bore women a grudge. Most men, as Prince Andrew was to tell his sister, cannot harmonize their natures by instinctive submission. Their self-assertion creates a discord which has to be consciously resolved, until, after many relapses, a new harmony becomes habitual to them and the tension is released. But with Tolstoy the tension never was released, and so everything which tempted him to relax, women and music for example, more and more allured and terrified him.

In a fragment, *The Dream*, recently published but written about this time, he embodied the conflict between man's desire to influence the world and shape its thought, and woman's indifference to such desires through her perfect self-sufficiency. Her 'look had in it at once gentle ridicule and faint regret. Not that she had understood my words, or wished to understand them. It was merely that she was sorry for me. . . . She herself was happiness throughout, and had need of none. For which very reason I felt all at once, that I could not live without her.'

Nevertheless he could not love Valeria Arsenev for herself, for her eager beauty and her pleasure in life. She must fling her youth into the moral whirlpool in which he himself was struggling. 'Two things I implore you,' he wrote: 'work, work at yourself, think with greater steadiness, make yourself give a sincere account of your feelings . . . the only possible, entirely true, enduring, and highest happiness is obtained by three things: work, self-renunciation and love. I know it, I bear in my soul this conviction, but I live according to it only for a couple of hours in the course of a year. . . .'

Much of such counsel was admirable in itself, but through it all we feel him seeking to impose himself and his problems on a girl whose nature he could not allow to develop in its own way. It may be that she was shallow and frivolous, and that his stern announcement – 'I do not love tender and lofty things, I love honest and good things' – was justified by her affectation or sentimentality. But honesty need not exclude tenderness or poetry unless a lover is afraid of his feelings. Tolstoy was so afraid of them that, disappointed in his efforts to reform Valeria Arsenev along lines which he had laid down for himself, he allowed their engagement to lapse.

In art, however, he married her. For in *Family Happiness*, written two years later, he completed as an artist the situation which, as a moralist, he had curtailed.

§ 5

The first awakening of love is like the coming of spring to the natural world. It quickens the senses to a new awareness. The blood flows strongly, like the sap in the trees, and the lover projects his enriched awareness of health and freedom into the world about him, which takes on an enchanting freshness and, like himself, is full of infinite possibilities, unsuspected before.

Again and again Tolstoy was to re-conceive this moment, and *Family Happiness* is perhaps the most perfect record of it, which he ever wrote. But it is a study too of the inevitable decline of a love, however lyrical, which has no moral centre, and which therefore pursues a seasonal course from spring rapture to autumnal regret.

Nature was always to Tolstoy a partner in rather than a background to human destiny, and in no story is she more exquisitely involved in its drama. She conspires with the swelling passion and takes her colouring from its mood. As the girl sits in the shade of lime-trees waiting for her lover who has yet to declare himself, they are gathering

the harvest in the fields, and the creaking wagons, the
peasants moving in the distance, the sultry heat and the
singing voices, all enrich her expectancy, while the late
summer, in which this young love rises to its climax,
steeps it in the pathos of beauty doomed to decay.

Again, while she plays Mozart to her lover, the clear
summer night looks in at the open windows, the full moon
rises higher and shines more brightly and then the garden
is seen bathed in it. 'The lilac bushes, already beginning
to lose their leaves, were bright all over in every twig.
The flowers, all drenched with dew, could be distinguished from one another. In the avenues the light and
shade were so mingled that they seemed not trees and
little paths between, but transparent, quivering, and
trembling houses,' while out of the darkness rose 'the
fantasticaily shaped top of the poplar, which seemed as
though, for some strange inexplicable cause, it had halted
near the house, in the dazzling brightness above it,
instead of flying far, far away into the distant dark-blue
sky.'

Here, as so often again, Tolstoy embodied that exquisite rapture of the senses which reaches out beyond a
radiant awareness of the physical world to a height,
bounded indeed physically, but remote and immaterial.
And in a love of this kind between a man and a woman
there always comes, as he was to write many years later, a
moment when, for the woman at least, it 'has reached its
zenith, when it is unconscious, unreasoning, and with
nothing sensual about it,' when her whole being is
'stamped with those two marked characteristics, purity

and chaste love – love not only for him but for everybody and every thing, not for the good alone but for all that is in the world.'

Such was the smile in the soul of Katusha, before the sullen lust of Nekhlyudov stripped it of all but fear; such before the intrusion of a worldly young officer was the quiet peace at the heart of Liza in *Two Hussars*, as she sat at her window listening to the nightingales that sang in the moonlight and felt that 'life is a sweet and joyful thing for one who had some one to love and a pure conscience.' And such was the mood in which the girl of this story saw, as it seemed to her for the first time in her life, the sunrise after the night when she was convinced that Sergei Mihalovitch loved her. 'And such a night and such a morning,' as Tolstoy makes her say, 'I have never seen again.'

Yet, until her marriage, no flaw appears in this ecstatic naturalism, in which the intoxicated senses embrace everything in their delight, and judgment is not sublimated, but submerged in a mood of pure acceptance. It appears indeed to be ultimately moral, to make it so easy to be perfectly sinless, to love every one and to be loved by them. Even religion is in league with it. 'When the priest at the end of the service said, "The blessing of God be with you," it seemed to me that I felt instantly passing into me a physical sensation of well-being, as though a sort of light and warmth had rushed into my heart.'

And with this comes too a perfect self-assurance, that sense of commanding and commanded impulse which every artist and athlete experiences in moments of perfect functioning, which belongs to the horseman sitting his horse as though he were one with it, and which reveals itself in the inevitable but wholly unselfconscious style of all Tolstoy's best writing, to which we might apply the words of his heroine – 'I can't understand how I came by such composure, such decision, such exactness in my phrases. It was as though it were not I, but something apart from my own will was speaking in me.'

Disillusionment, however, inevitably follows marriage. The very satisfaction of the senses proves their limitation; engrossed now in a particular person, they no longer embrace the world at large or suggest a 'pure condition of soul'; and thus stripped of much of their sentimental glamour, they are felt only as the mediums of a restricted physical actuality. 'Loving was not enough for me after the happiness I had known in learning to love him. . . . I really was happy; but my torment was that this happiness cost me no sort of effort, no sort of sacrifice, while energy for effort, for sacrifice was fretting me.'

To be enervated and at last rendered hysterical by a sensuous attachment, unsupported by moral effort, was to be the tragedy of Anna Karenina. And in *Family Happiness* Tolstoy traced the same process working itself out in circumstances less violent and fatal.

The nature of the young wife and, through her, of her husband gradually deteriorates. Her energy, lacking moral direction, makes her restless and the 'quiet family life in the country with continual self-sacrifice, continual love for one another, and a continual sense in all things of a kind and beneficent 'Providence,' of which she had dreamt so expansively before her marriage, merely frets her taut nerves. Inevitably she is drawn to Petersburg, as Madame Bovary was drawn to Paris. There amid a vain fashionable activity she can indulge her senses more variously and so deaden her self-disgust.

But in doing so she alienates her husband. He grows detached and soured and their relations become stereotyped in a kind of disapproving friendliness. Like Anna Karenina too she is indifferent to her child because towards him also she feels no sustaining moral relation.

The climax of her demoralization comes when a coarse man makes love to her and she feels not only the vanity of a society beauty but an undeniable animal attraction. The last veil is stripped from the sensational passion which had seemed so eternal in her engagement days. It is revealed as a crude and carnal egotistic craving, like that which underlay all the false glitter of the society life from which she now turns in disgust.

She goes back to her old home, hoping there to recapture the enchantment which she had known. But what was once bathed in a warm light is now all cold. 'Everything was the same; the same gardens one could see from the window, the same path, the same seat out there above the ravine, the same nightingale's songs floating in from near the pond, the same lilac in full flower, and the same moon over our house and yet all so terribly, so incredibly changed! Everything so cold that might be so precious and so near one's heart! . . . I, too, am still the same, but I have no love nor desire of love, no longing for work, nor content with myself. And so remote and impossible seemed to me now my old religious ecstasies, my old love for him, and my old intense life, I could not have understood now what had once seemed so dear and right to me — the happiness of living for others.'

It is the same cry of disenchantment, the same confession of spiritual paralysis, which every Romantic has uttered, who has dreamed a merely sensuous dream, however paradisal, and woken, jaded, to the facts of life. No longer can the girl find in Nature a moral stimulus. She has learnt, as Coleridge learnt, that we receive from Nature only so far as we give. And so it is to a God, vaguely conceived in and above Nature that she appeals to 'restore me what was once so good in my soul, and teach me what to do, how to live.'

And Tolstoy, with that instinctive symbolism of which he was such a master, sets the concluding discussion between husband and wife on the possibilities of a new relationship against the background of an unsettled spring evening. On the same veranda where they had avowed a spring-like love with rapture in an autumnal setting, he conducts a resigned autumnal argument in a spring-like setting.

'Love is left, but not the same; its place is left, but it is all wasted away; there is no strength and substance in it, there are left memories and gratitude, but . . .' Outside in the garden the scent of lilac and bird-cherry was so strong 'that it seemed as if all the air was in flower; it came in wafts, now stronger and now weaker, till one longed to shut both eyes and ears and drink in that fragrance only.' But Nature can no longer seduce the disillusioned senses.

The young wife accepts her middle-aged husband's resignation and is content to regard him henceforth 'not as a
lover, but as an old friend.' Passion with all its possibilities of ecstasy and self-disgust is forsworn. No longer
craving the intoxication of love, she is delivered from its
terror. At last she can look into her husband's eyes as one
unexacting human being into another's, and a new feeling
of love for her children and their father 'laid the foundation of a new life and a quite different happiness.'

Such is the conventionally moral conclusion which explains the title of *Family Happiness*. And we have traced
the development of this early story at such length, because
it contains in germ all the elements of Tolstoy's later attitude to love, women, and marriage. The Masha of this
story, like the Natasha of *War and Peace*, escapes from
the unrest of her instincts into the nursery. Failing as a
lover, she is made to find peace and preoccupation as a
mother.

No one will deny that such an issue is true to life. It is
or was the normal issue of unsatisfactory mating. But
Tolstoy increasingly propounded it as the only moral relation possible to men and women in marriage. He could
not believe that love between a man and a woman might
be a self-sufficient ideal, which parenthood enhanced
without superseding, because of his view of woman's
innate inferiority as a merely instinctive being, and his
fear of her physical attraction. As the hero of his short
story *Oasis* says: 'Of women I knew only that they were
dangerous, and I was afraid of them,' and it is only when
his wife is dead and so has ceased to excite desire, that

Pozdnyshev, in *The Kreutzer Sonata*, can recognize in her a human being.

It was impossible, in Tolstoy's view, to love at once passionately and humanly, instinctively and intelligently, and since marriage, beneath a veil of sentiment, was an animal relation, motherhood was its only justification. It cost effort and sacrifice: it was the price which Nature exacted for the pleasures of the senses and by which she sought to restrain their selfish indulgence.

But motherhood, unless it is an extension of a truly human relationship already existing between husband and wife, can never be ideal, and is often as animal and egotistic as the passion in which it originated. Tolstoy, as we shall show, demonstrated this with approving, but to our mind pitiable, logic in the person of Natasha, that eager, adorable girl who ends as the tenacious matron wholly preoccupied with baby-linen. And the whole weakness of the moral, which, however subconsciously, he wished to be drawn from the fate of Anna Karenina, lay in his indifference to the loveless nature of her marriage, as an ignorant girl, and to the fact that such marriages, whatever be the consequences of breaking them, are essentially immoral.

He himself too was eventually to experience in his own home the limitations of the primitive and tenacious maternal instinct, which he sentimentally applauded as 'that wonderful and highest manifestation of Divinity on earth,' and to rebel as ineffectually against what he considered the selfishness and materialism of family life as against the consecrated license of marriage.

But the one revolt was the inevitable consequence of the other, and both were rooted in a sense of physical enslavement, which led him to try and moralize the instinctive instead of recognizing intelligence as a necessary factor in any ultimately moral and distinctively human relationship.

'Love without marriage,' he was to confess in the person of Levin, 'did not appeal to him.' But the secret of love with marriage, independent of the family which he exalted above it, he never really discovered. During the next twenty years he became far more deeply disillusioned of the senses and of the life of Nature which he loved but could never completely live, until he arrived at that conviction of the senselessness of life from which he wished to free himself by noose or bullet.

Family happiness, of which during these years he had his full share, could not save him from this. It afforded him in fact no such stable moral satisfaction as he suggested in the story which we have examined. It merely enlarged, as he discovered, the province of his egotism; it did not liberate him because it was the extension of an imperfect relationship. Here again he never learnt how the acquisitive instincts which he admired and even sentimentalized in all who obeyed without question the physical compulsion of Nature, but hated in himself, could be allied with a conscious creative purpose and so cease to tyrannize.

This indeed was the end which he was to seek with more and more anguish. But although he increasingly hated the senses, fearing the abyss of senselessness which gaped beneath their indulgence, he hated as much the conscious intelligence which showed him this abyss. But since the conscious intelligence has itself evolved from Nature, there can be no harmony for those who reject its critical questioning, as there can be no richness of life for those who content themselves with its negations. In a perfect art of life, as in all other perfect arts, criticism is implicit in a creative act. Only so can a man be liberated from sensual or mental egotism and the physical claims of Nature be reconciled with human ideals.

This fusion of the dual faculties of experience Tolstoy could never achieve and yet, without achieving it, he could never rise above the alternations of carnal pleasure and mental disgust. And it was because death annulled the former with a dread finality that it became increasingly the pivot of his inquiry and his despair.

§ 6

Under two aspects Death appealed to Tolstoy. When he was charged with the joy of living and felt himself part of an immense whole directed by a single will, death, which was also an expression of that will, had no terrors, but even heightened his enjoyment by associating it with danger. To quote from *Family Happiness* – 'I was so full of joy . . . and so tenderly I looked on myself and every one, that the thought of death came to me like a dream of bliss.'

Equally it attracted him, when wearied by the strife of thought and appetite, as a great liberator. In many places throughout his work he describes the approach of death as bringing with it an ecstatic indifference, a final relaxation. The images of life pass through the mind without evoking any feeling whether of pity, anger, or desire. Everything at last seems insignificant and the self dies before consciousness fails. Hence, he would say, that 'peace of the brow – that strange calm of the smooth forehead,' which strikes the onlooker so wonderfully in a dead body.

And later, in describing how he was attacked by a bear, lay under him and looked into his warm, large mouth, with its wet, white teeth, and felt he was about to die, he wrote – 'I often remembered that moment afterwards; and now whenever I think of death, I picture that situation to myself, because I have never been nearer to death than then. I recall it, reflect on it, make comparisons, and see that death – real, serious, and all-absorbing death – is, thank God, not dreadful. Everything becomes torpid then, and all that causes fear ceases to growl above one's head, and one's soul is easy and at peace.'

In both of these aspects, it is to be noted, death was conceived as purely physical, and if it was insignificant in the rush of life and might ultimately reduce the claims of life to insignificance, there were intermediate periods when it could only be regarded as a terrible fact. In such periods Tolstoy's vivid physical imagination intensified his suffering in exactly the same way as it intensified his appetites. His horror, as a boy, of his dying grandmother's swollen white hand and as a man of the corpses of Sebastopol was intense in proportion to his avid physical awareness. His revulsion from the body in decay

corresponded with his attraction to it in its strength, and
his own health which flowed and ebbed between extreme
exhilaration and threatened consumption paralleled, if it
did not condition, his feelings.

It has even been argued that the crisis which occurred
in middle-life was physical rather than spiritual in origin,
that it was dictated by the fact that he was 'no longer
expanding, but contracting, that his muscles were growing weaker, and his teeth falling out.' And Tolstoy himself has told how to his wife his continual talk about God
and religion was a sign of ill-health for which a doctor
should be consulted, 'whereas I knew I was ill and weak
because of the unsolved questions of religion and of God.'

It is indeed impossible to dissociate the spiritual from
the physical, nor is a spiritual conversion the less real or
necessary because a man can no longer enjoy the pride of
his body. One of the purposes of this book is to show
that there comes a point in human development when to
live the life of the Natural man is either impossible,
meaningless, or odious. The cause of this need not be so
much physical decline as mental and moral growth which
disturbs the bodily economy.

Such it was with Tolstoy, although a connection between his thought and his health may be traced throughout his life. And it was, as will be shown, when he was
ageing, that he became most oppressed by an animal
dread of decay and expressed his dread most coarsely.
For it was not only a sentimental regret for the decline of
beauty, exclusively associated with youth, which affected
him, but a sensuous loathing of wrinkles and unpleasant

breath, sweat, bad odour and loss of bodily shape, which he arbitrarily associated with advancing years. This coarse hatred of the physical was the exact counterpart of his coarse love of it, as when he delighted to come fresh from the fields and join his family circle, reeking of manure.

But already in the same year (his thirty-first) that he wrote *Family Happiness* he had, as a writer, presented death under three aspects. *Three Deaths* is rather a set of calculated variations on a given theme than an intimate expression of Tolstoy's own emotions towards it. He was to express that later in describing Prince Andrew's semi-mystical experience of death in *War and Peace*, in the harrowing realism of *The Death of Ivan Ilyitch*, and the wintry beauty of *Master and Man*. But objective and experimental as *Three Deaths* is, it presents death on three levels which were also characteristic of Tolstoy's view of life.

We are shown first the pampered, middle-class lady, stricken with consumption, who will not admit that she is dying but thinks by going abroad that she will recover, and who, when at last she is prevailed upon to receive the last consolations of religion, tries still to derive physical rather than spiritual hope from them, and dies painfully, protesting 'My God! why must it be?'

Uncle Fyodor's is the second death. He lies disregarded on the top of the stove: he has lain so for two months coughing away his life, unclean and untended. But he is a peasant, who, having lived with nature and endured much, like the Nikita of *Master and Man*, 'was

patient, and could wait for hours, even days, without growing restless or irritated. . . . The thought that he would
die . . . came upon him, seeming not very unpleasant,
nor very awful. Not unpleasant, because his life had been
no unbroken feast, but rather an incessant round of toil of
which he began to weary.'

The contrast between his acceptance of death and the
lady's feverish struggle for life is indeed exactly similar to
that which Tolstoy drew many years later between Nikita
and Vasili, although the issue was different.

The third death is that of a hewn tree. Here death is
divested of all feeling or suffering. It is clean and decisive.
It is a fact stripped of the sickness and sentiment which
clings like a fungus to distorted humanity.

But what Tolstoy emphasizes in each of these examples
is the isolation which death imposes on its victims, the
same isolation which the egotist knows, whenever he
ceases to find satisfaction in physical life. And the lady
alone feels it because she is an egotist. 'None of them care
anything about me,' she complains. 'They are all right,
and so they don't care. O my God!' And her doctor and
husband, rubbing their hands together over a case of wine,
justify her complaint.

Uncle Fyodor does not suffer in this way, but his situation is outwardly even more forlorn. No one thinks of
him, unless it be to wish that he would have done with
dying, while Fedya is callous enough to claim his boots
because he cannot want them again.

And lastly Nature is wholly indifferent to the hewn tree.
Indeed, 'the trees, more joyously than ever, extended their

branches over the new space that had been made in their midst.' As in *Hadji Murad*, where the nightingales which hush their songs while the mountaineers are done to death, start their trills once more as soon as the firing ceases, Tolstoy emphasizes the indifference of Nature to death by associating it with her unquenchable impulse to life.

Death, then, as he already felt, becomes agonizing to man in the degree to which he is conscious of this indifference. And he becomes so conscious when he outgrows an instinctive submission to life without discovering a spiritual serenity to take its place.

How agonizing such an intermediate state could be was now first deeply impressed upon Tolstoy in the autumn of 1860 when he witnessed the death of his brother Nicholas. From this moment, as he was to write later in *Anna Karenina*, he became horrified, not so much at death, as at life. The horror, as has been sufficiently shown, was already in his heart, but from this time it crept more and more into his consciousness until it became eventually an obsession. For his agony was now both physical and mental.

'All who knew and saw his last moments,' he wrote of his brother, 'say: "How wonderfully calmly, peacefully, he died"; but I know with what terrible pain, for not one feeling of his escaped me.' And if death proved terrible to his brother whose character he felt to be loftier and purer than his own, who actually practised the humility which he himself could only preach, how more than terrible must it prove in his own experience! Nicholas in his last hours had said that nothing was worse than death, had revealed his conviction that death was the end of all. 'And if he found nothing to cling to, what can I find? Still less!'

So Tolstoy argued a month after the event, an event which, in his own words, tore him terribly from life. For if there was nothing worse than death, there was also nothing worse than life. Life in fact was death. As he was to write in his essay, *On Life* – 'Life runs onwards towards destruction of our animal being; yet people vainly strive to preserve only that. Such success as is possible in that direction brings first satiety, then increasing pain, and it finally fails at death. The fear of death accompanies desire for a rich life.'

Yet one who desired this 'rich life,' who was possessed beyond hope of deliverance by his animal being, was doomed from the moment of birth to dissolution, was the slave of a ghastly physical dispensation.

And the more conscious he became, the more intolerably this enslavement weighed upon him: the more the question 'Why?' dinned in his ears: the more imminent seemed the inevitable departure: the more certain seemed it that the destination was nowhere. 'Whence? Why? Whither?' – such were the questions of which Tolstoy was more and more to demand of life an answer, because, unanswered, life *was* death. Death spoke mockingly to him of life, and life of death. They flowed into one another. For a good life is the condition of a good death and fear of death is the proof of a disjointed life.

For long Tolstoy did not recognize how intimately

they were involved, but instinctively he acted upon the truth of their connection. All his struggles with himself, with his sensualism and his pride were struggles with the fact of death in his own life. For 'death was not so far off as he had been in the habit of thinking. He felt it in himself too.' It was this that drove him to physical work and to emulation of the peasant, who subdued his body by toil and acquired the habit of self-renunciation by necessity. Thus he strove to ease the pressure of egotism, both mental and physical, which by isolating made life a constant rehearsal of the last agony of death; and thus he came at last to denounce as vicious and valueless the whole physical world in which he felt himself to be snared.

But it was long before he arrived at this ultimate denial or realized the intimate connection between the terror of physical death and his self-loathing, the consequence as it was of the conviction of moral Death which followed not only sensual aberrations but also every self-limiting act. And only when marriage, philosophy, and every kind of physical activity had failed to smother his fear, did he seek definitely to banish death from life by divorcing spirit from flesh. He never succeeded in banishing it, because life forbids such a divorce. A death-tormented man he always remains because he was a self-divided one.

Every man of genius has of course experienced the sense of isolation alike from God and his kind which Tolstoy knew. It would seem indeed to be a necessary condition of all absolute experience. Religion, as Professor Whitehead has recently written, 'is what the individual does with his own solitariness. It runs through three stages if it evolves to its final satisfaction. It is the transition from God the void to God the enemy, and from God the enemy to God the companion.' And the second stage cannot be evaded. The most poignant cry in the history of the world, 'My God, my God, why hast thou forsaken me?' proves that even the man who knew God more intimately than any other experienced it.

But Tolstoy felt the indifference and hostility of life, not through the mortal agony of spiritual loneliness and bodily suffering, but through the moral agony of spiritual weakness and bodily appetite.

And the death of his brother Nicholas first made him fully conscious of this agony – 'The truth I have learned in thirty-two years,' he wrote, 'is that the position in which we are placed is terrible.' And earth-bound as he was, it seemed to him that one thing only was left, 'a dim hope that there, in Nature, of which we become part in the earth, something will remain and will be found.'

He would have done well to remember this in later years. For there can be no real victory of the spirit which is not founded in Nature; her forces, so cruel as mere forces, are yet the agents of light as well as of darkness, of the purest human consciousness as of animal nescience. Nature in her purely physical aspect is indeed indifferent to our ideals. But our ideals derive from her too. They are in harmony with Nature, but not merely with that Nature 'of which we become part in the earth.' It was because Tolstoy's conception of Nature was physical that he could not find in her the something which he sought and so at last was driven to deny her.

The power to transform the forces of Nature into ideals of conduct and perfect creative expression, to pass from a rule of physical law into a realm of spiritual liberty, in which the law is not transgressed but is interpreted at once intelligently and morally, is the final patent of man's humanity. Nature cannot be indifferent to such ideals, because she is at the base of them.

Tolstoy then was right to hope that in Nature something would be found, as he was right later to condemn all art, which drew feebly upon the organic sources of life. But his estimate of the truth or falsehood of art by its appeal to the peasant betrayed how limited his conception was of truth to Nature, and how arbitrary his exclusion of some of the highest human faculties from the sphere of her originating influence. And in the peasant's attitude to death, which he already contrasted with that of the pseudo-civilized, the same limitation existed.

Uncle Fyodor accepted death without a struggle, because life had never allowed him to be self-indulgent. But it had also never allowed him to be finely self-expressive. He had escaped being morbid by being, to some extent, stunted.

That already Tolstoy hoped to discover the same peace by the same denial of the value of life is proved by the fact that he wrote in the Diary which he kept in the Caucasus – 'There is something especially gratifying and grand in indifference to life: and I enjoy the feeling. How fortified against all things I seem so long as I can feel firmly persuaded that I have nothing to look for save death!'

But there is a higher conception of death than this and it is the only conception which will bring lasting peace to one who has grown conscious of himself. Those who have loved life well, who have wrung from it all its joyous significance and realized all its spiritual possibilities, love death as a culminating expression of such a life.

For in every great spiritual experience the body seems to die, because it lives ideally. It passes out of our consciousness and we become, while still ourselves, one with the creative mind of the universe. Yet this life of the spirit does not, in Tolstoy's sense, 'depend on the death of the body,' but on its perfeét quickening. In this life, at least, the body co-operates with and sustains the spirit.

Yet to have known this experience often and intimately not only robs the thought of death of its terrors but may even make it a source of joyous expeétation. Death invites us because it suggests a complete identification with the reality which we have known in our most creative moments. Such questions as whether our personality survives cease to trouble us. A material longing for personal survival is displaced by a conviétion of spiritual immortality. For a positive disinterestedness is the quality of all pure spiritual experience, and so far as personality consciously intrudes upon such experience, it limits it.

Such an ultimate affirmation of self is the condition of perfeéted consciousness and is of another order than the natural man's resignation of self. It is a positive love of death corresponding to a positive love of life, as the peasant's acquiescence in death corresponds to his acquiescence in life. And only by this extension of conscious personality into creative consciousness can the man who has ceased to be instinctively loyal to Nature reconcile himself with the fact and the thought of death.

Tolstoy could forget himself in the rush of physical life but not in the ecstatic poise of spiritual experience or of perfect moral relations. Consequently much of his moral teaching was merely physical hygiene in disguise – excellent counsel indeed for bodies jaded and enervated by indulgence, but affording no more than a basis for moral perfection, which depends on the cultivation of the mind as well as on the health of the body, and on the co-ordination of the two.

The vigorous body of the peasant, hardened by constant manual labour, and the lack of grasping egotism which often goes with it, are moral as all that lives and dies according to nature is moral. But this is not the highest morality nor can a man who has outgrown a physical acquiescence relapse into it without denying the particular divinity within him. Such a relapse is forbidden to all in whom reason has lit her fatal and sublime lamp.

Its light may be dimmed, but it cannot be put out. Hard physical labour may temper the appetites of those whose minds it has stunted, and it may materially assist towards the balancing of more highly developed natures. But it cannot silence the mind which has begun to question.

Tolstoy was slowly to realize this, but it led him to deny Nature instead of seeking how she might co-operate with human understanding. And so the discord remained and the fear of death which was the penalty of discord. For him 'the busy dance of things that pass away' was an absolute tragedy, because he could not realize in his own being the idea of life of which all beauty is a recurrent image.

The One remains, the many change and pass;
Heaven's light forever shines, Earth's shadows fly;
Life, like a dome of many-coloured glass,
Stains the white radiance of Eternity,
Until Death tramples it to fragments. – Die,
If thou would'st be with that which thou dost seek!

Tolstoy could never travel Shelley's way; the body ruled him too powerfully for him to spiritualize it. And yet for one so conscious of himself there was no other way of liberation. Only by loving life disinterestedly could he cease to fear death. But to come to terms with life was as impossible to him as to come to terms with the society and the age in which he lived. He was too conscious of the vileness of the body when it is exploited by the mind, to come to false terms.

Therein lies his nobility and the searching truth of much of his denunciation of our predatory civilization. But by this great refusal he rejected also the terms of a true acceptance. For to hate the body is as fatal to self-emancipation as to indulge it.

§ 7

Previous to his brother Nicholas' death Tolstoy had been engaged in educational experiments at Yasnaya Polyana and had travelled abroad. With the former we have not space here to deal in any detail. Tolstoy, both in his theory and practice as a teacher was indebted to Rousseau, but he was impelled also by his own particular conviction of the innate value of the peasant and his own dislike of 'the privileged Liberal circle' which sought to impose its knowledge and its errors upon 'the people, to whom it is a stranger.'

The Liberal, on the other hand, might well have replied that Tolstoy's professed humility towards the inspired ignorance of the people was not really disinterested, that he was seeking salvation for himself in a more primitive strata of life, where by associating with peasant children on a level of assumed equality he might regain that sense of innocence so dear to him in memory.

To confuse the childlike with the childish, the innocence of perfect insight with that of ignorance is an act of treachery to the mind towards which all who are weary of mental warfare and sceptical, as they well may be, of a barren intellectualism whether literary or scientific, are sorely tempted. Childhood with its instinctive self-absorption, its tireless curiosity and its disinterested affection, is indeed an image of perfect living, but one upon which the grown man cannot model himself truly, if, in the process, he seeks to cast off the burden of experience.

Tolstoy became disenchanted of the village school of Yasnaya Polyana, as he had of his Caucasian life, primarily because his educational theories were based on a half-truth. And the value of his experiment and his theories lay rather in his generous recognition of the instincts upon which all true education must be built than in any clear view of how the building should be done. Modern educationists have reaffirmed scientifically his efforts to rescue originality from the dead hand of external discipline. But the evils of false discipline do not justify anarchy and the spectacle of the village children kicking in a heap on the floor when they were not interested, although it testified to the free play of youthful instincts which he sought to foster, provided little evidence of their education.

Many years later he was to complain that conventional education 'consists of those forms and that knowledge which will separate a man from others. Its object is the same as that of cleanliness; to separate one from the mass of the poor, in order that those cold and hungry people may not see how we make holiday.'

That a false class bias has influenced education, no one will deny. But cleanliness is no less a virtue, although it separates a man from others. And the same is true of intelligence. Both may be used as weapons of class arrogance and division, as in the ceremonial cleanliness of the Pharisee or the elegant cynicism of the pseudo-aristocrat. But the cure of this lies in the more intelligent education both of the poor and the privileged, and not in a denial of intelligence.

And it was scarcely true that conventional education, even in Russia, 'never produced men of whom humanity had need, but only those of whom a depraved society had.' Tolstoy, for reasons already cited, detested the official, although as an artist he was to admit that even a Karenin, beneath the masque of officialdom, could be pathetically human. But his experience of state methods, peculiarly callous and brutal as they were in Russia, had convinced him that sympathy and imagination could not survive official routine. As the official remarks in *Resurrection*: 'in my position I do not permit myself to swerve an inch from the letter of the law, just because I am a man and might be influenced by pity.'

And Tolstoy's intolerance of such an attitude was justified by such incidents within his own experience as the fate of a soldier, who under great provocation had struck his officer, and who was executed after Tolstoy had pleaded unsuccessfully against the death sentence. The action of peasants who did all they could for the prisoner until his execution was indeed in striking contrast with the barbarity of such military judges.

Such incidents help to explain why he could never believe that public service might appeal to men as an ideal, as it has in England even in the past, and will, we are convinced, increasingly do in the future under the influence of Socialist aims and thought.

For officials, as a class, reflect the tone of the society which they serve. And Russian autocracy was corrupt. Even in England the public servant, like the public schools from which he has mostly been drawn, has too often combined with a real sense of responsibility and human tact the arrogance and insensitiveness of a privileged ruling class.

But no one could say that the public schools have never produced Englishmen of whom humanity had need or that the only hope of producing such men lay in abandoning intellectual effort or training.

'Go to the people,' wrote Tolstoy, 'to learn what they

want! If they do not value the art of reading and writing which the intellectuals force upon them, they have their reason; they have other spiritual needs, more pressing and more legitimate. Try to understand these needs and help them to satisfy them.'

In itself such advice was good and applied equally to those in all classes, who could derive little benefit from a literary or scientific education, but much from a more practical one. Always however with Tolstoy it contained the implication that the peasant's anti-intellectualism was an absolute virtue, that not only was it 'harmful to force upon the people a culture they do not demand,' but that culture itself was valueless because the people spurned it.

The false culture of privileged Russian society was indeed valueless, but that there was no intrinsic virtue in ignorance and mental sloth, he himself had already found in his dealings with the peasant. The practical and the spiritual needs of humanity have been served quite as much by men with minds quickened and enlarged by 'the art of reading and writing' as by those who have laboured at lowly tasks in simple faith. And among those who have so laboured the finest have not scorned knowledge but have been like Burns' father as Carlyle described him: 'a man of thoughtful, intense character, as the best of our peasants are, valuing knowledge, possessing some and open-minded for more, of keen insight and devout heart, friendly and fearless; a fully unfolded man seldom found in any rank in society and worth descending far in society to seek.'

Humanity in fact owes as much to Caxton as to Hodge, and it would be as harmful to starve potential organizers, thinkers, poets or scientists of the culture they need as it is to force upon others a culture they do not demand.

The truth was that Tolstoy could not dissociate culture from the luxurious and selfish refinement which masqueraded under its name in Russia. In condemning the abuses incidental to the advance in man's mental control of life, he failed to appreciate the immensely beneficent uses to which such control could be turned, and by sanctifying ignorance he was, like the Church which he was later so rightly to attack, helping to preserve the conditions that made the poor the slaves of, and to that extent participators in, a predatory civilization.

But it was above all because he could not cultivate himself in the sense of directing his instincts rationally that he idealized the peasant who was saved by circumstances from a false refinement and from those dire problems of conduct and conscience which rational growth involve.

Yet arbitrary and hateful as class distinctions have been, only fanaticism can deny that mankind reveals many levels of consciousness, ranging from the savage to the saint, and from the simpleton to the genius. Man's moral value does not of course necessarily coincide with his mental equipment. The highest morality is in the last resort the highest intelligence, but intelligence need not be moral at all.

So far as a man loses the instinctive virtues in developing his intellect, he loses as much as, if not more than, he gains. And the education of a privileged class has undoubtedly in the past tended to entail such loss. But the aim of the educator should surely be, not to preserve the instinctive virtues at the expense of intelligence, but to develop the two in harmony. Only by such education can men be freed from the class limitations which impoverish alike the socially favoured and the socially oppressed. Men will vary then not according to class consciousness but real consciousness. Both the peasant and the scientific expert can serve the needs of humanity, but their moral worth, their standing in a true scale of culture, will depend upon the degree to which they are intelligently humane.

Tolstoy, however, loved the natural too dearly and hated the restrictive tendencies of reason too fiercely to realize that the vicious elements in both could only be removed by the union of the two. And so when eventually the peasant child, like the 'intellectual,' failed to satisfy his need, he imputed it to his own corruption. But what he called corruption was in fact intelligence. He could not for long adapt himself to the peasant's primitive outlook, because in such an outlook his critical being was not expressed.

Yet when he travelled in Europe, in France, Germany, Switzerland and England, countries in which a sympathetic observer might, even in 1857, have detected at least the germ of a more human and responsible conception of life at work in the still barbarous body of society, he saw only legalized and rational cruelty. Two incidents in particular confirmed his scepticism of the 'progress' preached by intellectual Liberals – the spectacle of an execution and the treatment of a poor musician by prosperous English tourists in a Swiss hotel.

To take another's life impulsively in battle cannot shock

the sensibility so much as the spectacle of an execution from which there is no escape in action. Yet although there is to-day a strong, and in our opinion convincing, moral argument against all taking of life, it is surely less morally reprehensible to execute a proved criminal, in the supposed interests of society, than to kill fortuitously in battle an opponent with whom you have no personal quarrel and of whose merits you have no personal knowledge.

But to Tolstoy legalized murder was far more terrible even than murder by battle. He had indeed already come to condemn the latter, but he was still to describe it exultantly as an artist and applaud the heroic qualities associated with it.

Nothing, however, in his view could justify capital punishment. It was savagery divested of all the qualities which appealed to the savage in himself; and to the rational arguments advanced in its favour he could not listen. At the same time the rational arguments which he later advanced against it were very unconvincing. He was to argue, for example, in *The Kingdom of God is Within You* that murderers commit their acts of violence because the law acts with violence against them. 'We cannot give up the use of violence,' he supposed them saying, 'because we are surrounded by violent ruffians.' This argument, applicable as it is to modern war, defies the facts and the psychology of murder.

But Tolstoy's horror of capital punishment was essentially physical, not rational. 'I understood, not with my mind but with my whole being,' he wrote later, 'that no theory of the reasonableness of our present progress can justify this deed; and that though everybody from the creation of the world, on whatever theory, had held it to be necessary, I knew it to be unnecessary and bad; and therefore the arbiter of whatever is good and evil is not what people say and do, and is not progress, but is my heart and I.'

The ambiguity of this appeal to the individual heart, as to a faculty opposed to the head, was to characterize all Tolstoy's teaching, and, as will be shown, explains the perversities which marred later his really profound inquiry into the credentials of art.

The quality, however, of his feelings, as he watched the head of a living man being severed and heard it thump into a box, may be estimated from what he wrote years later of an impending execution. 'The image of the woman Sophie Perovsky especially oppressed me. I pictured clearly to myself how she placed her head in the noose, and how she involuntarily adjusted it, moving her head till the noose lay under her windpipe; and then, when the stool had been pushed from beneath her feet and the cord pressed the soft gristle of her throat tight to the hard vertebræ of her nape, she suddenly felt a rush of blood to her head and writhed with her whole body. . . . I suffocated and repeatedly swallowed saliva to assure myself that my throat was not yet squeezed up. . . . I saw those protruding eyes fixed in amaze on the inexorable nearness of something terrible, and the blue face under the black cap. . . . The horror of it all! The horror!'

The vivid physical imagination shown here explains the violence of Tolstoy's revulsion against capital punishment, as indeed all his other revulsions. If he had written, 'I understood not with my mind but with my whole body,' he would have described the experience more exactly. It was because he experienced the victim's sensations with a morbid intensity unrelieved by even an element of rational detachment, that he felt that nothing could justify this deed. He felt it physically rather than morally.

The incident of the poor musician described in *Lucerne* seemed to Tolstoy another proof of the fatal warping of natural sympathies by Western education. But the in-difference of the English tourists in a luxurious hotel towards a poor but talented man who had tried to please them with his art was typical only of insensitive pluto-cracy. To condemn the progressive tendencies of Western civilization on the evidence of the manners of a class de-moralized by unearned wealth and social privilege, was altogether too sweeping. And Tolstoy's own treatment of the old musician was strangely lacking, as Kropotkin has pointed out, in real charity. In his anxiety to reprove the offending tourists, he was himself guilty of the insensitive-ness against which his reproof was directed. To make a public object lesson of an injured man by ostentatiously entertaining him in the circle which had humiliated him was an act of which the really humane Tchekhov, for example, would have been quite incapable. He would have sympathized too deeply with the victim to victimize him anew, thanking God that he was not as these Sadducees.

Such incidents as these could not of course have dis-illusioned Tolstoy of the West, had he not approached it with a conviction that 'the instinctive, primordial cravings

. . . are the best,' and that reason deadened these cravings while supplying nothing to take their place. This view of reason as inevitably the negation of instinct and of instinct as always beneficently inspired, is entirely alien to the practical and meliorative spirit of the West.

In later life Tolstoy held it more temperately, but his bias against attempts consciously to control and direct instinct always remained. At this time he wrote, 'Civilization is *good*, barbarism is evil; freedom *good*; slavery *evil*. Now this imaginary knowledge annihilates the instinctive, beatific, primitive craving for the *good* that is in human nature. And who will explain to me what is freedom, what is despotism, what is civilization, what is barbarism? . . . One, only one infallible guide we have – the universal Spirit which penetrates all collectively. . . . And this one unerring voice rings out louder than the noisy, hasty, development of culture.'

So far as culture destroys 'the universal spirit which whispers to us to draw closer to one another,' Tolstoy's attack upon it was justified. But so far as this universal spirit is confined to 'instinctive, primordial cravings,' it whispers also other less benevolent injunctions. The principle of internecine conflict is at least as evident in Nature as that of mutual help, and only by his reason can man learn to discriminate between the creative and destructive impulses which he inherits from her. Certainly he may use it merely to exploit the latter, and we know now that the savage possesses virtues and a native insight into the laws of life for which the science of civilization is in some ways a poor substitute.

In 1857, too, it is well to remember, the claims of science were as uncritically championed as opposed. And Tolstoy would have been right if he had only contended that a mastery of the material forces of life did not necessarily increase human happiness and might very well diminish it, or that natural and human evolution, even if they overlapped, were distinct in kind. Instead, however, he claimed that the two tendencies were finally and fatally opposed, and the fact that science could not in itself ensure moral progress and might indeed facilitate human suicide, led him to sanctify the sometimes inspired and sometimes vicious ignorance of savagery.

It mattered not that he had already disproved the primitive in his own experience. His dissatisfaction with the artificial life which seemed to him the only existing substitute for it compelled him to continue his attempts. Thought, as he knew it and as he observed it in those who claimed to be most civilized, either poisoned men's roots in natural life or enabled them to exploit their most vicious appetites. It was a disease which separated man from his kind, dried up his generosity, and intensified his egotism. That it was a disease through which man had to pass to achieve a finer health than the purely physical, that reason could not become organic without first being disorganic, he never contemplated.

The conditions in the Russia of his day confirmed his blindness to the possibility of such an evolution. For he not only shared the Slavophil view of Russia as presenting a problem different from Europe, but he claimed that she, with her mass of peasants uneducated and uncivilized in the Western way, was in advance of Europe. As he wrote later, 'You dream that so we should walk behind Europe, though in fact, as far as the people's consciousness goes, we are a thousand miles ahead of Europe.'

This conviction was grounded both in a reasonable hostility to the Russian ruling class which reflected all the worst qualities of European culture and in his instinctive sympathy not only with the Russian peasant, but with the wild nomads whose life he had shared and in whose festivals he was to take part. So much more real, for example, did the struggle for life under primitive agricultural conditions or the horse-races of the Bashkirs seem to him, despite the flies and dirt, than the fraud and stupidity of English Parliamentary debates as described by Dickens. And if these were the results of submitting to the rationalizing influences, which, since the Renaissance, had been the dynamic of European culture, why should Russia travel the same road?

Few of course will deny the folly of attempting to impose an alien culture on a people, whose development, if it is to be real and stable, must be autonomous. But the potentialities of human nature are essentially the same in Russia as elsewhere, and the mass of the people there are still primitive in their faith and their passions, because a corrupt autocracy, supported by an equally corrupt Church, thought it to their interest to keep them so. That they so often combine a simple and ecstatic religious faith with a capacity for sordid cruelty merely proves the fallibility of 'primordial cravings' in themselves. And those who applaud the Russian peasant's simple faith have no right to complain of his barbarism. For the two are complementary.

The Russian soul may indeed be, as Dostoevsky believed, more universal in its aspirations and its sympathy than any other, at once more deeply rooted in earth and more absolute in its spiritual demands. It may be its destiny 'to show to Europe a way to escape from its anguish . . . to instil into her a brotherly love for all men's brothers, and in the end perhaps to utter the great and final word of universal harmony.'

But the new consciousness to which Tolstoy fruitlessly aspired and which Dostoevsky conceived in anguish is not sought only in Russia. Modern literature elsewhere reveals men struggling to reconcile an instinctive love of life with an intellectual rejection of it, as modern life elsewhere reveals the conflict of individual and social impulses. The forces in opposition may vary in strength and proportion, and in the Russian soul the conflict may be more extreme and elemental. But there as elsewhere the solution, the reconciliation in man of the two aspects of God, His force and His reason, cannot be achieved by a denial of one of them, by idealizing in short the primitive man who is as prone to simple savagery as simple wisdom.

The conviction then of the absurdity of the belief in 'progress' which haunted Tolstoy during his travels in Europe was essentially irrational. For it was the principle of conscious reason which he rejected as well as the

> barren optimistic sophistries
> Of comfortable moles

who were content to believe that 'all evolves and I evolve with it.'

But the necessity of reason is not disproved by its misuses or of civilization, because in the process of its development it makes men consciously vicious. Without a consciousness of vice man cannot consciously strive after virtue. It may even be that some men, as Dostoevsky believed, must *will* vice, must *consciously* outrage their finer instincts, must challenge pain and degradation by seeking it, before they can emancipate their soul from their senses. But Tolstoy knew too well in himself how hard and bitter was the conflict between man's animal inheritance and the demands of his humanity to admit its necessity.

It was easier to invest the primitive man with an unerring craving for good and to contrast his healthy integrity with the meanness and sickliness of the selfishly cultivated. As a modern poet has written,

> Life murmurs from the waste
> Beneath the mind . . . who made the reasoning part
> The jailer of the wild gods in the heart?

And it was convenient to suppose that the wild gods were also the good gods, infallible in their commands.

Europe then outraged the natural man in Tolstoy rather than the moral. Loth to confess how great a part intelligence must play in any high morality, he comforted himself by observing how false were its claims to an absolute prerogative. He thus denied evolution as a social, political and historical theory, some twenty years before he denied it in reference to himself.

Certainly in Germany after visiting the Wartburg where Luther was confined after the Diet of Worms and seeing the room in which he began his translation of the Bible, he noted in his Diary – 'Luther was great.'

But he did not realize the extent to which the Western Civilization which he rejected was the logical outcome of that great protesting personality. Luther indeed was primitive enough to please him, but although in some ways he plunged men back into barbarism, he also released the reason of the West.

And possibly Tolstoy himself may prove to have been the Luther of a later age. For he too was to challenge the established Church with the sword of its own Scriptures, was to despise the wisdom and the graces of humanism because of its corruptions, and was to plough the soil from which a new humanity might spring rather than realize that humanity in himself.

But if Wartburg was to inspire the later Tolstoy, it was the neighbourhood of Geneva which satisfied him most at this time. There, in the same village where Rousseau's Julie lived, his being melted into Nature as Rousseau's had. There beauty and nature seemed indeed one, no longer divided by a conscience which measured virtue or a reason that sifted truth. There the wild gods smiled blandly and the heart might escape its jailer.

Tolstoy rejected the West, not only because the path it had chosen was too difficult, but because the seductive countryside upon which it had turned its back was too inviting.

'I love Nature,' he wrote from Switzerland, 'when, though it surrounds me on all sides and extends unendingly, I am part of it. I love it, when on all sides I am surrounded by hot air, and that same air rolls away to unending distance, and those same sappy leaves of grass which I crush as I sit on them, form the green of the boundless meadows; when those same leaves which, fluttering in the wind, run their shadows across my face, form also the dark blue of the distant forests; while the same air one breathes makes the deep, light blue of the immeasurable sky; when you do not exult and rejoice alone in Nature, but when around you myriads of insects buzz and whirl, and beetles, clinging together, creep about, and all around you birds overflow with song.'

St. Francis preached to the birds and doubtless would have done to the beetles too, if the occasion had arisen. But while he called himself their brother, he never forgot that he was their elder brother. But to Tolstoy the greatest happiness was to become as they and the sharpest pain to awake to his wounded manhood and know that he had eaten of the tree of good and evil and was banished from their world.

It was because the West reminded him of this banishment that he turned his back upon it in disgust. Baffled alike in his attempts to revert to the primitive and to relate the primitive to the rational, with his love of life darkened by his dread of death, Tolstoy at the age of thirty-two had already approached the abyss into which seventeen years later he was to gaze appalled. All the elements of the terrible drama, which Mihailovsky was later to describe him as carrying in his soul, had even now taken shape and substance.

And with him 'one asks oneself what such a man is going to do, how can he live, how shall he avoid that poisoning of his consciousness which at every step intrudes into the pleasures of a satisfied need?'

Already this question had become paramount with Tolstoy, and each attempt which he made to answer it had failed. No physical activity, it seemed, could quell his accusing egotism, while every mental activity exasperated it. Only in the act of writing was the tension relaxed, which possibly explains the surprising fact of his defence of art for art's sake in a paper which he read to a literary society shortly before his brother's death.

But that death had deprived him even of the happy refuge of art. In its shadow, deepened by a suspicion of consumption in himself, literary activity began to seem but self-indulgence. It too brought little moral satisfaction because it reflected only his moral confusion. Even to remind 'Society' that its pleasures and amusements were not the pleasures and amusements of all mankind, to explain to it 'the true sense of the phenomena of progress,' to wake up, if only in the few 'the conscience of the feeling of justice,' was in some sense to live a lie, to gratify his vanity and evade his own inner problem by presuming to solve that of the world at large.

The complete failure also of his practical efforts to champion justice as an Arbiter of Peace between landowners and emancipated serfs emphasized his want of adaptability and threw him back in disgust and defiance upon himself; while such incidents as a Police raid upon his house and schools during his absence added to his conviction of the viciousness of Government.

Already, then, in 1860 the need which Tolstoy felt of personal salvation was so acute that it promised rapidly to 'destroy all other interests, just as the creeper suffocates all other plants.' Already too he had begun to define this need in his relation with peasants and women, art, science and government, war and the fact of death.

But there was still one relation which might bring him peace, where all others had failed — that of marriage. He hesitated to try it. All the doubts which had assailed him during his engagement to Valeria Arsenev returned. So late as August, 1862, he wrote with prophetic insight in his Diary — 'Ugly mug! Do not think of marriage; your calling is of another kind.'

But in the following month he was married to Sophie Behrs, a girl of eighteen, with whose family he had long been intimate, and for nearly fifteen years he tried to forget that his calling was of another kind.

PRELUDE TO BATTLE

PRELUDE TO BATTLE

§ I

IT is scarcely fair to judge Countess Tolstoy by the Auto-biography which she wrote in old age under a deep sense of injury. But so far as it confirms impressions of her character derived from other sources, it may be relied upon.

Few women can have had more of a vocation for marriage and motherhood. All her claims to literary and artistic interests were, we feel, subservient to this. Like many very practical and hard-working women, she was too engrossed in the fact of living to ponder the truth of life, and at heart she considered any such pondering a weakness or even a pose. Orthodox herself in religion and practically humanitarian, she could not understand a nature unable to accommodate itself to a standard faith or to forget the causes of poverty and oppression in particular acts of charity.

Her admirable efficiency was due to her acceptance of facts and insensitiveness to ideas, and no one could have exemplified more convincingly what Tolstoy had written to Valeria Arsenev, 'one can live splendidly in the world, if one can work and love, work for that which one loves, and love that at which one works.' But she also exemplified what Serpuhovsky says to Vronsky in *Anna Karenina*, 'Women are more material than men. We make something immense out of love, but they are always *terre à terre.*'

Tolstoy's denial to women of a free intelligence, his

conception of them as made only for child-bearing, was dictated by his own crude servitude to their physical attraction, but it was doubtless also confirmed by observance of his wife's nature. All his intimate pictures of women date from his marriage, and although he could draw women of a simple and saintly piety after the model of his Aunt Tatiana, he never drew one whose intelligence was not subservient to her instincts.

It is interesting therefore to note that shortly after his marriage he wrote a farce, entitled *The Contaminated Family*, in which he attacked with rather laboured humour the new ideas on woman's emancipation, suggesting, as Tennyson did in *The Princess*, that such women must be merely intellectual poseurs really interested in nothing but love-making and dress, and that all rationalists were prigs and egotists, suffering from the 'accursed stamp of intellectuality.' In maliciously caricaturing the 'intellectual' who wishes to educate the girl he is going to marry, he may have forgotten his own moral efforts in this direction. But the bias against the free woman, which was also to underly his treatment of *Anna Karenina*, was typical, and in preventing a really human conception of marriage, made inevitable his final flight from family life.

His wife's perfect absorption, however, in physical life and her practical energy enabled him for a period to temper the introspection which was sapping his instinctive strength. The process, as we shall see, went on in a subterranean fashion and particularly in the two great novels which were to be the glory of the period. But it went on,

for the most part, subconsciously. He too became physically absorbed in his art, as in life. He ceased thinking of
it as a lie because it was associated with incessant family
activities.

The physical gaiety of the man, his native kindliness,
his unquenchable animal spirits found at last a natural
expression. Preoccupied as we are in this book in tracing
his inner drama we have little space to give to this side of
his nature. It is well therefore to emphasize here that
always, even in old age, he was capable of an ebullient
good humour, of tricks and jests, and spontaneous horse-
play. It was not a subtle humour, as may be judged from
its literary expression where it is generally either sly or
proverbial, but it could be rich, vital and earthy. In the
man it was a happy outflowing of the same urgent physical
energies which in passive moments tortured his conscience.

His early married life was so happy because these
energies could find an uncensored outlet. There were
drives, walks, music and singing. There were private
theatricals for which he wrote a farce at which he laughed
until he nearly died. And among the visitors there was a
preponderance of youth, of youth as lyrical as his wife's
younger sister, Tanya, whose wild impulsive gaiety was to
be immortalized on Natasha's lips.

Incessant action too forbids thought and Countess Tolstoy was indefatigable. If he stopped working, she felt
dull, because there was nothing for her to copy in the few
hours which she could spare each day from the demands
of a regularly increasing family. 'Prepare, prepare work

for me,' she would insist, and in responding Tolstoy had little time in which to weigh, as later in an essay on Zola he was to weigh and find wanting, the worth of work as an end in itself.

Marriage then seemed to justify his egotism by extending its range, to acquit pleasures which his conscience had previously condemned as gross and self-indulgent, because they involved responsibilities and a life of incessant activity. He was too absorbed in developing and working on his estate and in providing for the future of his children to accuse himself of interested motives, although the history of Levin remains to prove that subconsciously at least the self-accusation still continued.

For about fifteen years, however, it could not subdue his happiness. He was playing too vigorously the part of an Old Testament patriarch to let the ethic of the New Testament disturb him. He allowed the elementary forces of life to dictate his conduct and his expression and consequently he wrote with the same instinctive fertility with which he lived.

§ 2

That literary creation was to Tolstoy akin to physical activity explains the obliviousness with which he devoted himself to it at this time as it does his revulsion from it later. We have already remarked the physical quality of his perception. The characters also to whom he attributed excellence were those who surrendered with an unconscious wisdom to forces beyond their control, whether it was the commander-in-chief Kutuzov or the peasant

Platon, while he delighted to disparage the officious and heartless self-assertion of a Napoleon or a petty staff-officer.

But his style even more intimately reveals an instinctive dictation. His description of the ease of perfect self-expression as of something apart from his own will speaking in him was applicable even to his later didactic writing, in which he was to confess that his thoughts had led him into positions which he had never contemplated.

Writing, in fact, afforded him the same satisfaction as hunting or scything, until conscious thought destroyed the unity of the experience. In it he relieved the tension of his being by expressing it. So long as he kept within certain physical limits he perfectly harmonized his faculties, and by so doing forgot himself.

All his best writing is devoid of self-consciousness. It is vividly realistic, yet we are not conscious of its realism. Its detail is a necessary, but never intrusive, element in an organic act of expression. Tolstoy observes with the uncanny precision of a wild creature whose life depends upon quickness of vision; he selects those details which are completely relevant, but both processes are instinctive, and perception and conception coincide. This coincidence was only perfect, however, so long as his perception was predominantly physical. His style degenerates, becoming even vague and diffuse, as soon as he deserts the concrete.

His habit of delineating character by reiterating certain

bodily peculiarities has been noticed before, and it is deeply significant. We know Vronsky, for example, by his white teeth, Karenin by his cracking fingers, Natasha by her restless, impulsive movement, Kutuzov by his lethargic stoutness, Napoleon by his puffy chest and yellow skin. Through these physical characteristics, examples of which could be multiplied, Tolstoy conveyed a psychological conception far more vividly than by any rational analysis.

But this method was so successful and so necessary because the characters which he was expressing were conceived physically. He applied it equally well to horses, to Vronsky's race-horse in *Anna Karenina* or the suffering horses in *Polikushka* or *Master and Man*. He was a master in fact of animal psychology, but his art falters, is at once less realistic and less real, as soon as he tries to express spiritual psychology. His women are so real because they are physically conceived. Anna Karenina, for example, is less a character than an exquisitely alluring body, and the same may almost be said of the enchanting Natasha as it may, in a grosser sense, of the peasant woman in *The Devil*.

This applies less to his men, because they were so often mouthpieces of his own dilemmas and aspirations and as such are artistically inferior. Certainly he could create peasants, because they too revealed an animal fidelity to life, but he inclined to idealize these falsely. Platon, for example, in *War and Peace*, is not artistically quite convincing. He is less a person than a personification of selflessness as Tolstoy conceived it, although he has cer-

tain physical features, notably his compact rotundity,
which do convey the idea of natural integrity which he is
meant to embody.

Tolstoy's powers and limitations as an artist illustrate
in fact from another angle his problem as a man and a
moralist. His failure to experience spiritual truth is
proved by his inability to express it, while his miraculous
delineations of the physical prove the power of his animal
nature.

To create characters in the round, a writer must be at
once interested and disinterested. His sensitiveness to life
must equal his need of self-expression, and his creative
range will depend upon the extent of the province over
which he can preserve the balance between external and
internal experience.

Tolstoy could only preserve it perfectly on the physical
or semi-physical level. When he writes of Nature, he is
both himself and Nature. He does not describe her; he
experiences and re-conceives her. When he writes of
animals, it is the same. He writes of horses as the perfect
horseman rides them, subduing himself to the rhythm of
their being. Similarly he expresses the speed and excitement of a hunt or a race or the subtle tortures of bodily
pain. Ivan Ilyitch's sufferings, for example, affect a
sensitive reader with actual nausea.

As a diviner of sensations he was supreme. For he
loved physical life at once so avidly and so curiously that
he wholly identified himself with it, and thus even in his
relations with human beings there was a quality of animal
telepathy and magnetism, as when he wrote, 'I love tacit

relations of the sort expressed with the eyes and almost imperceptible smiles.'[1]

But physical life was the only plane of experience which he entered by an unconditional act of imagination. The very intensity of his physical insight deprived him as an artist of spiritual insight, just as the intensity of his appetites deprived him as a man of moral harmony. When he tried to create characters in whom experience had become conscious, he no longer shared in the life of what he described with his whole being. He believed that consciousness must attenuate a primitive unconsciousness instead of defining it, and in delineating such characters, his own conscious purpose did restrict and weaken his unconscious imaginative powers.

The many characters therefore who reflect this divided consciousness were never self-contained. Obsessed by his own problem, he lacked freedom of perception and more and more came to project into them his own isolated self-consciousness with its needs and prejudices, until they ceased altogether to exist in their own rights and became, like Prince Nekhlyudov in *Resurrection* a mere channel for ideas. This increases their interest from the biographical point of view, but it detracts from their artistic value.

[1] In this connection it is interesting to note that in proposing to Sophie Behrs Tolstoy employed a tacit method, writing the initial letters only of the sentence containing the question he was addressing to her, as he sat with her at a card-table, while she nodded her head as a sign that she had understood. A somewhat similar method of proposal exists among many primitive peoples. Among the natives of Kenya, for example, a suitor traces hieroglyphics in the sand, to each of which there is a countersign, as an indication of his state of feeling.

Tolstoy's characters then were restricted in type. He could create human bodies but not human souls, because for him the mind warred upon the body and destroyed its wholeness. His women were real, but they express only feelings and sensations, and his men were abstractions and tended even to be reiterated formulas in so far as they criticized their feelings and sensations.

Again and again he contrasted the primitive man with the falsely civilized, and the contented materialist with the self-centred and distracted idealist, but although his sympathies, as a moralist, were with those who carried the burden of a conscience, his powers as an artist were only fully realized in his delineation of the former. He could not create a really civilized character. Those few, for example, who care anything for art are, like the musician in *Albert*, demoralized by it, or, like the frequenters of Petersburg drawing-rooms, prostitute art to relieve their tedium. Those also whom he describes as seeking to perfect themselves can only do so by violence. Hating the intellect, they cannot bring it into a true relation with their instincts and thereby gradually extend their mastery over the subconscious. Consequently they are swept away by their ideas as incontinently as by their appetites. Indeed their ideas are often but abstracted appetites and their 'spiritual doubts and joys' are determined by physical fluctuations, 'eternal hesitations and oscillations of feeling' as Turgenev described them, culminating in a sort of sensational orgasm. Like stricken animals they look up to the sky, seeking by some elemental abandon to forget the wounded flesh which tortures them.

How imperfectly defined such experience was to Tolstoy himself is proved by the language which he employed to describe it. His style, so subtle, sensitive, and decisive on the plane of finite sensation, is cloudy, confused and even ungrammatical when he strives towards the metaphysical because he is expressing neither thought, working freely by its own laws, nor sensation precisely focused, nor the perfect fusion of the two.

So far as Turgenev wished him to accept the limits of his physical apprehension, he was doubtless right in begging him to be content to be 'the pure and powerful artist.' But no counsel could stay the forces which drove Tolstoy to try and extend these limits, to rebel against their confinement. As he was to write, 'One can live only while one is intoxicated with life; but the moment the intoxication is over one sees that all is merely deceit, a clumsy fraud.'

And if this applied to life, it applied also to art. There too disgust trod on the heels of physical satisfaction, and in trying to ascend beyond the reach of this disgust, he lost his animal grasp of things without achieving a spiritual insight into them.

His failure therefore to achieve a spiritual harmony in himself was reflected in his inability to create a completely human character. As he was to write: 'There comes, as it were, unnecessary and gratuitous suffering, passing into a new form of life, untried as yet by man as he is to-day. Something happens akin to child-bearing. All is ready for the new life, but this life still does not make its appearance.'

The new man, whom humanity needs, and whom in various degrees the great post-Renaissance writers, whom Tolstoy despised, have conceived, is born out of the animal. But he needs the intelligence as midwife. He does not deny his origin, but he consciously transcends it. He discovers a soul. The disinterested intuition of the artist is an expression of this soul as is the disinterested love of the saint. Tolstoy strove to achieve a soul, both as an artist and a man, but although in theory all was 'ready for the new life,' in practice 'it did not make its appearance.'

That was the cause, fifteen years after his marriage, of his profound disillusionment. But during these fifteen years he was too physically absorbed in creative living to face the fatal issue. He experienced what Mr. Shaw has described as 'the true joy in life . . . the being a force of Nature instead of a feverish, selfish little clod of ailments and grievances, complaining that the world will not devote itself to making you happy.'

As he wrote he did not try to force or bend to his purpose the events in the story; he followed wherever they led him. They led him more essentially into regions of his own past experience than into those of Napoleonic history. They led him to define more clearly than he had yet done his own needs and his failure to satisfy them. But until he was writing _Anna Karenina_ he was too actively absorbed in expression to be consciously troubled by the limited region over which his imagination was wholly master and by the spiritual problem of which his restricted imagination was the artistic expression.

§ 3

War and Peace, which occupied Tolstoy from 1864 to
1869, is less a work of art than a great natural growth. It
is also intimately personal. Tolstoy studied a whole
library of authorities, accumulated details military and
diplomatic and derived the Rostovs and the Bolkonskys
from his own family records. But the Russia which he
describes is not in any deep sense historically conceived.
It is essentially that of his own day and the characters are
projections of himself or are closely modelled on those
near and dear to him.

How close the modelling could be is proved by Vera
Nagorny, who in a recent article has shown that Natasha's
personality and history intimately corresponded with that
of his favourite sister-in-law, Tanya. For example, like
Natasha, Tanya was carried off her feet by one Anatole
S—— during an *entr'acte* at the Mikhaylov Theatre in
Petersburg; she screeched and shouted in the excitement of hunting and coursing; she became engaged to
Tolstoy's elder brother and the engagement which was to
last a year was most unhappily broken off; and eventually
she married and 'all her passion and love were turned towards her family . . . she was completely absorbed in
her children and her husband. She nursed her children
herself . . . and was almost morbidly attached to them.'

Many of the conversations too in the novel, as Vera
Nagorny shows, exactly reproduced the actual speech of
Tanya or the words which she confided to letters and
diaries. Again Levin's jealous ejection of Vasenka with-

out explanation in *Anna Karenina* corresponded exactly
with Tolstoy's treatment of an admirer of Tanya whose
cynical worldly attentions he resented.

Such material indebtedness, which characterized almost all Tolstoy's writing, in no way of course detracts
from his imaginative achievement, but it shows how
closely it was always related to the facts of life about him.
He was the least literary of writers and he was the most
autobiographical. *War and Peace* is far more an epic of
his own life than of European history. Even those of its
characters which are apparently historical, Napoleon himself, for example, and Kutuzov, reveal at every turn the
bias of his sympathies and antipathies. The very title of
the novel and the contrasted world of peasants and nobles
which it describes, symbolize the conflict of extremes in its
author's experience.

And here again, as in the first narrative of Sebastopol,
Tolstoy found in war an elemental inspiration. Imaginatively at least he could experience it with a zest uncompli-
cated by disgust. War exposes man to the crude realities
of life and death; it entails a sort of submission to the
elements, though they be diabolical. It challenges the
emptiness of an 'idle, insipid, affected' peace.

In *War and Peace* Tolstoy surrendered himself to the
tide of natural forces. He poured into the writing of it not
only all the physical rapture but also the moral discontent
of which we have traced the history. But for the most part
the two were not in conflict, his moral striving being itself
expressed as a sort of rapture, flowing into philosophical
digressions, often imperfectly related to the narrative, but

like the fatal sweep of events, reflecting an elemental impulse. In *War and Peace* he relieved himself of his moral obsession and deferred facing it, by pouring out his thoughts through the characters of Pierre and Prince Andrew.

These characters develop only in the sense that Tolstoy's own character developed, by stating ever more clearly and explicitly their problem and making more and more conscious attempts to solve it. In the process Tolstoy inevitably became increasingly aware of himself, and in *Anna Karenina*, which he wrote next, his thought had ceased to be fluid and intangible. His elemental inspiration had ebbed, had turned back upon himself, and in Levin we see the self-conscious Tolstoy who could no longer escape from actuality into sensational ecstasies.

In *War and Peace*, then, the moral elements of his nature, which were later to be crystallized in his didactic works, were in solution. Here, as perhaps in no other of his works, he expressed the whole of his nature with the completest freedom. It is less a mirror of history than of all the facets of his personality, of his search for the meaning of life and his conviction that it was only to be found through the annihilation of self, of his conception of women as beings, whether good or bad, equally subservient to the forces of life, and of men as striving uselessly against them, of his depreciation of intellect and science, his idealizing of the peasant and his contempt for 'Society' and the art which fed its corruption, and above all, of his dread of and exultation in death.

§ 4

The two characters, then, into which Tolstoy explicitly projected himself, were Pierre and Prince Andrew. In them he stated the problem of his nature under two aspects and propounded two conjectural solutions.

Both of them are divided beings in contrast with Princess Mary who has the integrity of a simple religious faith, Natasha who obeys the instincts which impel her towards motherhood, Princess Hélène who is contentedly carnal, the unregenerate Anatole Kuragin who 'was instinctively and thoroughly convinced that it was impossible for him to live otherwise than as he did live and that he had never in his life done anything bad,' and Nicholas Rostov who lived upon the same conviction, but without being vicious.

These characters, with the exception of Princess Mary, exist below the conflict of good and evil. Pierre and Prince Andrew are torn between them. In both the longing to achieve a disinterested standpoint above personal desire and disillusionment comes and goes, leaving the one to sensuality, the other to cynicism.

The kindly, clumsy, absent-minded Pierre embodied the sensationalist in Tolstoy, that part of his nature which sought a primitive satisfaction in the Caucasus and thought to combine this with moral self-respect in marriage. Prince Andrew represented the critical and self-conscious side to his nature which was to forbid this satisfaction. The two elements are not of course mutually exclusive in either character, but in the one the animal man predominates, in the other the intellectual, in the one the democrat, in the other the aristocrat, and neither really solves the problem of life because its solution depends upon a combination of the qualities which each singly possesses.

Pierre's life, like Tolstoy's own of which it was essentially a record, is shown as a succession of crises, each one of which is acclaimed as final for the 'strong, joyful sensations' which it brings and which delude him into the belief that he has attained at last 'complete peace of mind and inner freedom.'

Its drama begins in a surrender to carnal appetite which results in his marriage with Princess Hélène. Already he is uncomfortably aware that merely sensual pleasure is not for him, that it is for those who lack something which he possesses, but with an indulgent smile at his physical self, he capitulates to 'the whole charm and seductiveness of her body which he now saw and felt, and which now seemed only veiled by her garments. . . . And at the same instant Pierre felt that Hélène not only might but must be his wife, and that this could not be otherwise. . . . She was terribly near him. She had him already in her power, and there was no longer any barrier between them, except the barrier of his own will.'

And that barrier breaks at the first assault. And Pierre's virtues, his excellent heart, his sensitiveness to others' pain, which made him ready to cry himself at the sight of tears, his sympathy with another's standpoint (as when he thought before the duel with Dolokhov – 'I might have done the same in his place'), his expansive cravings for a higher life, were all qualities of this defect of will.

The man of strong will is often self-centred; he subdues everything to his own needs, and in defining his experience he narrows it. As a sensualist he seeks a precise gratification, as a thinker he sacrifices perception to logic.

But Pierre is generous and expansive even in his sensualism. He is ashamed of his appetites because he is intoxicated by them and he finds no security in his dreams of moral perfection for the same reason. His marriage with a woman inherently coarse despite her education in the most aristocratic circles sets him searching for a meaning in life which will justify the appetites that he has come to hate. For him, as later for Tolstoy, the problem of his own nature becomes a problem of faith in the universe and how to achieve it. In him Tolstoy asked imaginatively what fourteen years later he was to ask actually — 'What is bad? What is good? What should be loved and what hated? Why do I live? And what am I? What is life, what is death? What is the Power which governs all?' To answer these questions in the abstract seemed to him a necessary preliminary to practical regeneration.

This was the first stage in Pierre's attempt to spiritualize his passions. It was marked by his meeting with the old Mason Bazdeev and his enrolment in a Masonic brotherhood. The highest wisdom, the old Mason told him, was founded 'not on reason alone, not on those worldly sciences of physics, history, chemistry and the like, into which intellectual knowledge is divided.' It was rather 'the science of the whole – the science which explains the whole of Creation and the place man occupies in it. In order to receive in oneself that science it is necessary to purify and regenerate one's inner man, and therefore before knowing, it is necessary to believe and to perfect oneself. . . . God is not to be apprehended by the mind, but by life.'

These idealistic arguments, which subserviated knowing to being instead of really reconciling them, appealed strongly to the simple Pierre. Longing vaguely, but with his whole heart, to believe, he 'believed and felt a joyous sense of comfort, regeneration, and restoration to life.' Enraptured by these moral sensations he pictured to himself the 'blissful, irreproachable and virtuous future which seemed to him so easy.'

But in fact he lapsed as easily as before into lower forms of dissipation and he found, on joining the Masons, that they too were a brotherhood only in form and in no way personally reflected the ideals which they professed. The seven virtues, prescribed by the Masonic Order, were identical with those which Tolstoy had so often prescribed for himself with as little effect on his actual conduct. He, like Pierre, had tried to evade the personal problem by dreaming of the regeneration of the human race, by indulging his philanthropic aspirations as a landlord, and by drawing up lists of virtues which he contemplated with rapture.

The first attempt then at a solution failed with Pierre as with Tolstoy, because it was both abstract and sentimental. The second attempt was made at Borodino, where

Pierre's experiences on the Knoll battery correspond with Tolstoy's on the Fourth Bastion at Sebastopol. Pierre is diverted by war and its concrete horrors and heroisms from sentimental miasmas. 'Oh, to be a soldier!' he thinks as he falls asleep, 'to enter completely into that life in common, to be penetrated by that which makes them what they are. But how am I to cast off all the superfluous devilish burden of my outer man?'

In the unassuming simplicity of the common soldier Pierre saw embodied the seven virtues which the Masonic Order prescribed. The soldier, like the peasant, accepted the ruling of life and moreover accepted it with a certain gaiety. And in doing so it seemed to Pierre that he was accepting God's laws.

'The most difficult thing is the subjection of man's freedom to God's laws,' the voice had said. 'Simplicity is humility to God; you cannot escape from Him. And they are simple. *They* do not talk, but act. . . . Man can possess nothing while he is afraid of death, but he who does not fear it possesses all. If there were no suffering, man would be unaware of his limitations, would not know himself. The hardest thing of all . . . is to be able in your soul to unite the meaning of all. To unite all?' he asked himself – 'No, not to unite. Thoughts cannot be united, but to *harness* all these thoughts together is what is wanted! Yes, one must *harness* them, *harness* them!' Pierre repeated with inward rapture, feeling that only those words expressed what he wanted to say and solved the question that tormented him.'

But they only solved the question in theory. For the

common soldier succeeded in harnessing his thoughts together, because he had not come to know himself as Pierre had done, and in consequence had no need of the 'inward rapture,' which Pierre was always seeking. Significantly enough this solution came to Pierre in a dream, in which his thoughts seemed to be dictated by someone outside himself. It was an inspiring dream, but once again it could not transform his nature.

He would still feel suddenly overcome by a sense of 'confusion and helplessness,' and this inevitable revulsion from rapture was turned into utter disillusionment, when he witnessed, as Tolstoy had witnessed in Paris, the execution of prisoners on the retreat from Moscow. 'Though he did not render account of it to himself, his faith in the good ordering of the universe, in humanity, in his own soul, and in God, had been destroyed in him. . . . He felt that to regain faith in the meaning of life was not now in his power.'

He did not realize that the common soldiers who inflicted death as uncritically as they accepted it were no less the slaves of forces beyond their control than the men who shot these prisoners. And because he sentimentalized their submission in the one case as divine, there was no rational issue open to him from the horror inspired by naked brutality in the other. Lacking a reasoned distinction between natural law and God's laws, everything inevitably fell 'into a heap of meaningless confusion.'

Nevertheless, Pierre renews his faith through association with his fellow-prisoner, Platon Karataev, the little, round peasant soldier with his proverbs and cheerful trust in life and death, in whom Tolstoy embodied, as he was to embody so often again, his ideal peasant — that 'eternal personification of the spirit of simplicity and truth,' which he so impossibly aspired himself to be.

Platon comes very near being real. His folk-songs and sayings, his evening prayer, 'Lay me down like a stone, O God, and raise me up like a loaf,' his deep, natural, pleasant smile and gentle brown eyes, his touching oddities, are convincingly human. Yet as Tolstoy describes his character, we feel him to be less a man than an illustration of ideal simplicity: 'He loved his dog, loved his comrades, and the French, and loved Pierre who was his neighbour; but Pierre felt that in spite of Karataev's affectionate tenderness to him . . . he would not have grieved for a moment at parting from him.'

He is almost inhuman in his perfect humanity, in his freedom not only from the desire to dominate and possess, but from any earthly attachment. And yet we are to believe that he achieved this freedom not through any spiritual stress, but instinctively, that he was one who obeyed his instincts without being tied by them and in whom Nature expressed herself as innocently as in the child and as sublimely as in the saint. 'Every word and action of his was the manifestation of an activity unknown to him, which was his life. But his life, as he regarded it, had no meaning as a separate thing. It had meaning only as a particle of a whole of which he was always conscious. His words and actions flowed from him as evenly, inevitably and spontaneously as fragrance exhales from a flower.'

It is a perfect and poetic conception, the loveliest tribute which Tolstoy ever paid to the peasant of his dreams. But for him at least it was an ineffectual dream. And so in fact it is for Pierre.

The example of Platon and the privations of the Moscow imprisonment which they share together confirm in him the ideal of self-renunciation conceived at Borodino. He is convinced that he has at last obtained the peace and self-content which he had formerly striven in vain to reach. He no longer searches for an aim in life, and it is just this absence of aim which gives him the complete joyous consciousness of freedom which constitutes his happiness. He has learnt in his captivity 'not by words or reasoning but by direct feeling what his nurse had told him long ago: that God is here and everywhere. In his captivity he had learnt that God in Kataraev was greater, more infinite, and unfathomable, than in the Architect of the Universe recognized by the Freemasons. He felt like a man who finds what he was seeking at his very feet after straining his eyes to see it in the distance.'

Pierre's sufferings have in short converted him from the abstract to the concrete, but his perception of life in the concrete is as sentimental and as relaxed as it was in the abstract. The dreadful question, 'Why?' which had formerly 'destroyed all his mental edifices,' no longer exists for him, merely because he has ceased to ask it, not because he has discovered a really convincing answer.

Certainly he is more human, because he is more resigned, and the renewal of his love for Natasha and its realization in marriage sets the seal, as Tolstoy believed his own marriage had set the seal, upon the physical and moral dissipations which lay behind him.

His engagement is another such period of 'blissful insanity' as that which Masha knew in *Family Happiness*. Looking back upon it, Pierre is convinced that he was wiser then and had more insight than at any other time and that he understood all that was worth understanding in life. This 'blissful insanity,' however, cannot preserve his married life from the commonplace. No longer swept away by his emotions, he becomes the good-natured property of his wife, who, absorbed in babies, neglects herself, is untidy and even stingy, and treats him not as an intelligent human being, but as a domestic institution.

Clearly Tolstoy did not regret at this time such an anti-climax. He considered it in the order of nature that Natasha, having found a mate and become a mother, should lose all the grace and enchantment which was hers before, but for which she had now no material use. He applauded too her attitude towards discussions about women's rights. 'These topics were not merely uninteresting to Natasha, she positively did not understand them. These questions, then as now, existed only for those who see nothing in marriage but the pleasure married people get from one another, that is to say, only the beginning of marriage, and not its whole significance which lies in the family. But then and now these discussions and questions of that kind, which are similar to the question how to obtain the greatest amount of gratification from one's dinner, did not, and do not, exist for those who see the purpose of dinner in the nourishment it gives, and the purpose of marriage in the family.'

The use of such an analogy shows how completely physical Tolstoy's view of marriage was. If marriage is a mere physical necessity like a meal, eagerly anticipated by the appetites, a family is its only moral justification. But if it is a human and spiritual relationship, of which physical union is but one intimate expression, then the question of the standing of women and of their right to a free intelligence, is a vital one, since no really human relation can exist save between equals.

It was true of course that the women's rights movement was in some circles tainted by 'Society' corruption, that the pseudo-civilized woman was, like pseudo-civilized art, a luxury and a decoration, that her natural instincts were perverted rather than educated. But the rational champions of women's emancipation opposed this perversion with far more enlightenment than Tolstoy who wished to preserve women on an animal level, where indeed, as he was to show in *The Kreutzer Sonata*, they are not only enslaved themselves, but enslave man.

Pierre too is enslaved, if only by domesticity. Primarily, however, he is enslaved by himself. He has little more real self-possession at the end of the novel than at the beginning. Like Tolstoy he has soothed his agitations by marriage. But the peace is a conventional one, and unrest begins again to trouble him, impelling him to join the Secret Society which seeks to Christianize Russian society and government. He shares of course none of these ideas with Natasha, who, as Countess Tolstoy was later to do, tolerates his Christian ideals so long as he does not forget 'that we have other duties nearer to us, duties indicated to us by God Himself, and that though we may expose ourselves to risks, we must not expose our children.'

Thus the end of *War and Peace* shows Tolstoy already expressing as an artist the dilemma which he expressed more consciously in *Anna Karenina* when it had come to be a personal obsession. He had accepted marriage as a physical union rendered moral by its physical issue. But this acceptance was disturbed by strivings towards the 'infinite, eternal and absolute.' These, however, being sensational too, could not bring any lasting satisfaction.

If Pierre had represented the whole of Tolstoy's nature instead of its more expansive side, this dissatisfaction might never have become acute. But there was the other side, which Prince Andrew represented, to be taken into account. And it was the Prince Andrew in him which ultimately converted the vague agitations, embodied in Pierre, into a hatred of the senses and even of such a 'virtuous' indulgence of them as marriage had seemed to offer.

§ 5

In Prince Andrew then, who 'united in himself in the highest degree those qualities which Pierre lacked, and which might be described as will power,' Tolstoy isolated the critical and self-conscious elements in his own nature. Prince Andrew has the male qualities of pride, disdain, self-possession and intellectual doubt, while he lacks

Pierre's flutteringly feminine sensibility. His handsome, neat figure, his stern well-defined features and quiet movements, all typify this self-possession which is also self-confinement.

Already at the opening of the story, through his marriage with a pretty but empty-headed little woman, he is disillusioned of society women and of women in general. 'Selfish, vain, stupid, trivial in everything – that,' he remarks, 'is what women are when you see them in their true colours!'

He sees through sentimentality, as Tolstoy himself did when he was not intoxicated by feeling, shrugging his shoulders and frowning 'as lovers of music do when they hear a false note,' and even his sister's faith is disabled for him by an element of this quality. And when she tries to convert him to it, 'there was a look of tenderness (he was touched) and at the same time there was irony in his face.' As with Pierre his nature is put into solution by the experience of war. A nervously emotional and softened mood follows the Council of War before Austerlitz, engendered by the thought that he may possibly be killed on the morrow. But the pride of the soldier eager for glory subdues the inner voice suggesting death and suffering. After he falls, however, with the standard at Austerlitz he experiences his first extension of vision as he looks up at the sky and contrasts its infinite calm with the frenzied faces of the gunners. 'How is it,' he thinks, 'I didn't see that lofty sky before? How happy I am to have recognized it at last! Yes, all is vanity, all is falsehood, except that infinite heaven. There is nothing, nothing but that.

But even it does not exist, there is nothing but quiet and peace.'

Such indifference, however, is not enlightenment. It is merely a surrender of will through weakness, resulting from loss of blood, suffering, and the near prospect of death. Everything becomes insignificant instead of significant. And here Tolstoy was expressing, what he came later to define intellectually, that life has no meaning. And in moments of exhaustion peace, comparable to that of conventional piety, may indeed be the reward of ceasing to make any effort to comprehend. But the incomprehensible ceases to comfort as soon as vigour returns and transformed then into the meaningless, it brings, not peace, but a sword.

Such is Prince Andrew's experience. He forgets the lofty sky and returns to himself and his discontent. The death of his wife under pathetic circumstances intensifies his cynical attitude to life, and, to kill thought in action, he devotes himself to the management of his estate, in which, unlike Pierre, he is very competent, but not idealistic.

Pierre, meeting him in the full tide of his Masonic enthusiasm, tries to convert him to his vague ideals of equality, brotherhood and love. Their argument on the ferry is the one place in the novel where the two sides of Tolstoy's nature come into immediate conflict, in which the aristocrat in him debates with the democrat, the emotional idealist with the sceptical realist. And the debate is wholly inconclusive because the two sides cannot achieve contact.

Prince Andrew perfectly enunciates the negative argument against the 'good-natured fussy shallowness' of sentimental reformers. 'Why raise the peasant from his animal condition?' he asks. 'Animal happiness is the only happiness possible and you want to deprive him of it. Physical labour is as essential to him, as much a condition of his existence, as mental activity to me. The only men who will benefit by the liberation of the serfs are the owners who perish morally through being able to inflict punishment justly and unjustly.'

To this static and selfish view of life, which Tolstoy himself had shared to the extent of showing no interest in the liberation of the serfs, Pierre can only oppose a vague conception of a reign of goodness. And the same opposition of extremes characterizes their discussion of death. To Pierre's true contention that if you live in the whole, you cannot fear to become part of it in death, Prince Andrew answers: 'It is not arguments which convince of the necessity of a future life, but this: when you go hand in hand with someone, and suddenly that person vanishes *there, into nowhere*, and you yourself stop before that abyss, and look in. And I have looked in. . . .'

Here in fact Tolstoy dramatized the irreconcilable oppositions in his nature. Prince Andrew is affected by Pierre's enthusiasm. He looks up to the sky as at Austerlitz and recovers for a moment a joyful sensation. But it passes, even as it passed and recurred again in Tolstoy's own experience. For how could ideas which were no more than extended sensations stand up against the sensual fact of death?

The second vital point of contact between Prince Andrew and Pierre is indirect. It lies in their contrasted relationship with Natasha, through which Tolstoy expressed the two aspects of his attitude to women, his hatred of them, on the one hand, because of his sense at once of physical subservience and moral superiority, and on the other his admiration of their fidelity to Nature, culminating in motherhood.

Natasha from the moment of her appearance as 'a black-eyed, large-mouthed girl, not pretty but full of life, with childish bare shoulders, which after her run, heaved and shook her bodice' is incarnate Nature.

Her lyrical vitality, which overflows into song and dance and incessant movement, her 'recklessly bright eyes,' her unconscious coquetry, her impulsive self-abandonment, bespeak a finely-sensed but purely instinctive being. And in the issue, as Tolstoy tells it, all her graces express unconsciously her need of children, of serving life physically. And so when this need is satisfied, she is no longer shy and lively, no longer lovely in her animation. Then 'her face and body were all that one saw, and her soul was not visible at all. All that struck the eye was a strong, handsome, and fertile woman.'

Tolstoy would seem to have been convinced of the inevitable logic of this and even to have approved it. But an issue which so hurts the artist in us could not be as moral as he claimed. And Prince Andrew's relations with Natasha show that Tolstoy realized the weakness of one whose sense was with her senses all mixed in, even while he insisted that it was not in woman's nature to be otherwise.

A year after his conversation with Pierre, Prince Andrew drives the same way in spring. He sees a gnarled oak among smiling birch-trees and it seems to him to say, 'Spring, love, happiness! How is it you are not weary of this eternal, stupid, and meaningless fraud?' Knowledge for him has stripped life of all illusion. And then, as he drives up the avenue to the Rostovs' house, he sees running ahead of some other girls 'a dark-haired, remarkably slim, pretty girl in a yellow chintz dress, wearing on her head a white pocket-handkerchief from beneath which escaped loose locks of hair.'

She is life. She is happy like the birch-trees. And later, hearing her talking above him, as she leans out of the window in the moonlight, he is enchanted with life once again. As he drives back the way he came, the old oak is covered with sprouting leaves, and in him too spring puts forth new leaves and he longs to give himself to others.

Natasha also is possessed through her love by the spirit of life, so that she cannot believe in the possibility of evil, sorrow, or death. Yet this love because it is purely instinctive and craves an instinctive satisfaction cannot resist the strain of delay, imposed by a year's engagement, or the demoralizing atmosphere of a 'society' function. She is momentarily carried away by Anatole Kuragin's physical magnetism, and Prince Andrew's belief in life is destroyed, his nature frozen anew, by her disloyalty.

It was not in him to forgive, as Pierre would have done. His very virtues, his clear-sightedness, his self-control and consequent contempt for those who surrendered themselves blindly to the forces of nature, forbade this. Henceforth, turning away from life, which he can only regard behind its sensuous seductions as a valueless, physical process, he seeks truth, so far as he seeks it at all, through an understanding of Death.

For him death puts the agitations of life into perspective, but only, once again, by reducing them to insignificance. Before Borodino, for example, as he thinks of death, his past with its raptures and agonies is suddenly illumined by a cold white light without shadows. It is the light of the absolute, but of the absolute conceived as nothingness.

After being wounded, however, and when his hold on life is weakened, he regains something of the sense of innocence towards life which he remembered as a child, that feeling of love and happiness 'which is the very essence of the soul and does not require an object.'

This love which puts a man outside the play of physical forces, which frees him from 'the bondage of life,' Prince Andrew could only experience when his body was utterly weakened. His acceptance of death is not grounded in an acceptance of life, but in cessation of desire for it. And this is confirmed by his final relations with Natasha.

When she comes to tend him, she renews at first his desire for love and life. 'Love for a particular woman again crept unobserved into his heart and again bound him to life, and joyful and agitating thoughts came to his mind.' He is not reconciled with life, but bound once again to its wheel. He remembers Kuragin again with a twinge of jealousy and thinks with terror of going into the unknown.

And then the spirit of life in his body fails. Death resumes command, conquers his will to live and kills in him the possibility of pity or sympathy, jealousy or fear. He is not reconciled with death, but numbed by it. He can experience life disinterestedly, only when he has lost all interest in it. If he had lived, his possessive, imprisoning egotism would have returned to him.

And so neither Prince Andrew nor Pierre really solve the problem which Tolstoy formulated in their persons. Both remain divided beings. Pierre seeks escape from his discontent in vague mystical dreams or conventional domesticity. Prince Andrew escapes from the life which he could not love because he was too critically self-conscious into death in which all egotism is dissolved.

The problem in both cases was how to spiritualize the passions and in both it was insoluble. In Pierre the senses overran intelligence, in Prince Andrew the two were morosely opposed.

Tolstoy realized wherein the solution lay, but he gave it a false moral twist. 'It is now necessary,' he wrote, 'that man governed by his senses, should find sensuous pleasure in virtue. It is impossible to eradicate the passions; so we must only try to direct them to a noble aim, and it is therefore necessary that every one should be able to satisfy his passions within the limits of virtue.'

Noble aims, however, and 'virtue' spiced with pleasure cannot transform disunity into unity, a critical denial of life into a creative affirmation of it. It is intelligence which has created the discord, and only intelligence, instinctively inspired, can heal it.

And because Tolstoy's morality denied intelligence, he could never reconcile his passions with real virtue. He could only, like Pierre, try to escape from them into a vague mysticism or to satisfy them within the limits of conventional virtue in a fertile marriage, or, like Prince Andrew, deny them that in their death he might find life.

Throughout *War and Peace* he continually disparaged a controlling and directing intelligence. Kutozov is greater than Napoleon because he is resigned to events, of which man is the slave, as the individual is of illogical emotions, 'irrational, inexpressible thoughts, secret as a crime, which alters his whole life.' 'We are forced,' Tolstoy wrote, 'to fall back upon fatalism as an explanation of unreasonable events (that is to say, of events the reasonableness of which we do not understand). . . . The higher the human intellect rises towards the discovery of those purposes, the more obvious it becomes that the ultimate purpose is beyond our comprehension.'

Science therefore being 'the pseudo-knowledge of absolute truth' was worthless. Doctors, because they knew little, had no curative power, but were only of use because they satisfied a 'moral need' of the invalid and his friends. Government being often corrupt and partisan, must be dispensed with. Politicians who pursued 'glittering prizes' and generals who coveted decorations served no purpose in peace or war but to sit on the shoulders of the patient common soldier.

These views, still fluid in *War and Peace* but to become the dogmas of the later moralist, were all part of Tolstoy's disparagement of intelligence, and it was a disabling dis-

paragement alike in his efforts for social and personal
salvation, because it entailed a merely destructive attitude.

The fact that there are forces in life which the individual cannot control does not justify him in ceasing to
attempt to understand and direct them. In life as in art
the problem for man is how to rationalize 'the irrational,'
express 'the inexpressible' and advance continually his
control over the unconscious and the elemental. The
control may be false and exclusive as Tolstoy saw. At the
present stage of our civilization it is almost invariably so,
and all the abuses and pretensions which he so finely
exposed are the consequence of this.

But although Governments have served the interests of
a class, disregarding in peace as in war the worth and the
rights of the common man, they may yet express the will
and the moral purpose of the people; although science
has confused pseudo-knowledge with truth, it has also
cleared the path towards a surer apprehension of truth;
and although Napoleon was to some extent the slave of
fortuitous and complicated events, he also was an inspired
and effective strategist.

And, finally, although women respond more blindly
to Nature than men, they may also be human and intelligent beings. For it was, as we have argued, by his denial
of free intelligence to women and his acclamation of those
who were 'simple and submissive to God's will,' or, in
other words, who obeyed blindly the demands of their
physical being, that Tolstoy perpetuated the enslavement
which he hated.

Some years later he was to write that the 'wonderful

nonsense called "women's rights" ' had arisen and was
entirely preached by women who artificially made themselves barren and bewitched men by their shoulders and
curls. And in contrast with these he belauded 'those
women and mothers who, having the power to avoid
childbirth, simply and consciously submit to that eternal,
immutable law, knowing that the hardship and labour of
that submission is their vocation.'

The contrast was a false one because it was based on a
complete misconception of what 'women's rights' implied.
The claim behind this movement was that woman should
be treated as a human and responsible being and neither as
a child-bearing chattel nor as a pampered mistress. To
be the one, which Tolstoy favoured, is to live on almost
the same physical level as to be the other which he
abhorred. The best modern woman does not desire to
evade her vocation as a mother, but refuses to succumb
to it as a mere maternal animal. 'Woman,' Tolstoy was to
argue, 'having forgotten her law, has believed that her
strength lies in the fascination of her witchery, or in her
dexterity in the pharisaic pretence of intellectual labour.'

This is true to an inconsiderable extent. The prostitute, whether married or unmarried, is almost always un-
intelligent, and women's demand for education (which
was not pharisaic as Tolstoy supposed in his contempt for
all mental culture) ran and runs equally counter to
enslavement as a mistress and as a mother.

In the same book Tolstoy drew a touching picture of
mothers who for months and years did not have an undisturbed night's sleep, but 'sometimes, and often, do not

sleep for whole nights together, but walk up and down with numbed arms rocking the sick child who is tearing your heart.'

To accept such conditions seemed to him to be obeying a 'reasonable perception of life,' when in fact a certain exercise of reason, and a certain application of the science which he despised, would have rendered them superfluous to the gain both of the mothers and the children.

In writing thus we have advanced beyond the point which Tolstoy had reached in *War and Peace*. But such false acquiescence in physical necessity, sanctified as 'God's will,' underlies his handling both of the characters and events in this great novel. And while his nature expanded in the process of writing it, as it did in the other activities of his early married life, it expanded only to contract more painfully.

Prince Andrew was dead in the novel. But he was alive in his creator's being. And as Tolstoy's energies ceased to flow outwards in unimpeded expression, they gradually turned inwards in critical discontent. And in this discontent the vague moral agitations of Pierre combined with the critical egotism of Prince Andrew. They combined first in the character of Levin in *Anna Karenina* and then, when art could no longer relieve the tension, in the explicit and distracted *Confession* of Tolstoy himself.

§ 6

Tolstoy began to write *Anna Karenina* in 1873, eleven years after his marriage, and completed it four years later. He began it without any preparation, having previously contemplated another work on the scale of *War and Peace*, but of the time of Peter the Great. Its central theme was suggested by a local tragedy which had occurred the year before, when a lady named Anna who lived with a neigh-bouring squire had been driven by jealousy to commit suicide by throwing herself under a train. Tolstoy had been present at the post-mortem and knew all the details of the affair.

Anna Karenina, however, if more objective than *War and Peace*, is nevertheless saturated with Tolstoy's 'peculiar egotistical self-consciousness.' It is in fact only more objective because Tolstoy had begun to define his sympathies and antipathies more exactly and could no longer abandon himself to the abstract and sensational as he did in the person of Pierre.

During the first ten years of his married life, while *War and Peace* was being written, he may indeed be said to have renewed in some ways the fluid attitude to life which he had known before he experienced the shock of Sebas-topol and of his brother's death. But from 1873 the horrifying thoughts of life and death, submerged for some years by the new joys and duties of marriage, rose again to the surface of consciousness, and the paralysing ques-tions began to present themselves more and more fre-quently – 'What am I? Where am I? and why am I?'

Before he finished writing *Anna Karenina* he ceased to project these questions into the characters of a novel and addressed them directly to himself. As with Levin, 'all the traces of his past life seemed to seize him in their grasp. "No, you cannot escape from us," they seemed to say. "It is useless your trying to be different from what you always have been, with your doubts, your perpetual dissatisfaction, your vain efforts at bettering yourself and your everlasting expectation of happiness that does not come and never will come." '

He was ceasing in fact to be able to live in the present, as his wife could do, but while one inner voice kept telling him that he need not be a slave to the past but could make what he would of himself, another mocked his recurrent feeling that some change was going on, some modification in his nature which would save him from a revival of the old discord.

Levin is the medium through whom these two voices speak. He is conscious of the antagonisms in his nature to a greater degree than either Pierre or Prince Andrew, and he seeks even in his later Christianity a more practical solution of them. And while in Pierre's marriage to Natasha Tolstoy expressed his hope that he had found peace, in Levin's to Kitty he confessed that he had not. In his presentation too of Anna he clearly voiced for the first time his sense of passion as a false and implacable foe to the higher life.

Like all of the characters through whom Tolstoy explained himself Levin is an egotist, and his strongest impulse is to escape from a 'refined, complex, internal life' into one that is external and physical. He even contemplates mating with a peasant woman, as Tolstoy himself more than once did later in his revolt against what he considered a selfish family life.

As always a love of the physical and a hatred of the

sophisticated blends in the impulse. 'The young peasant woman moved about lightly and merrily . . . the curve of her back, encircled by a red belt, looked wonderfully graceful as she bent down, and so did her full bosom under the thin white kerchief as she straightened herself up again.'

Levin loves her body for itself, but he loves it also for what it represents. It speaks to him, as the wild, coarse voices of the haymakers and their lusty laughter do, of a life unburdened by egotism and absorbed in communal toil. And that is why he finds in scything with his men a perfect happiness. The more he thinks of his work and of trying to improve it, the less straight his line grows and the more tired he feels. But as the work goes on there comes a time of complete oblivion when he loses all consciousness of what he is doing and the scythe seems to cut of itself. The co-ordination between his muscles and his mind has become instinctive and he loses himself in a larger rhythm.

But Levin, like Tolstoy, could only drug himself by such activities. He confesses that he is tied to another kind of life by his love of Kitty. 'No,' he said to himself; 'however good this simple life of work be, I cannot return to it. I love *her*.' He does not yet realize, however, that the impediment lies in himself rather than in the accident of his social standing and his marriage. He feels only a strong desire to live a 'pure, simple, delightful life of work.' But his ideas, as he admits, are vague. And when he asks, 'Well, what shall I do?' he can only reply, 'I shall reduce them to order later on.'

Throughout *Anna Karenina* Tolstoy shows him reducing them to order and in the process dimly realizing that
salvation for him cannot lie in a simple return to the
physical.

Nevertheless, Levin's opinions are dictated by an arbitrary opposition of the primitive and utilitarian to the
civilized and decorative, and since Tolstoy expressed
publicly for the first time through them the false antithesis
which was to restrict later his influence as a critic of
society, it may be well to define here in what it consisted.

Levin remarks to Stepan that in the country 'our one
object is to get our hands so that we can work with them.
For that purpose we cut our nails short and are not afraid
to turn up our sleeves . . . there is something barbaric
about it, just as there is something barbaric about our
dinner. In the country we eat merely to satisfy our
hunger, in order to make us more fit for work; here you
try and prolong your appetite as much as possible, so you
eat oysters. . . .'

'Quite so,' Stepan Akadyevitch put in; 'to make a
pleasure of everything we do seems to me the whole aim
and object of civilization.'

'If that's the sole aim of civilization, then I'd sooner
be a savage.'

'But you are a savage as it is. All you Levins are
savages.'

In this conversation two forms of barbarism are
opposed to each other, and the suggestion is that there can
be no compromise between them. Civilization on the one
hand represents the selfish and so barbarous pursuit of

pleasure of which all its refinements, its music and dancing, drawing-rooms and dresses, are the indulgent expression. A natural and moral life, on the other hand, is
guided simply by biological necessity. It consists of
practical work and only of such satisfaction of the
appetites as conduces to practical efficiency.

All Levin's views reflect an incapacity to believe that
there might be a good life beyond the mere response to
practical necessities, and that in such a life 'to make a
pleasure of everything' need not imply indolent self-
indulgence, but creative self-expression.

Humanity, as he sees it, is divided into two classes, a
small, luxurious, and predatory one which seeks only self-
gratification, and a large one of workmen and peasants
who by their unremitting and selfless toil supply the
means for this self-gratification.

No one will deny that this was true of the Russia of
which Tolstoy wrote, or that it is still true to some extent
of European society in general. And so far as Levin con-
fines himself to attacking such inhuman exploitation, we
agree with him enthusiastically. We agree with him when
he argues that before rational farming can prevail or
before even schools can help the peasants, there must be
an economic change 'that will make the peasant richer
and then schools will spring up of their own accord.' We
agree with him when he says of war-mongering politicians and journalists – 'What they were preaching was
the very same mental pride that had ruined him. He
could not agree with the statement that a few dozen men
. . . had the right of saying that they and the newspapers

were expressing the thought of the people – a thought that found expression in bloodshed and murder. He knew full well that the masses amongst whom he was living, of whom he felt himself a part, could not wish for war, or advocate it for any general purpose.'

But we do not agree with him when he complains that 'a workman who can read and write is hopeless. He will think it beneath him to mend the roads, and if you put a bridge across he will be sure to steal the planks.'

Such a view, which did embody what was to be more and more Tolstoy's own opinion, reflects the false bias against civilization noted above. Because civilization, as represented by the 'educated classes,' was corrupt, education itself was corrupting, and a man could only preserve his virtue by confining his attention to the immediate objects of sense and his activities to work and practical use.

These views were of course based on Tolstoy's own experience. He hated civilization because it had merely taught him how to gratify his senses, as he hated science because it had undermined his instinctive faith without supplying him with a higher one. And so he failed to see that the conscious and artificial might be a necessary, if debased, phase in man's development from the instinctive and utilitarian, in his liberation from that life of physical necessity, which expressed humanity only in its primitive stage.

In *Anna Karenina* this prejudice appears not only in the views of Levin, but in Tolstoy's handling of the central theme of the book – the supposedly 'divine' vengeance which pursues the breaker of a marriage-vow.

In Vronsky's St. Petersburg world, we are told, humanity was divided into two distinct classes, the dull and old-fashioned set who believed in respectable married life under the condition that 'girls must be innocent and women modest and that men must be manly and temperate,' and the licentious set who believed that men should be generous, bold, gay, unashamed of their passions and laughing at the rest of the world. By these it was thought ridiculous to fall in love in a conventional way and be loyal.

The assumption is that virtue is confined to the former and vice to the latter, when in fact the conventional marriages were often respectable rather than pure, the innocence of the girls was an enslaving ignorance, and the manliness of their husbands a tedious patronage. The consequent revolt against them might indeed represent no more than an outburst of licence, but it might also involve a true protest against relationships, which beneath a masque of propriety were neither vital nor human nor moral.

Such a relationship was Anna's with the middle-aged man whom she married in ignorance as a young girl. *Karenin* is less a man than a ministerial machine. He is too cold and fastidious to be crudely possessive as Mr. Galsworthy's Soames, but his attitude to his wife, as to life in general is, like that of Soames, possessive. He cannot perceive and enjoy beauty disinterestedly. It may be that Anna, before meeting Vronsky, had not realized how revoltingly loveless her marriage with such a man was. Doubtless she accepted the general opinion of it as

eminently respectable, and only later when 'recalling the
feeling that had existed between them – a feeling that
had also been called love – she shuddered with disgust.'

Nevertheless a nature so 'large, fresh, rich, generous
and delightful' must have unconsciously suffered in such a
marriage and fretted for a truer and cleaner relationship.
And it is because her marriage is empty and false, and not
through any inherent viciousness in her nature, that she
surrenders so easily to Vronsky.

From the moment, however, of her association with
Vronsky we feel in Tolstoy's expression of her character
an undertone of that fear and hatred which was to
culminate twenty years later in the frenzy of Pozdnyshev.
He suggests not merely that, under existing social conditions, an illicit passion must demoralize because it
desocializes, but that the passion was inherently evil.

The Anna whom we first know has bright grey eyes
under thick long lashes, 'a peculiarly restrained, vivacious
expression' and a 'scarcely perceptible smile that played
about her rosy lips.' Like her brother Stepan 'she seemed
overflowing with radiance, which against her will shone
out in her glance, her smile.' Her movements are more
graceful than Natasha's, and she is 'complex and poetical'
as well as 'natural and simple,' but she differs from her
only in the fact that she is more conscious of the life by
which she is possessed.

But this in Tolstoy's eyes is her sin. Without this consciousness, he suggests, the nursery would have satisfied
all her needs. And from the moment that she enters the
ballroom where her destiny is decided, she becomes a fatal

Aphrodite, a Lamia endowed with 'an almost infernal seductiveness.' The passion which burns in her bewildering eyes is an unholy fire. It fascinates but to consume, allures but to enslave. Vronsky is unmanned by it. His expression is like that of an intelligent dog who is conscious of having done something wrong. He has no will of his own in her presence. And she has little will herself. The very thought of Vronsky fills her with an inhuman physical ecstasy akin to high fever. 'She almost laughed aloud with joy that suddenly took possession of her. Every nerve in her was alive. She felt her eyes opening wider, her hands and feet could scarcely keep still, something caught her breath, every form and sound in the carriage struck her with amazing clearness. She could not tell whether the train was going backwards or forwards or had come to a standstill.'

But this is not the purely instinctive possession by love which Tolstoy so often sentimentalized. Anna knows that she is possessed, and hates, while she loves, her enslavement. And her very ability to hate the physical enslavement of her passion for Vronsky, while yet preferring it to the lie of her marriage with Karenin, proves her to be on a higher human level than the Natasha of *War and Peace*.

Her tragedy therefore is essentially due, not to the fact that she broke a conventional marriage vow, as Tolstoy suggests, but that she is moral enough to know that a love dominated by physical attraction and selfishly indulged is debasing.

If she could have lived as Vronsky's wife and the

mother of his children instead of as his mistress in a world of enchanted dreaming and horrible awakening, her moral sense would not have infected her with neuroticism and hysteria. But her irrational refusal to demand a divorce from Karenin when he would have granted it, a refusal dictated by her instinctive attachment to her son, made this impossible.

And so between her natural virtues and her moral fineness she is forced into a position where both are outraged, and the elements of strife and hatred, which are latent in every passion which has a strong physical foundation, gradually emerge, and in the form of jealousy sap her fineness and integrity before she casts her body underneath the train.

No one will deny the artistic power and inevitability with which Tolstoy develops the tragedy. Yet beneath the art there is a moral confusion and insensitiveness which interferes with our acceptance and even makes us feel at times that the tragedy is engineered to suit a thesis, and certainly that the suggested moral is a false one.

The two conceptions of love which he brings into conflict are not the moral and the immoral as is generally supposed, but the legal and the illegal. Neither represents a really human attachment, but of the two Anna's relation to Vronsky is truer in its passion, finer in its feeling, and more informed with humanity and intelligence than her relation to Karenin. Her tragedy therefore, from an essentially moral standpoint, lies in the fact that the truer relationship, which might have blossomed within its limits into something fine, is distorted and poisoned by the circumstances of the falser one, into which she had ignorantly entered.

But this is not the tragedy or the moral which Tolstoy wishes to enforce. His implicit argument is that a marriage, whatever its nature and however entered, is divinely consecrated and that physical submission by women to their husbands is a law of life and not of a given society. The woman therefore who transgresses this law, not only by breaking her marrige vows but by becoming conscious of herself as a human being with rights and individuality, tastes and distastes, is inevitably punished by God as well as by Society.

Consequently Anna's tragedy in Tolstoy's view lay, not in the fact that she contracted a loveless marriage, but that she broke it, not in the fact that she was moral enough to hate her enslavement by instinct while lacking the power to free herself, but that she had developed a moral sense at all.

Hence the imperfect impression which the story makes upon us. The conventional moral which Tolstoy emphasizes conflicts with the essential moral which our reason acclaims. Tolstoy in fact expressed here implicitly what he was later to announce explicitly, when he wrote, 'I cannot but consider holy and obligatory only the first marital union which a man has formed.'

This view reflected the arbitrary opposition of the primitive to the civilized, which we have defined. Between domestic conformity and prostitution Tolstoy could see no alternative. It mattered not whether an ignorant girl had been trapped or pushed into marriage with a man, who shocked and disgusted her by his violence; or whether either she or her husband had realized too late a hopeless incompatibility of temperament. He could not recognize the spiritual waste involved in such marriages, and not only for the husband and wife but for the children who were supposed to justify them, because his conception of women was material.

The loveless marriage of a young girl was not tragic to him, because he treated women as the mere physical mediums of the life force. His admiration for their qualities as mothers was accompanied by a contempt for them as merely instinctive beings. And yet he dreaded their capacity to be something more, and called down fire from heaven upon all who dared aspire to intelligence and through it to humanity. For intelligence, in his view, could only increase woman's power over man by enabling her to exploit her allurement consciously. And from that prospect he turned away in physical terror, tortured by memories and fearful lest he should fall again.

§ 7

Ironically enough, however, Tolstoy emphasized the binding morality of marriage in the very novel in which he first betrayed his moral dissatisfaction with his own. The physical foundations of his life were quaking at the very time when he was arguing that a physical union once formed was holy and obligatory.

When Levin returns home after the marriage ceremony he feels that there is something that needs investigating, 'not now, of course, but sometime later,' and in the first

few months of his marriage he is described as awaking
from a Capuan life and reproaching himself for his happiness. The horror which he experiences when witnessing
his brother's death is combined with admiration for his
wife and his old nurse who seem to know without the least
doubt what is life and what is death. 'Though they could
not have answered, nor even comprehended, the questions
that presented themselves to Levin, neither the one nor
the other had any doubt about the meaning of the pheno-
menon. . . . As a proof that they understood what it
meant, they were never under an uncertainty as to what
to do with the dying and were not afraid of them. . . .
Had Levin been left alone with his brother, he would have
looked at him in terror and sat waiting in still greater
horror for what was to come, without being able to do
anything for him. . . . But Kitty did not consider all these
things. She had no time to think of herself, for she was too
occupied with the patient.'

It is from this time that Levin begins seriously to investigate the painful discord in himself and to strain all
his mental powers in order to put himself right. And
gradually he realizes that however deeply he may bury
himself in the soil, however fully his life may be occupied,
it has no meaning for him whenever he thinks of it.

The meaning of life and death which he credits his wife
with having is due to the fact that so far as she thinks at
all, she thinks in action. For her the meaning of life is
simply the fact of living. And while he feels that women
and peasants who believe in this way are 'the best people
he knows,' he is irretrievably divided from them. 'With-

out knowing who I am and why I am here, life is impossible. And I cannot know it, consequently I cannot live,' he would say to himself. . . . And though in good health and happily married, Levin was several times so near to killing himself that he had to hide a rope so as not to hang himself, and would not go out with a gun for fear of shooting himself.'

The inevitable moment in fact was approaching in Tolstoy's life when his critical consciousness would assert itself definitely against the physical life which had absorbed him since his marriage.

In 1874 he had visited the Petrovsky Fair, as was his yearly custom, and had thrown himself with zest into the pagan sports and festivities. At the same time he had stayed at a neighbouring Monastery, where a hermit resided who was 'saving his soul' by a solitary and ascetic life. And as he was completing *Anna Karenina* three years later and the labour became more and more tedious, the need to save his soul, like the hermit, began to darken the pleasure he derived from expressing his body like a Bashkir.

'Something very strange began to happen to me. At first I experienced moments of perplexity and arrest of life, as though I did not know how to live or what to do: and I felt lost and became dejected. But this passed, and I went on living as before. Then these moments of perplexity began to recur oftener and oftener, and always in the same form. They were always expressed by the question: 'What is it for? What does it lead to?'

The need of knowing grew upon him as the pleasure of

being declined. This pleasure had never indeed been all-sufficing. There had always been 'trivial signs of indisposition,' but for fifteen years he had been too active to notice them seriously. Now, however, he was increasingly conscious of a mortal disease.

The crisis was not yet. But Levin's search for a solution of his sufferings and still more the solution which he claims at the end of the novel to have found, foretold it.

The problem, as Levin realizes, is to reconcile his thought which denies life with his instincts which accept it. 'He was living well and thinking badly. He had been living unconsciously on the spiritual truth he had imbibed with his mother's milk, yet in his thoughts he had not only refused to acknowledge them, but had cautiously avoided them altogether.'

His assumption, however, here and in all his arguments is that the commands of instinct are always virtuous and that reason is evil because it runs counter to them. It was instinct which told him, as for centuries it had told peasants, the poor in spirit, and the wise, to live, not for himself, but for God. This knowledge could not be explained through reason, because it was beyond the sphere of reason. 'Reason discovered the theory of the struggle for existence, and the law demanding that I should gratify my own desires at the cost of others. To love my neighbour could not have been discovered by reason, because it is unreasonable. . . . The knowledge has already been revealed to my heart, so why do I persist in trying to express it by means of reason, and through the medium of words that are foreign to it?'

So Levin argued, and his 'secret of happiness came back to him, clear and strong. . . . He had no need to arouse it by reflection; the feeling had become independent of thought.'

It had; and as such, as Tolstoy was to discover, it lent him no lasting support.

For feeling 'independent of thought,' as faith uncorrected by scepticism, has no centre, no critical criterion. Levin knows this when he says – 'without the idea of a God we cannot build up anything.' But he fails to distinguish an idea from a feeling. A conception of what is good or evil is essential to a really creative life, and thought must enter into such a conception. An instinctive response to life is not enough; for natural life *is* ruled by the impartial struggle for existence which Levin hated reason for discovering, and it is only by recognizing the fact that we may learn to transcend it. Reason by exploiting and individualizing the forces of which it has become conscious may, and often does, convert the impartial struggle for existence, by which the natural world preserves its equilibrium, into a vicious discord. But the struggle exists and feeling, independent of thought, cannot transform it into something higher. Until we have learnt that to love our neighbours is not unreasonable, but in fact the most reasonable relation possible, we are likely to hate them instinctively as often as we love them.

And Levin, in the concluding paragraph of *Anna Karenina*, although he tries to convince himself that he has found the secret which will solve his inner contradiction, betrays his doubt. 'This new feeling,' he confesses, 'has

not changed me, made me happy all at once. . . . I shall
probably get angry with Ivan, the coachman, the same
as ever, embark upon useless discussions, express my
thoughts irrelevantly as before; there will always be the
same dead wall between my soul and that of others, even
with my wife; I shall probably go on accusing her in my
anxiety and repenting of it afterwards. I shall continue
to pray without being able to explain to myself why, but
my life, my whole life, independently of what may happen
to me, every minute of it, shall no longer be senseless as
before, but every moment, every action shall be invested
with meaning.'

Despite the defiant conclusion, the note of despair
sounds ominously in these words. And indeed the crisis
in Tolstoy's life was at hand. It was, as has been said, only
the culmination of many lesser ones, of all those cessations
of life and reanimations through which he had passed in
fifty years. But always before he had recovered the blind
instinctive force which drove him on. And now it was not
merely to falter, but to fail.

And since he attributed to instinct the source of all life's
meaning, its failure emptied life of all significance. He
was not only faced with his own solitariness, but with his
own and the whole world's senselessness. For in denying
the rights of reason to its due share in experience, he had
denied the very reason of his being.

¶ PART FOUR

THE BATTLE JOINED

THE BATTLE JOINED

§ 1

FROM the completion of *Anna Karenina* early in 1877, Tolstoy, suffocated by 'the fumes . . . of what is going on inside,' devoted himself to religious reflection and to a close study of the Gospels. He had indeed begun to observe Church rites and fasts a year previously and had derived a delusive comfort from them. Until he was fifty, as has been shown, he strove with some success to forget his divided being in a life of sensation, idealized in various ways. And so long as his muscles were growing, his memory was being enriched and his appetites defied the staleness of satiety, it was natural to believe in a cheerful evolution to better states as the universal law. The voice of resilient instinct which assured him that his nature was changing, that a new life and a new being were being born in him by divine dispensation could still convince him, although again and again its assurance had been disproved.

But 'a time came when the growth within me ceased. I felt that I was not developing, but fading; my muscles were weakening, my teeth falling out, and I saw that the law [of evolution] not only did not explain anything to me, but that there never had been or could be such a law and that I had taken for a law what I had found in myself at a certain period of my life.'

From this time, therefore, he became obsessed by 'a consciousness of inevitable impending destruction' and sought in Christianity 'the only possible means of safety in this position.'

Still, of course, and to the end of his life, the physical cessations and reanimations continued. Strahof, for example, wrote of him in 1879 – 'I found Tolstoy in excellent spirits. . . . With what vivacity he is carried away by his ideas! Only young people seek truth as ardently as he; and I can say positively that he is now in the very bloom of his strength.'

It was in fact because the tide of physical life never ceased to flow in him uncontrollably that he both loved and hated the instincts which accepted its compulsion. Henceforth, however, he hated them far more persistently than he loved. He hated his body because it told him more often of death than of life, and he could only recover hope in Christianity by compelling it into a service of hatred against the body and every expression in public and private life of the pride and pleasure of the body.

In *Memoirs of a Lunatic* he later recorded, more graphically perhaps than in any other of his writings, the despairing sense of death which now continually possessed him. The writer of the *Memoirs*, who is of course himself, describes how, when he had been married ten years, he was going to buy an estate, when a feeling of the utter futility of all such transactions came over him. He wakes up in a square newly whitewashed room in an inn feeling: 'Why am I here? Where am I going? Just as I am I must be for ever. . . . I am unbearably weary of myself. I want to go to sleep, to forget – and I cannot, I cannot get rid of self.'

The feeling of dreary horror gradually increases. '"What nonsense!" I said to myself, "Why am I so de-

jected? What am I afraid of?" "You are afraid of me" –
I heard the voice of Death . . . "I am here."

'I shuddered. Yes – Death! Death will come; it will
come and it ought not to come. Even in facing actual
death I would certainly not feel anything of what I felt
now. Then it would be simply fear, whereas now it was
more than that. I was actually seeing, feeling the approach of death, and along with it I felt that death ought
not to exist.

'My entire being was conscious of the necessity, of the
right to live, and at the same time of the inevitability of
dying. This inner conflict was causing me unbearable
pain. . . . To feel my life doomed to be taken from me
was a terror shutting out any other thought. . . . And
acid hatred deprived me of every spark of kindly feeling.
Just a dull and steady hatred against myself and against
that which had created me. What did create me? God?
We say God. . . . "What if I tried to pray?" I suddenly
thought.'

He prays, and by diverting his thoughts from himself
gains some relief. But it is transient, because even in the
act of prayer he is conscious of opposing himself to God,
of blaming Him and flinging angry questions at His head.
And so the despair and horror return, and again he re-
volves in the vicious circle of love of life and hatred of the
death to which life points.

From this circle he seems to discover an outlet, when
lost in the forest he resigns himself absolutely to life, ceasing to demand an answer to his questions or to reproach
God for His silence. 'My soul was full of joy. . . . I

was not quite happy, but I knew there was a joy within me which I would understand later on. . . . Since that I have grown even less interested in the management of my affairs and in family matters. These things even became repulsive to me. Everything was wrong in my eyes. . . . My wife was vexed with me and abused me. But I was full of joy.'

He went to Mass, and as he was leaving the church, beggars were standing on the steps. 'It became instantly clear to me that this ought not to be, and in reality was not. But if this is not, then there is no death and no fear, and nothing is being torn asunder within me, and I am not afraid of any calamity which may come.

'At that moment the full light of the truth was kindled within me, and I grew into what I am now. If all this horror does not necessarily exist around me, then it certainly does not exist within me.'

This short story illuminates even more vividly perhaps than the *Confession* which Tolstoy was shortly to write, how starkly opposed were now the two forces in his nature and also the purely evasive method which he was still at first to adopt in seeking an issue from the conflict.

For his first interpretation of Christianity was only the old naturalism in disguise. He resigned himself to God as he had resigned himself to the Caucasian forest, hoping to become like 'a mosquito, or pheasant, or deer.' He ceased to question, and when some ugly actuality forced itself on his attention, he closed his eyes and comforted himself with the delusion that 'in reality it was not.'

For reality, he felt in himself, must be blameless. But

he only felt this by turning a deaf ear to that part of him which argued otherwise. And, as ever, the excluded faculty reasserted itself. It reasserted itself in particular, as we shall see, when he went to Moscow in 1882 and was appalled by the conditions of its slums. And when this occurred evasion was no longer possible. The 'reality' of his emotional dreams was too rudely shattered by actuality for him to cling to it.

And so from indulgence in a passive and personal Christianity, in a dream of ideal innocence in which he could forget the ugliness of fact, he was driven to formulate an aggressive and social asceticism. He no longer closed his eyes to brutal actuality, but he bid men desert an actual world in which such brutalities could exist, and recover either as peasants or ascetics the innocence of which he dreamed and for which he longed. He bid them not only deny all the organizations which, in his opinion, had corrupted the inherent virtue of humanity, but, if possible, deny also the desires by which humanity perpetuated itself.

The last thirty years of his life were thus divided between struggles to heal the dissonance in his own nature and in that of the society to which he belonged. The causes of the two dissonances were, as he rightly saw, identical. And his deep significance lies in the fact that he was thus representative not only of certain temperaments but of a morbid phase of civilization which still persists.

Only, however, after he had sought salvation for himself and dreamed that he had found it, did he turn again to the world. And in his conflict with the world he fought over again, with a deeper desperation, his conflict with himself.

§ 2

The five years, then, immediately following the completion of *Anna Karenina* were devoted to a search for a meaning in life which would enable him to continue to live. This search is described in *A Confession*, which he wrote in 1878.

He began inevitably by reviewing his past, of which his present was only the logical culmination. He had been reared in conventional orthodoxy, and he saw now that the reason why such religion ceased to have any hold on him from the age of sixteen was that it was unreal. The orthodox were frequently 'dull and cruel people, who considered themselves very important.' Their Christianity was one of outward form, and they were often morally inferior to unbelievers.

To that extent he had been right to dissociate himself from them, but in so doing he had lost all faith apart from animal instinct and a desire, largely dictated by vanity, to perfect himself. He had been led too by the contempt of his class for moral goodness and its respect for ambition, power, covetousness and lasciviousness, to abandon himself to war, adultery and dissipation, while self-display had been the dominating motive even of his writing.

And so, it seemed to him, he had lived until his marriage, not without spasmodic moral strivings but unsustained by any clear moral purpose. And then the inner questioning had grown louder and more insistent, until he reached the point, already defined, when before he did anything, he found it imperative that he should know why he was doing it. His inability to answer this question destroyed all his initiative, as man and artist. For since he had expressed himself instinctively in art, as in life, it too appeared 'an adornment of life, an allurement to life,' and as perishable and fraudulent as all other appetites. He had been relying on his animal faith, and when this no longer existed, he had nothing left to live on. Each step in knowledge led him to the conviction that the truth was death and that life was meaningless.

The common-sense argument – 'You cannot understand the meaning of life, so do not think about it, but live' – offered no escape from his dilemma. For it was his reason that denied life and it was therefore his reason which must accept it. As a character in one of Eugene O'Neill's plays remarks of life – 'It isn't enough to be her creature, you've got to create her, or she requests you to destroy yourself.' Tolstoy could not create her, because he had ceased to believe in her instinctively and could only deny her rationally.

He still believed in her enough, however, as a creature to refuse to destroy himself. And he began to seek in the field of rational argument a justification of life. He sought it in the sciences and philosophies, and both only seemed to confirm the senselessness of life.

The problem of experimental science was 'the sequence of cause and effect in material phenomena.' It contented itself with analysis, with the mechanism of existence, the work of the nerves or the interplay of forces. But explanations of the physical working of life did not help a man to live. They merely confirmed the inevitability of death. They did not show how a man might be free, but only defined the conditions of his slavery. It was a knowledge of the whole, as a means to wholeness in himself, which Tolstoy sought, and science reduced life with wonderful subtlety into its constituent parts.

And so its words seemed to him to have no meaning. He could find no relation in its activities between the infinite whole which he sought, and the finite complexities which it traced. As he was to write later in *A Confession* — 'What is there for me to be proud of in the fact that I know down to the smallest detail the meaning of each hieroglyphic, and yet am not strong enough to understand the hieroglyphic inscription?'

'They hope to understand it,' I said.

'Hope, indeed! It is time they understood that this hope has lived through three thousand years of history, and we have not moved a hair's breadth forward towards the knowledge of the nature of justice, or freedom, or the meaning of human life!'

Such an exaggeration is an index of Tolstoy's inability to adapt himself rationally to life. He desired an infinite satisfaction and science dealt only with the finite evidences of the senses; and between the two he could see no possibility of a relation.

He turned then to philosophy, and here too he found men merely putting the question, 'Why?' and failing to answer it. They might speak of an essence of life, existing within all that exists, and name it 'idea,' or 'substance,' or 'spirit,' or 'will,' but the reason of it all and the relation of this essence to human life remained as obscure as ever. To be told that he was the medium of an essence helped a man to live as little as to be told that he was a transitory cohesion of particles.

Philosophy, therefore, which reduced life to the abstract, availed Tolstoy no more than science, which reduced it to the concrete. He could not believe that science might help eventually to explain the nature of the infinite through the finite, and philosophy that of the finite through the infinite, or that the approach to life which each represented might and must be reconciled in a creative consciousness.

And so reason seemed to lead nowhere, and only the ignorant, the hedonistic, those strong enough to destroy life, having understood that it was evil, or weak enough to cling to it in spite of this understanding, could continue to exist.

And yet he was dimly conscious of the invalidity of his thoughts. 'How can reason deny life, when it is the creator of life? Or to put it the other way: Were there no life, my reason would not exist; therefore reason is life's son. Life is all. Reason is its fruit, yet reason rejects life itself. I felt that there was something wrong here.'

This indeed was the crux of the matter. Reason denied life because it had lost its organic relation with life. And yet an organic relation of a kind could persist in reason's despite. 'Reason worked, but something else was also working which I can only call a consciousness of life.'

But it was here again that Tolstoy made his cardinal mistake. He failed to distinguish between a creature response to life and a creative consciousness of it. He believed that his sufferings were due to pride of intellect, in which all of his own narrow circle shared. But 'the real labouring people,' for whom he had such a 'strange physical affection,' did not suffer so. Their relation with life, he felt, was organic, and without inquiring what sort of an organic relation it was, without remembering how often he had tried to recover this relation and how invariably he had failed, he determined that he must 'seek meaning not among those who have lost it . . . but among those milliards of the past and present, who make life and who support the burden of their own lives and of ours also.'

Once again he sought peace by a relapse into the primitive, and from primitive faith as from primitive life he found himself debarred by the critical intelligence which he hated but could not silence.

'My position was terrible. I knew I could find nothing along the path of reasonable knowledge, except a denial of life; and there – in faith – was nothing but a denial of reason, which was yet more impossible for me than a denial of life. . . . By faith it appears that in order to understand the meaning of life I must repudiate my reason, the very thing for which alone a meaning is required.'

From this contradiction there were two possible exits. Either reason was not so rational as he supposed, or what seemed irrational was not so irrational as he supposed.

And pondering the first of these alternatives, he saw that so long as reason considered either the finite or the infinite exclusively, it could not answer his question, which was 'What meaning has my finite existence in this infinite world.' And 'however irrational and distorted might be the replies given by faith, they have this advantage, that they introduce into every answer a relation between the finite and the infinite without which there can be no solution.'

Simple people preserved this relation instinctively, and their very credulity helped them to preserve it. Their faith did not depend upon the legends and fables which they associated with it, but upon the fact that they lived it. From which Tolstoy concluded that he had erred not so much because he had thought incorrectly, as because he had lived badly, and that faith was justified even if it could not be rationally explained, when it was confirmed by the lives of those who professed it.

It was not so confirmed by the lives of Orthodox Churchmen of his own class, and this accounted for the slight hold such faith had had upon him. Their creed was something separate from their lives, which did not correspond to the principles which they expounded in their teachings. They lived to satisfy their desires, while they preached that a man should live for others. At most therefore their faith supplied them with a refuge from the evils of life which their own selfishness helped to create.

Among simple, unlettered folk he found also much superstition, but this did not prevent their whole life from being 'a confirmation of the meaning of life which their faith gave them.'

To accept their faith, therefore, because it worked, and to work and live like them to make it real, seemed the only possible exit from his dilemma. And consequently the life of his own circle became more and more distasteful and lost all meaning in his eyes. 'I understood that it is *all* merely self-indulgence, and that to find a meaning in it is impossible; while the life of the whole labouring people, the whole of mankind who produce life, appeared to me in its true significance. I understood that *that* is life itself, and that the meaning given to that life is true; and I accepted it.'

So Tolstoy argued, and upon the conviction which he had now reached he was to base the tremendous assault upon the predatory and parasitic nature of modern civilization that was to occupy him for the rest of his life. The distinction that he drew between the life and faith of the simple and the life and creed of the privileged commands agreement. But once again it led him to deny the consciousness which he hated rather than to relate it positively to the instinctive life which he loved.

The faith which the peasant possessed and expressed in a life of toil was rather an acceptance of necessity than an affirmation of God in the highest sense. The infinite which he related to his finite existence was the life-force of which he was the passive instrument. And the problem before Tolstoy, as before all who have put their reason to the service of self-indulgence, is how to express the life-force, not as a slave, but as a free being. Tolstoy turned his back upon the falsely civilized and sought to recover the creative faith of the simple and unlettered; but it was a reversion which the forces of evolution disallowed even in one so physically constituted.

To become truly civilized was the only fertile solution of his discords, as of those of the world at large, and in a true civilization the self is neither renounced nor indulged. It is expressed, not in servile obedience to the life-force, in an unquestioning creature faith, but in a rational creativeness in which the life-force is informed with, but not perverted by, intelligence, and is defined in perfect personality. For the highest life does not consist, as Tolstoy claimed, in 'moving away from self towards God,' but in discovering and developing the God that is in self.

'The aim of man in life,' he wrote, 'is to save his soul, and to save his soul he must live "godly," and to live "godly" he must renounce all the pleasures of life.' But the aim of man is rather to find his soul, and he will find it not by denying the faculties which make him distinctively human, but by developing them to the utmost degree. And only by such development can God completely realize Himself in man, and man in God.

It may be that such development is beyond the powers of certain natures; that they can only approach God by trying to become His creatures. The physical forces in Tolstoy's nature were so powerful that they dictated a physical faith. He was convinced, for example, that man to be happy should 'produce his living as the animals do, but with this difference, that he will perish if he does it alone; he must obtain it not for himself but for all. And when he does that, I have a firm assurance that he is happy and that his life is reasonable.'

But a man can be disinterestedly productive in many ways. He can serve the spiritual needs of humanity as a poet or its physical needs as a plumber. While it is true that a peasant or an artisan lack the means to be social parasites, a creative life of thought is as possible as a creative life of manual labour. The great artists of the world, and the great thinkers, have expressed the life-force as disinterestedly as the peasant, and have known far more vividly than he the joys and the pains of service.

Tolstoy, however, could not dissociate consciousness from egotism. He could only renew his relation with life by returning 'to what belonged to my earliest childhood and youth . . . to the belief in that Will which produced me, and desires something of me.'

And possibly the discord in him, as in the Russia of his day, was so aggravated, the perversion of intelligence so vicious, that true civilization could only be born through a return to the primitive. Fearful of everything which 'inflamed' in him 'excessive desires,' he turned perforce to 'a laborious, frugal, rough life which moderates the lusts,' and built his faith upon physical necessity.

We criticize, therefore, the solution which he now claimed to have found, not because it failed to answer the needs of his personality (although we shall show that in many ways it did), but because he was to insist that it was the only solution which could answer the needs of humanity, and was to compel the teaching of Christ into conformity with it.

For the peasant not only had faith in life but was an Orthodox Christian. And so Tolstoy himself for a time

tried to submit to the Church, to fast and take the sacrament. But he could not silence his critical powers to this
extent. The ceremonial, try as he would to read meaning
into it, remained for him quite unreal, and more and more,
as he observed the brutalities which the Church justified
or condoned, he became convinced that its ritual was a
mere distraction and narcotic. And yet the peasant found
in the Church's teaching something that corresponded
with his faith, which led Tolstoy to write – 'That there is
truth in the teaching is to me indubitable; but it is also
certain that there is falsehood in it, and I must find what
is true and what is false, and must disentangle the one
from the other.'

This was the great task which absorbed all his powers
for eight years and which he never really relinquished.
In it he sought not only to discover the essentials of
Christ's teaching which had become overlaid by Church
dogmas and a worldly ecclesiasticism, but to define and
confirm the peasant faith which he had accepted by obtaining for it the sanction of the divinest man in history.

His aim was now to transform the moral truth which he
had always felt in primitive life, 'from dim, indefinitely
conceived suppositions and wishes into firm and definite
expressions inevitably demanding corresponding actions';
to convert, in fact, a peasant faith into a code of conduct.

But since this faith entailed a condemnation of all those
who failed to produce their living 'as the animals do,' and
yet had its roots in a hatred of his animal nature, it more
and more divorced him from his wife and family. As he
wrote in *A Confession* – 'The two drops of honey which

diverted my eyes from the cruel truth longer than the rest: my love of family, and of writing – art as I called it – were no longer sweet to me.

'Family' . . . said I to myself. 'But my family – wife and children – are also human. They are placed just as I am: they must either live in a lie or see the terrible truth. Why should they live? Why should I love them, guard them, bring them up, or watch them? That they may come to the despair that I feel, or else be stupid? Loving them, I cannot hide the truth from them: each step in knowledge leads them to the truth. And the truth is death.'

But his wife was not placed just as he was. Her life was not and could not be poisoned by the thought of death. Absorbed in family life, she could not share the 'feeling of fear, orphanage, isolation in a strange land, and a hope of help from some one,' which drove him to deny his own class, to denounce the Church which she respected, and no longer practise the art for which he was famous.

'He reads,' she confided to a friend, 'and he ponders until he gives himself the headache, and all to prove that the Church is not in agreement with the teaching of the Gospel. He will hardly find a dozen people in Russia whom the matter could possibly interest. But there is nothing to be done. I have only one hope: that he will be done with it all the sooner, and that it will pass off like an illness.'

It was, however, no passing distemper, but a mortal disease. And although Tolstoy strove for thirty years to cast it off, and in the process profoundly stirred the conscience and exposed the hypocrisies of Christian Europe, he remained always the stricken man, of whom an observer wrote at this time – 'He looks overwhelmed. A double furrow traces symmetrical lines in the large comely face. There is so much goodness, such tenderness, in the great dog-like muzzle, in the eyes that regard you with so frank, so clear, so sorrowful a look. They read your mind so surely. They pity and implore.'

§ 3

Tolstoy began his work on Christianity, as he had begun *War and Peace*, by studying the authorities. The fruits of this study were published later in *A Criticism of Dogmatic Theology* and *A New Translation and Harmony of the Four Gospels*. But, as with *War and Peace*, subjective interpretation quickly superseded objective study, and was first crystallized in *What I Believe*, which he wrote in 1883.

'Every man of the present day,' he was later to assert, 'if we go deep enough into the contradiction between his conscience and his life, is in a state of despair,' but suddenly, as it seemed to him, he heard the words of Christ and understood them, 'and life and death ceased to seem to me evil, and instead of despair I experienced happiness and the joy of life undisturbed by death.' But like all his sudden convictions of joy and serenity, the mood passed, and he saw that it was necessary to reinforce his instinctive faith with an ethical structure, which would stand firm against the fluctuations of mood.

In *What I Believe* he defined such an ethic in five dogmatic commandments, which he claimed to embody the essence of Christ's teaching, and he showed with withering logic that the Church which pretended to be Christian transgressed each one of them.

He had already, however, in the previous autumn taken a house in Moscow, and his experience of social conditions there renewed and intensified the despair which he had somewhat appeased. To relieve it he extended his attack upon theology and priestcraft, and assailed, in *What Then Must We Do?* and seven years later in *The Kingdom of God is Within You*, the whole predatory system of society which perpetuated war between classes and between nations.

We are not concerned here to argue at any length the extent to which Tolstoy distorted Christ's teaching, but rather to show how his interpretation of the Gospel reflected his own inner needs, while failing to satisfy either them or the needs of the world at large.

Christ's teaching by its very nature provokes and requires a personal response. His language was that of the poet, and the characteristic of great poetry is to be so profound and yet so ambiguous that each man can wrest from it what his nature demands. Tolstoy himself, in a tolerant moment, admitted that 'Jesus did not lay down rules of life,' agreeing in the abstract with Matthew Arnold who wrote – 'The most important and fruitful utterances of Jesus . . . are not things which can be drawn up as a table of stiff and stark external commands. . . . The very *secret* of Jesus, "He that loveth his life shall lose it, he that will lose his life shall save it,'' does not give us a command to be taken and followed in the letter, but an idea to work in our mind and soul, and of inexhaustible value there.'

Christ in fact revealed, often in the form of paradoxes, what the poet reveals through imagery, a profound intuition of life. His truth therefore cannot be expressed in terms of logic without some loss of its reality.

But ideas 'to work in our mind and soul' were too vague and too corruptible a medium of salvation to satisfy Tolstoy. Ideas to him, as has been sufficiently shown, had induced only a sentimental self-abandonment, and he needed rather a strictly defined ethical code which he could enforce upon his senses. Moreover he saw how cleverly the Christian Church had exploited the ambiguity of Christ's life and teaching for its own selfish ends, and although he replaced one set of dogmas by another, there can be no doubt that he approached far nearer the reality of Christ's teaching than the Church which he attacked.

Those too who complain of his literalism, of the fact that he subserviated Christ's teaching to his own peasant faith, to his belief in the virtue of illiteracy and his hatred of the flesh, must admit that there are elements in the Gospel records which support, if they do not justify, such treatment. Christ was limited, not in his spiritual insight, which was beyond time, but occasionally in his application of this insight to the affairs of men, by the circumstances of his time and environment. He lived in a peasant community, sharing, it would seem, to begin with, the current expectation of a cataclysmal and immediate coming of the kingdom in a political sense. And even when the kingdom of his expectation had become a change of heart, a new order of consciousness in man, he still believed that it would be sudden and cataclysmic, a spiritual seizure, overriding and transforming in a moment all the recalcitrant forces in human life.

Although therefore the Western Churches have tried to reconcile his teaching with their own practical and compromising attitude to life, it is impossible to read the Gospels with an open mind without finding in them elements of Eastern nihilism.

Tolstoy, like other ascetic devotees, could not have so successfully based his own denial of the physical and the rational upon scriptural quotation, if these elements had not existed there. Christ's spiritual insight was such that his teaching may reinforce and crown a positive ideal and may be applied to circumstances which he could not visualize and an evolutionary view of human history which he was too spiritually possessed to contemplate. We believe too that his unique reality lies in the fact that in his being the conflicting ideals of self-assertion and renunciation – the symbols of West and East – were resolved, and that his characteristic paradoxes expressed this resolution.

But if Christ himself brought these opposites into union, his followers have been able to dissociate them. And so far as his teaching has divorced the spiritual in man from the physical and the rational instead of reconciling them, so far even as it has separated the timeless from the world in time, it has, in our view, embodied an ineffective ideal, and one which is less valid to the needs and purposes of human life than that which Keats expressed when he wrote – 'How then are these sparks which are God to have identity given them – so as ever to possess a bliss peculiar to each one's individual existence? How, but by the medium of a world like this? This point I sincerely wish to consider, because I think it a grander system of salvation than the Christian religion – or rather it is a system of Spirit recreation. This is effected by three grand materials acting the one upon the other for a series of years. These three materials are the *Intelligence* – the *human heart* . . . and the *World*. . . . Do you not see how necessary a world of Pains and Troubles is to school an Intelligence and make it a Soul . . .? As various as the Lives of Men are – so various become their souls, and thus does God make individual beings, Souls, Identical Souls of the sparks of his own essence.'

In the soul of Christ himself, for those at least who seek it, intelligence and humanity were reconciled perhaps more perfectly than in any other man. He did not deny his passions or his reason because he feared them, as Tolstoy did in his name; and yet his very innocence of earthly passion, his assured and almost effortless spirituality, and his claim that his kingdom was not of this world, have made his superhuman acceptance of life the cause of a false denial in others, of a false divorce between the spiritual and the material, and a substitution of negative prohibitions for positive principles.

What was recently written of the influence of the purest

of Christian saints is to a less degree applicable to that of
Christ himself. 'It is because the basis of negation, however beautifully transcended in the life of St. Francis and
his followers, never disappears from view that his influence
among us to-day is mainly sentimental, is neutralized, that
is to say, by a host of unrecognized withdrawals. . . . It is
clearer to mankind now than it was then that life is, in one
aspect, all material: and that the transition from the
material to the spiritual is not a passage from one world
to another, but a substitution in the soul of a changed
attitude to the same things . . . more and more we realize
that the example we chiefly need is the example not of
abnegation but of use and fulfilment; it is, indeed, infinitely more difficult to create harmony than to refuse to
touch the instrument with which it is to be made: and the
task of religion, we increasingly perceive, is not to show
us how to escape the world but how to avail ourselves of it
most fully and most completely.'

Even if these words are inapplicable to the teaching of
Christ himself, they are particularly relevant to Tolstoy's interpretation of that teaching, which is our concern
here. The basis of his negation was not indeed mediæval
saintliness, but a mediæval fear which arbitrarily denied
that certain material attachments could be avenues of
spiritual experience and tried to simplify life by rejecting,
instead of mastering its complexity.

Against a sentimental withdrawal from life into a region
of dreamy mysticism he did indeed inveigh with all his
powers, but his own withdrawal from a modern 'world of
Pains and Troubles' was also in its essence sentimental,

while his denial to certain physical relations of the possibility of spiritual significance was not Christian, but sensual. It was a sensualist who wrote – 'Sexual love, marriage, is a service of self, and consequently in any case an obstacle to the service of God and man, and therefore, from a Christian point of view, a fall, a sin.'

Such a conviction, which was to become more and more pronounced and created, even more perhaps than his hatred of property and privilege, the discord in his family life was as alien in its animal realism to true Christian morality as the sentimental eroticism which he rightly denounced. Upon it he based the generality that 'Christian morality is not merely independent of pagan philosophy, but it stands in complete contradiction to it.'

Certainly the Manichean element in Christianity has been due to the stress of its reaction against Paganism. The ascetic has always feared the lust of nature too much to accept her strength and sanity. He has not dared to admit that the senses are the nerves, as the intelligence is the lens, of the soul, but for three hundred years the conviction has grown that the natural is essential to the good and the beautiful, and Christianity itself, although it has always lagged behind the most creative spirits, has increasingly tended to absorb into itself the sane and vital elements of paganism.

But Tolstoy rejected such a synthesis because he could not realize it in himself. For him Christianity was necessarily opposed to paganism, as spirit was to flesh. He wrote, for example, in a letter – 'There are moments when one ceases to believe in spiritual life. This is not unbelief, but rather periods of belief in physical life. . . . A man suddenly begins to be afraid of death. This always happens when something has befogged him, and he once more begins to believe that bodily life is real life . . . he suddenly succumbs to the seduction of illusion, and feels frightened.'

The awful issues of life and death therefore resolved themselves for Tolstoy into an unequivocal conflict. He could not ponder them calmly or admit that we know in part and see in a mirror darkly. Nor could he rebuke the indifference of men to the things which essentially concerned them with the wisdom of one who saw how complex was human life and how hard it was to apply rigid rules to its conduct.

Certainly the cruelty and immorality of the ruling classes in Russia, and the consequent 'crushed and stupefied condition of the working masses' justified almost all he wrote of them. But it was fundamentally his own sensuality which made it impossible for him to accommodate his Christianity to modern life. He could only balance the physical forces in his nature by an extreme denial of them, and he attacked 'personal life' so fiercely because it represented for him only acquisitive instinct and carnal desire.

And it was because he lived in terror of surrendering to his lower nature that he rejected all compromise. 'Once you let yourself lower the ideal,' he wrote, 'to suit your weakness, there is no finding the line at which to stop.'

Admittedly the familiar and convenient worldly argu-

ment that ideals are impracticable lent support to his contention. But the only way to disprove it is to accommodate
the ideal to life and gradually prove its practicability. The
danger of compromising the ideal in the process is
obvious, but a fanatical absoluteness is not only dangerous,
but useless. Such absoluteness, dogmatized in some particular duty, has caused most of the crimes done in the
name of God. And upon the average individual its effect
is more deadening than quickening.

Tolstoy admitted in one place that an average Christian
began by saying that the ideal was unattainable and so
excused himself from striving to approach it. But he refused to recognize the consequent necessity of adapting
the ideal to each individual case. He claimed that
humanity had reached that point in its evolution when,
having passed through an animal and a social stage, it was
ripe for the Christian ethic which he preached. He disregarded as a moralist, what he admitted as an artist, that
although the moral sense of mankind as a whole had advanced, yet it was necessarily composed of men at very
different stages of development, and that the ideal which
corresponded with his own needs could not be summarily
imposed either on those in advance of himself or on those
behind.

In contending that as soon as a man argues, he acknow-
ledges that he is a rational being and so must cease automatically to be an animal, and long to be a Christian in the
absolute sense, he neglected the fact that the first use to
which men commonly turn their reason is to justify their
animalism, and that such men often continue to find

in the calculated satisfaction of their instincts an adequate reason for their being.

It may be that 'only in worldly life do the powerful enjoy and delight in the fame and power of personal life'; yet thousands still enjoy such a life without a twinge of conscience, and although they admit the fact of death, they are too unimaginative to be troubled by it. Self-consciousness in its early stages increases the pleasure a man derives from his instincts; it is only when he has passed beyond this stage that he comes to hate what he loved and seeks to transcend his egotism.

But Tolstoy assumed that all but a small minority in the modern world had, like himself, reached this point of self-hatred, and in civilization he saw, not the gradual evolution of man from barbarism through vicious self-love to a reasonable humanity, but a perverted and irretrievable viciousness. It was a physical, no less than a moral disease, and of those who suffered from it he wrote — 'They are nearly all subject to nervous, digestive, and sexual illness from gluttony, drunkenness, debauchery, and doctoring, and those who do not die young spend half their life in being doctored and taking injections of morphia, or are shrivelled cripples, unfitted to live by their own exertions, and capable of existing only like parasites or like those ants who are fed by slave-ants. Consider their deaths: this one shot himself; that one rotted with syphilis; another old man died from the effects of a stimulant,' and so on through a list of the most obscene diseases.

It is true that in time Nature revenges herself on those who misuse her, that self-indulgence leads to physical degeneracy; but Tolstoy's suggestion that a social parasite, or indeed all who in the modern world do not live as Christians, are necessarily neurotics or worse, is a gross exaggeration. Nature loves the unconscious pagan best, but she is apt to favour even the self-regarding pagan more than the saint or the genius who struggles to transcend her limits and so disturbs her equilibrium.

It is these, of whom Tolstoy was one, who are conscious of disease. But because civilization in his own experience had merely aggravated the predatory instincts, to combat which he had formulated a Christian ethic, he considered it the final negation of Christianity.

And in support of this ethic, as later in support of his moral conception of art, he claimed the testimony of inspired primitives. 'Not Christ only,' he wrote, 'but all the Hebrew prophets, John the Baptist, and all the world's true sages, have spoken of that same state, culture, and civilization as an evil, ruinous to mankind.'

Certainly modern civilization, as Tolstoy knew it, was un-Christian, but its very rational viciousness, culminating as it did in the European War, was in process of compelling a rational as distinct from a sentimental acceptance of Christianity or a primitive denial of evolution.

The fact therefore that Tolstoy failed to reconcile Christianity with a true civilization alike in himself and in his teaching, limits both the wisdom and relevance of his interpretation of the Gospels. Yet it was no small service to break through the mists of dogma and superstition, the accretions of legend and idolatry, which had obscured Christ's human reality and turned his teaching into a mockery and a fraud. And although Tolstoy was incapable of that spiritual rebirth by which man, following in Christ's footsteps, can and must strive to *be* God, and in the light of which alone can Christ's teachings be fully understood, he prepared the way for it by insisting so relentlessly upon its physical basis.

In exposing the animal in man, beneath all its disguises, he helped, in his own despite, to liberate the human. And above all he established the idea of the Kingdom of Heaven in its rightful place on earth. Jesus, as he wrote, 'understood his teaching not as a distant ideal for humanity . . . nor as a mystical poetic fantasy . . . but as a real thing, and a thing which would save mankind. . . . He did not dream on the cross, but died for his teaching.' Or again – 'If only people would cease destroying themselves and expecting someone to come and help them – Christ on the clouds with the sound of trumpets, or an historic law or a law of the differentiation and integration of forces. No one will help them unless they help themselves.'

For Science, as Tolstoy saw, although it attacked the Church for substituting something external for the use of reason, was doing the same thing in reason's name. 'In the Church teaching this external thing was – revelation; in the scientific teaching it is – observation.' The one lie conditioned the other. And Tolstoy too in concentrating on the practical side of Christ's teaching neglected its imaginative and mystical reality, and by neglecting this, which was beyond the reach of his understanding, falsified to some extent its moral meaning.

But orthodox Christianity had committed the far graver error of falsifying Christ's mysticism by separating it from its proper roots in conduct. The idea of the Kingdom of Heaven had proved an invaluable phantom with which to divert men's attention from the stark facts of life and to console the victims of human injustice with promises of divine compensation. The view that 'after this life true life will begin,' or that the oppressed, in Burke's words, 'must be taught their consolation in the final proportions of eternal justice,' provided a convenient excuse for tolerating the abuses of this life, and the Church's doctrine of the Fall and of Redemption served, as Tolstoy showed, to perpetuate it. Because Adam fell, it was suggested, life in the world was irreparably bad. And against this fate man's own reasonable efforts to improve human life were impracticable. Nevertheless a blissful life was obtainable, both now and hereafter, not however by man's exertions, but by a divine dispensation, a 'something outside himself,' bought automatically for man by Christ's death, provided he loyally accepted the Church's creed.

Certainly the Protestant Churches of to-day do not interpret the doctrine of the Redemption in this way, nor do they generally claim to be infallible mouthpieces of the 'Holy Ghost' and support their claim by repression and persecution. That they have ceased to do so is, however, chiefly due to man's rational refusal to tolerate such a claim, and fifty years ago, even outside the Russo-Greek Church of which Tolstoy wrote, such an interpretation and such claims were generally prevalent. Nor is the English Church of to-day, whose pulpits rang with incite-

ments to fight and to hate during the war, and one of
whose bishops has recently expounded how the rich may
enter the Kingdom of Heaven by 'wise investment,' since
this is 'the modern equivalent to selling your goods and
giving them to the poor,' innocent of the sin of making itself agreeable to the world, and of encouraging an external and fugitive worship of God, and of playing the
Pharisee to Christ.

A Church which blesses battleships is still akin to the
one which blessed brothels, and although it is perhaps
more concerned with social justice and less fearful of
knowledge to-day than ever before in its history, Tolstoy's assertion retains still a large measure of truth –
'All that is really alive – and does not linger on in angry
dejection, not really living but merely hindering others
from doing so – all that really lives in our European
world has rejected the Church, and all Churches, and lives
its own life independently of the Church.'

Admittedly Tolstoy's attacks on the Church's dogma
are often irrelevant for the English reader because the
theology against which he fulminated is already dead or
dying. And it may be that he even exaggerated the corruption of his own Church, like Kondratyev in *Resurrection*, who, 'wishing to revenge himself for the deception that had been practised on him and on his ancestors,
was never tired of venomously and angrily ridiculing
priests and religious dogmas.' Moreover he himself may
justly be accused of discouraging reasonable efforts to
improve human life, and of misinterpreting 'the Fall' as a
final evil instead of a disturbing condition of man's ad-

vance. For while he attacked the Church for arguing that
there were only two paths open to men – either to believe
and obey the powers that be and participate in organized
evil, or to retire to a monastery and vegetate – he too in
practice, if not in theory, renounced constructive
Christianity in the selfish world which the Church
cravenly accepted, and withdrew to the peasants in the
fields.

Nevertheless, for thirty years he strove most nobly,
within the limits of his nature, to show that religion, if it
is to be real, concerns 'life such as we have on earth, with
all its joys and beauties, with all its struggles of reason
against darkness,' and to extricate what Jesus taught himself, as 'a poor man who eighteen hundred years ago was
taught, was beaten, and executed,' from what worldly
interest had ascribed to him.

And while his interpretation of the five essential commandments which he derived from the Gospels were too
often narrow and negative, they yet remain the foundations upon which a positive and fearless Christianity must
build. To this extent Tolstoy was not only a destroyer of
false shrines, but a builder of the temple of truth.

§ 4

The five commandments which Tolstoy enunciated in
What I Believe, and upon which he based henceforth all
his criticism of life were these: 'Do not be angry; do not
commit adultery; do not bind yourself by oaths; do not
defend yourself by violence; and do not go to war.'

The first of these commandments presupposes the

fourth and the fifth, and need not be considered at any length separately. In it Tolstoy expressed in its simplest form his condemnation of the self-assertive attitude, the idea that 'a man must maintain his dignity and preserve his rights against others (which can only be done by humiliating and offending others),' whereas no man has any rights, being equally unimportant in the eyes of God. 'He only is inferior to all and most ignoble who desires to set himself above others,' and of this false pride anger is the crudest expression. It humiliates and is humiliating.

Even in his interpretation of this commandment Tolstoy was more concerned to deny the passions than to develop the reason. There is an ultimate sense in which no man 'can be superior or inferior to another,' but there is also a relative sense in which such grades exist, not indeed the arbitrary grades of class or riches, but those of real moral value, and it is possible to combine a recognition of these distinctions with a perfect respect for the inherent worth and individuality of every personality, to refrain from anger, not through self-abasement, but through wisdom and magnanimity. Humility of course is an ingredient of such wisdom, but it combines also with a sort of pride, with a positive conception of what it is to be really humane.

Far more marked, however, was the negative element in Tolstoy's interpretation of the second commandment. 'Men and women,' he wrote, 'knowing it to be the law of man's nature to live in couples, should unite with one another in couples and never under any circumstances infringe these alliances; so that the whole evil of strife

caused by sexual relations is removed by the fact that
there are no solitary men or women left deprived of
married life.'

Apart from the numerical fallacy of such a solution, the
assumption that marriage must inevitably remove the evil
of strife caused by sexual relations was quite unjustified.
At best it would only confine it within the limits of family
life. Married life, as Tolstoy was already discovering
himself, can be a state of solitude and of perpetual strife,
can even be as 'cruel and inhuman' as he described
divorce. Only indeed by denying the qualities which
make men and women distinctively human, by reducing
marriage to mere animal mating, could such a solution
ensure the harmony which Tolstoy claimed for it.

This is not to deny the truth of his condemnation of
sexual licence, and of an idle, rich existence with its refined sexuality, but his fear of everything which excited
sexual desire, as of 'every act which has for its aim to
adorn or *show off* the body,' led him to dismiss marriage
as a mere bodily bond, although it was a bond against
which he himself increasingly chafed.

Here more clearly than elsewhere it is evident how
blindness to the imaginative reality of Christ's teaching
falsified Tolstoy's moral interpretation of it. Christ's
statement that he who looks at a woman to lust after her
has already committed adultery in his heart expresses a
spiritual and creative conception of the relation of men
and women as distinct from a physical and negative one.
It is not in fact marriage which necessarily justifies passion, but freedom from the desire to master and possess.

Tolstoy admitted this in treating of these words of Christ, but he preferred to concentrate on another text ('he who puts away his wife . . . causeth her to commit adultery'), because he assumed that men in general were incapable, like himself, of an unpossessive love. Yet to teach men to regard as essentially inviolable, not only the bodies of women, but their personalities, whether in marriage or not, is certainly more in accord with the spirit of Christ's teaching than to denounce divorce under any conditions as criminal.

For that matter it is easy to discover attacks on family life in the Gospels, and Tolstoy himself was to cite these in support of his own desire to break away from it. He in fact who denounces divorce under any circumstances must also hold a low view of the possible relationship of a man and woman in marriage, and, like Tolstoy, consider it 'impossible to participate in the family and *also* in the source of life – in God,' unless indeed he claims in defiance of facts that every marriage is divinely ordained. For only if marriage is regarded either as a purely physical or inevitably spiritual relationship, can the right to divorce in certain cases be denied. And yet it was just because Tolstoy regarded it as the former and could not conceive how it might evolve into a franker, cleaner and freer relationship that his higher nature rebelled against it.

The same denial of evolution conditioned his interpretation of the third commandment. Upon it he based his attack on all the civil institutions of the State, and particularly the Law Courts, and his claim that no Christian could participate in them.

'All state obligations,' he wrote in *The Kingdom of God is Within You*, 'are against the conscience of a Christian – the oath of allegiance, taxes, law proceedings, and military service.' And since he made no distinction between degrees of violence but condemned all the life of the State as based upon it, his third commandment is ultimately involved with the two which follow it, non-participation being but one aspect of non-resistance.

A criticism, however, of his convictions must turn upon the very distinctions which he refused to make, and behind them on our conception of the nature, and belief in the possibilities, of human evolution.

Tolstoy's attitude to the Russian State and to his own passions was the same. In both he could only oppose an extremely vicious force by an extreme denial. In view of the terrible selfishness of Russian Society, he thought, as for a time it would seem, though in a more spiritual sense, Christ thought, that the day was at hand. 'Our life,' he wrote, 'has reached the extreme limit of misery and cannot be improved by any system of organization . . . no external reformation of life will render it less miserable.' Deliverance for the individual lay only in following the light of truth that was in him and in withdrawal from contamination by those who lived by legalized violence, hypocritically disguised. That this light might be brought into public life and gradually transform it, he denied.

And possibly, so far as Russia was concerned, he was right. To read his descriptions of shooting and floggings of peasants who had merely expostulated against being exploited is to believe that from such organized brutality there could be no issue but the revolution of force which has occurred or the immediate revolution of consciousness in which Tolstoy believed.

But in this belief he was himself guilty of that substitution of the miraculous for the rational, of which he rightly accused the Churches. Through eighteen centuries, he argued, Christianity had penetrated into the consciousness of humanity, until 'every man of the modern world recognizes that our salvation lies in fulfilling the law of Christ . . . Christianity cannot, as its Founder said, be realized by the majority of men all at once; it must grow like a huge tree from a tiny seed. And so it has grown, and now has reached its full development, not yet in actual life, but in the conscience of men of to-day.'

But was the day of rebirth so close at hand? Do men even at the present day 'genuinely hate oppression, inequality, class distinction, and every kind of cruelty'? Are the pagan ideals of pride and wealth worshipped only by a few, and by these uneasily, or do the majority still applaud a leading politician's view of 'glittering prizes' or a leading journalist's idea of 'success'?

It is upon our answer to these questions that our agreement or disagreement with Tolstoy's teaching must turn. For he addressed not only Russia, but the whole Western world.

If the seed of Christianity has grown, even now, to the dimensions which he claimed for it, then we may believe that the world is ripe for Christian anarchy. But if it has not yet reached its full development, if it is still imperfectly assimilated, then no credulous assumption to the contrary will ensure its practical realization or deliver men from the duty of patiently striving to bring public as well as private life into conformity with it.

We may agree with Tolstoy that Christianity corresponds with the needs of the mind and the whole nature of man, and that the living force of it 'has gained more and more upon the extinct Judaism and Heathenism.' But has it yet possessed the whole nature of more than a minority? For to do this it must satisfy not only men's instincts but their minds. They must see that there is, as Tolstoy claimed, true worldly advantage in Christ's unworldliness, that a selfish, destructive attitude to life is not so much vicious as irrational and essentially impractical. This recognition has begun to exist to-day, if seldom among orthodox Christians, with regard to war. More and more men do ask now with Tolstoy how politicians and generals 'can let it go on, not from higher considerations only, but from regard to their own safety.' And so almost all that he wrote on this subject is relevant to the life of to-day.

But men's reason was not convinced then, nor is it now, that in many civil matters the violence of government was greater than the possible violence of individuals, subject to no external restraint. That, as Tolstoy argued, was the justification of government, and he claimed that it had disappeared. 'The state organization based on violence, the aim of which was the security of personal, family, and social welfare, has come to the point of renouncing the very objects for which it was founded — it has reduced men to absolute renunciation and loss of the welfare it was to secure.'

In Russia for the majority of the population this was true, and in Europe generally, so far as foreign relations were concerned. But we do not believe it to be true of all state organization. Our own governments, for example, may have legislated and our own Law Courts administered justice in the interests of class and property, but they can do so with less and less impunity. Slowly we are beginning to exert a rational control over the instrument forged originally to assist survival in a savage world. And there is surely more hope of Christianizing society in this way than in abandoning the instrument as inherently vicious and uncontrollable.

For, as Tolstoy wrote, the Kingdom of Heaven is in the *understanding* of men, 'the divine light that dwells in man is *reason*, and one must serve it only, and by its aid seek for what is good.' But to assert, as he did, that a Christian, if attacked by a lunatic, must suffer himself to be killed rather than employ force in self-defence, is to deny the divine light, and confuse a quixotic irrationality with the imaginative reason, of which Christ was the voice. Elsewhere he wrote – 'I cannot employ any kind of physical force against anyone, except a child, and then only in order to save it from immediately impending danger.' And by this admission, later withdrawn, he unconsciously revealed the weakness of his position.

For if force is justified to preserve a child against dangers due to its ignorance, it is also justified against adults who share the ignorance of children. Doubtless

Tolstoy would not have admitted that such adults exist. He was convinced that in all men, as in himself, there was a 'gradual transition from the personal, animal conception of life to the social conception of life, and from the social conception of life to the divine conception of life,' and that mankind had now reached the final stage when it was ripe for perfect liberty.

But such a view, as we have said, was as blindly optimistic as his view of the necessary viciousness of government was blindly pessimistic. The more a true Christianity comes to possess the consciousness of men, the more reason must tend to replace force, not only because democratic governments, however grudgingly, must respect public opinion, but because the fear which dictates force, the fear of being exposed to 'savages inside and outside of civilized society,' must automatically decrease in proportion as the individuals who compose every society become too intelligent to be savages.

But the process is evolutionary, and it is as sentimental to believe that the majority of men are already ripe for the 'divine conception of life,' or that all criminals are only such because of the criminal nature of the State, as it is to deny that man may slowly learn the advantage as well as the righteousness of being rational and humane.

There can be, in short, no such *moment*, as Tolstoy conceived, when public opinion has become strong enough to replace every kind of force, but a continual advance of reason upon force and a continual transformation of destructive into creative force; and it is thus, and not by a sudden ecstatic conversion that the world may advance 'to a consciousness of the moral, living side of Christianity.'

Government in fact has not so much brutalized men as expressed their brutality or their fear of brutality, and it may equally come to express their civilization. That its spirit will always fall short of the best spirit of the age is possible, but it cannot resist the compulsion of an enlightened public opinion.

Admittedly such evolution can only occur if the government is, however imperfectly, representative, and in Russia it represented only a small and vicious minority, and was so rigidly constituted that it was scarcely susceptible to any progressive influence. But even if there could be no relation, except a degrading one, between the moral aspirations of the individual and such a government, this did not justify, although it helps to explain, Tolstoy's absolute condemnation of all government. And his condemnation was dictated by something deeper and more personal than the facts of Russia, by his refusal in fact to admit that only reason, patiently applied to life, can solve the contradictions between our rational and our animal natures.

He complained, for example, that man has merely set to work 'to use his reason in discovering the historic laws of his animal nature and of that alone.' But man cannot transcend these laws until he has discovered them. Until he has analysed his impulses, he remains their slave and cannot clearly distinguish whether the 'principle within him,' applauded by Tolstoy, 'which cannot be checked or governed by anything,' is divine or not.

'Judge not, that ye be not judged,' quoted Tolstoy, and on the strength of this text denounced every law court. And so far as the Law has been and is punitory, so far as it has dealt not good but evil to those whom it has called enemies of society, it is un-Christian. Yet the truth that 'there is but one way to end evil – by rendering good for evil to all men without distinction' cannot become effective until it has convinced not only the ethical instinct but the reason of man. Such has been and is the service of science, which has explored the psychology of the criminal, which has shown the extent to which society is responsible for his creation and proved that the qualities which have made him unsocial are often valuable and may be turned into creative channels.

It is only by such disinterested analysis that Christ's teaching may cease to appear 'as the expression of an impulsive enthusiasm, having no direct application to life,' that his inspired madness may be revealed as inspired sanity, and his creative conception gradually possess the consciousness and dictate the conduct of mankind.

But although Tolstoy agreed that the Christian religion could not be imposed but could only be freely assimilated in two ways, one spiritual and internal, the other experimental and external, he refused to admit their interdependence. And the same divorce between internal and external characterized his view that man could only become free by a change in his conception of life as distinct from a change of external conditions; and so, that even if a government could be persuaded to change the material conditions of life by economic reform, it would lead to no improvement.

If Tolstoy had really endured poverty as well as admired it, he would not so easily have dismissed the material aspect of life as of no importance to the moral. It is of course true that 'the meaning of life cannot consist . . . in what we possess and what we acquire – what is not ourselves,' and that the poor, through their very lack of possessions, live more in accordance with this truth than the privileged.

But we cannot possess ourselves in conditions of bitter need. It is as hard for the slum-dweller as for the rich man to enter the Kingdom of Heaven. Environment and conditions of labour do profoundly affect the possibilities of spiritual freedom, and stark poverty, when it is not voluntarily and ecstatically accepted, demoralizes even more perhaps than great riches.

Tolstoy wrote that the higher men climbed in the scale of worldly fortune the less they saw of the light of the sun, of the fields and the woods, and of wild or domestic animals. But although the agricultural labourer sees these things, he is generally too sweated to experience them. To strive therefore for his economic betterment is as necessary as to emphasize the fact that a true life consists in what a man is and not in what he has. But Tolstoy arbitrarily divorced the fact from the truth. Near the end of his life, for example, he announced in a cablegram to America – 'True social amelioration can be attained only by religious moral perfecting of all individuals. Political agitation, putting before individuals pernicious illusion of social improvement by change of forms, habitually stops the real progress, as can be observed in all constitutional countries.'

But to concentrate exclusively on the moral change in the individual is to play into the hands of selfish reactionaries as surely as to emphasize only the material factors is to encourage only a material revolution. It is by combining the two, as the best English Socialists have done, that we can best hope to change at once the monstrous conditions of wealth and poverty and the spirit which they express.

Tolstoy, however, was too tormented by the contrasted luxury and misery of the society in which he lived to work patiently for their reform. It was in 1882 when he went to Moscow that he realized its enormity to the full. 'At the sight of the hunger, cold, and degradation of thousands of people,' he wrote in *What then must We do?* 'I understood not with my mind or my heart, but with my whole being, that the existence of tens of thousands of such people in Moscow – while I and thousands of others over-eat ourselves with beefsteaks and sturgeon and cover our houses and floors with cloth or carpets – no matter what all the learned men in the world may say about its necessity – is a crime, not committed once but constantly; and that I with my luxury not merely tolerate it but share in it. . . . I felt and feel, and shall not cease to feel, that as long as I have any superfluous food and someone else has none, and I have two coats and someone else has none, I share in a constantly repeated crime.'

The shock, as the identical phrase describing it sug-

gests, was the same as that which he had experienced at the
spectacle of an execution. He felt the horror of it all with
the intensity of his wonderful physical imagination, crying
out with tears in his voice – 'One cannot live so; one
cannot; one cannot!'

And for the rest of his life he was as conscience-stricken
by the vices of society, in which he felt himself to be an
accomplice, as by the sexual licence of his youth which he
had never at heart outgrown. As he was to write in an
essay on 'Industry and Idleness,' 'You cannot be at peace –
cannot have pleasure which is not poisoned by this knowledge.'

Tolstoy was equally tortured by his consciousness of
social and of personal evil, because to him the two were
indeed one. In the evil around him he read the evil within.
The acquisitiveness of the world was his own, and he propounded the same physical solution for the one as for the
other. 'If a man really dislikes slavery,' he wrote, 'and
does not wish to be a participant in it, the first thing he
will do will be not to use other people's labour. . . . And
the rejection of all the customary means of exploiting
other people's labour will inevitably make it necessary
for such a man, on the one hand, to restrict his needs,
and on the other, to do for himself what others formerly
did for him.'

But in writing this he meant that a man could not avoid
exploiting his fellow-men unless he sustained his own life
by physical labour. He rejected in fact the possibility of
a just division of labour according to faculties. Once
again he was right so far as he applied his argument to

abuses. He wrote truly enough – 'However convincing may be the proofs of the division of labour among the cells of the organisms we investigate, man as long as he is not deprived of reason will still say that no one ought to weave cotton cloth all his life long; and that such an employment is not a division of labour, but an oppression of men.'

When, however, he wrote, 'Men live and support themselves by agriculture as is proper for all men,' his words were only relevant to primitive village communities, and excluded the possibility of participating in the struggle with nature, and supporting your own life and that of humanity, by spiritual and intellectual activity as well as by physical.

Because in Russia, and indeed in many other countries, those who professed to produce spiritual food in return for the physical food which they received, merely catered for a small, idle and polished class, or, in the case of priests, hypnotized the masses and kept them humble and stupid, in order to enslave them, Tolstoy refused to admit that a man could serve humanity with his brain unless he supported himself with his hands.

Again we may agree that many brain-workers take from society far more than they give, and that so long as one manual worker is underpaid, the wealth of high officials, leading lawyers, commercial and industrial magnates, and their like, is unjustifiable. We may agree too that it is as demoralizing for men to live only by mental labour as by physical, and that a contempt for manual labour is typical of a false refinement. But an artist, a scientist, or an organizing genius are not, there-

fore, morally compelled to devote so many hours daily to
work in the fields, nor will they necessarily serve humanity
the better by doing so.

And Tolstoy's views here as elsewhere were dictated
primarily by his own needs. 'What is most profitable for
all,' he wrote, 'is what I desire for myself: the greatest
possible welfare and satisfaction of all the needs of body
and soul and conscience and reason implanted within me.'

And he could only obtain this by doing enough manual
labour to appease his physical nature. 'For me,' he confessed, 'daily exercise and physical labour are as indis-
pensable   as   the   air. . . . Sedentary   intellectual   work,
without physical exercise and labour, is a real calamity.
If for a single day I do not walk, or work with my legs
and hands, I am good for nothing by evening. I can't
read or write, or even listen to anyone with attention; my
head whirls; there seem to be stars in my eyes, and I have
a sleepless night.'

Many others, like the present writer, must be under the
same physical necessity, without however agreeing with
Tolstoy's uncritical conclusions. And the intensity of his
hatred of towns, his view that they were places where
'nothing is grown, but everything is consumed,' had its
roots in the fact that in them he was always physically
unwell.

Again, of course the physical and the moral revulsion
were intimately connected. 'Town life, which had seemed
strange and foreign to me before, now became so repulsive that all the pleasures of the luxurious life I formerly
enjoyed became a torment to me. And try as I would to

find in my soul some justification for our way of living, I could not without irritation behold either my own or any other drawing-room, nor any clean, elegantly laid table, nor a carriage with well-fed coachmen and horses, nor the shops, theatres, and assemblies. I could not help seeing beside them the hungry, cold, down-trodden inhabitants of Lyapin House. I could not escape the thought that these two things were connected.'

And yet he did not press home the connection. His attempts at philanthropy failed, not because the poor cannot be bettered by external methods, as he argued, but because such methods have to be applied patiently, systematically and on a scale impossible to well-meaning individuals. He found among the very poor as among the rich that 'the unhappy were just such as exist among ourselves; people whose unhappiness depends, not on external conditions, but on themselves – a kind of unhappiness bank-notes cannot cure.'

In the last resort this is so. But it was their external conditions which prevented both the rich and the poor from achieving that view of life which brings happiness. The poor had always been too starved and brutalized to achieve it, the rich too pampered. Only by reorganizing the material conditions of life which allowed of these two extremes could the moral impulses in both classes be liberated. Only when a generation had grown up under conditions which did not allow men either to exploit or to be exploited, would it be impossible, for example, for one woman to lead her daughter to the taverns, another to take hers to Court or to balls, 'but both share the same view of life: namely, that a woman should satisfy a man's lusts and that for that service she should be fed, clothed, and cared for.'

Tolstoy's disregard of the necessary material basis to moral reform led him of course to denounce money as an absolute evil. 'I came to feel that in money itself, in the very possession of it, there is something evil and immoral: and that money itself, and the fact that I possess it, is one of the chief causes of the evils I saw around me.'

But money was not the cause of these evils. Rather it expressed them by its unfair distribution and the consequent unsocial uses to which it was turned. And just as it was the means by which men destroyed each other through wanton luxury and war, so it might be made to serve a creative purpose. Money represents power which must be mastered and transformed from an instrument of competitive violence to a medium of co-operative exchange.

That this can only be done when society comes to control its own economic forces is certain, but since Tolstoy denied, not merely the possibility of this, as it was reasonable enough to do in Russia, but even the fact that economic reform could serve a moral purpose, to possess money was for him to possess an absolute evil. It was not enough to cease to be luxurious and help the needy. He felt that only when he had nothing left could he be in a position to do even a little good or cease to feel ashamed and guilty, as one gratifying himself and practising a deception, in the presence of every poor man to whom he offered charity.

And behind the fine sincerity of such an attitude lurked the same disability to forget himself, which had always marred his relations with his fellow-men. He could only expose the sins of the world, he could not further its salvation, because he was thinking all the time about the salvation of his own soul. Despite all his arguments against the illusory nature of personal life, against the desire for personal gratification in this life and personal immortality in the next, he was ready to abandon everything in return for peace in his own heart.

All the fineness and all the futility of his moral and social philosophy were due to this inverted selfishness, which could never ensure the peace at which it aimed, because it denounced the forces that must contribute to a vital concord as inherently, instead of conditionally, evil.

§ 5

To be a Christian, therefore, as Tolstoy interpreted it, was rather to deny all force, than to direct it. His possessive instincts were too powerful for him to make them creative; and the value of *The Kingdom of God is Within You*, in which he embodied most fully his doctrine of non-resistance to evil by force, lies less in its negative doctrine than in its scathing attacks on the authorities, religious and secular, who perpetuated a predatory paganism by pretending that it was both necessary and Christian.

No other book has revealed with so intense a logic, such a richness of illustration, and such an outraged humanity, the extent to which the masses have been duped by men of the higher, dominating classes who have invested with all sorts of high-sounding names their own selfish, acquisitive impulses.

Tolstoy failed to reconcile the Sermon on the Mount with a true civilization, but he exposed, as no one had before, the vicious hypocrisy of those who pretended to reconcile it with Krupp cannons, smokeless powder, sectarian hatred, and sweated labour.

'We are all brothers,' he wrote in one of the most powerful passages of his great indictment, 'but every morning I must have a cigar, a sweetmeat, an ice, and such things, which my brothers and sisters have been wasting their health in manufacturing, and I enjoy these things and demand them. We are all brothers, yet I live by working in a bank, or mercantile house, or shop at making all goods dearer for my brothers. We are all brothers, but I live on a salary paid me for prosecuting, judging and condemning the thief and the prostitute, whose existence the whole tenor of my life tends to bring about, and whom I know ought not to be punished, but reformed. We are all brothers, but I live on the salary I gain by collecting taxes from needy labourers to be spent on the luxuries of the rich and idle. We are all brothers, but I take a stipend for preaching a false Christian religion, which I do not myself believe in, and which only serves to hinder men from understanding true Christianity. . . . We are all brothers, yet I take a salary for being ready to commit murder, for teaching men to murder, or making firearms, gunpowder, or fortifications.'

It matters not that Tolstoy hated European culture too much to do justice to its possibilities. Such words as

these will challenge the heart and satisfy the mind until a
sense of social responsibility has possessed the conscience
of men and they have reorganized their public and private
conduct to express it, until the pursuit of profit has been
subserviated to the needs of humanity and the sacredness
of life and of personality has been accepted as the foundations upon which any civilization worthy of the name must
be built.

But it was against war that Tolstoy spoke, here and in
the little known essay *Christianity and Patriotism* written in
the following year, with a force and an insight which are
the more convincing to-day because his predictions have
been so terribly realized.

In 1914, as Mr. Edward Garnett wrote in an introduction to this essay,[1] 'it was as though Tolstoy's warn-
ings had been written in ink which faded before men's
eyes when the Churches and the Clergy of all the com-
batant States began blessing the cannons and the bayonets,
and later the bombs and the land-mines and the poison
gas. Christ was mobilized by all the Churches, but not
Tolstoy.'

And if the last war served at least the purpose of shock-
ing the conscience of the civilized world, of revealing the
lies out of which it had grown and of proving by its scientific horrors that peace and co-operation, if only between
nations, was an immediate necessity of survival, the people
can still save themselves from their leaders only at the cost
of unceasing vigilance. Without this vigilance, 'The bells

---

[1] *Christianity and Patriotism.* By L. N. Tolstoy. Translated by Con-
stance Garnett. Introduction by Edward Garnett. (Cape.)

will begin ringing, men with long hair will dress up in gold-embroidered sacks and begin praying for murder. And the whole horrible business familiar for ages will begin all over again. The journalists will get to work, egging men on under the guise of patriotism to hatred and murder, and will be delighted at doubling their sales. The factory-owners, the merchants, the purveyors of army stores, will gleefully get to work, expecting double profits. . . . The higher officers of the army will get to work, receiving double salary and rations, and hoping to win for murdering men various trinkets greatly prized by them — ribbons, crosses, stripes, stars. The idle ladies and gentlemen will get to work putting their names down for the Red Cross, getting ready to bandage those whom their own husbands and brothers are going to wound, and imagining that in this they are doing a very Christian deed.

'And drowning the despair in their hearts with singing, debauchery, and vodka, torn away from peaceful labour, from their wives, their mothers and their children, hundreds of thousands of simple, good-natured men, with weapons of murder in their hands, will trudge off where they are sent. They will march; will be frozen, will be hungry, will be sick, some dying of disease; until at last they reach the place where they will be murdered by thousands, and will themselves, not knowing why, murder by thousands men whom they have never seen, who have done them no wrong, and can have done them no wrong.'

So it happened twenty years after these words were written, and unless they are inscribed on our memory it may well happen again.

Tolstoy not only tore aside the fabrications and the sentimentalities by which warmongers delude the masses, but he showed with the dramatic power of a great genius, what Mr. Norman Angell has proved by calm reason, that the world has outgrown war even from the point of view of material self-interest.

An aggressive Patriotism, as he argued, might have a meaning when each nation felt itself, as it were, an island in the midst of an ocean of barbarians, continually striving to submerge it. But such Nationalism no longer existed when the men of all nations were connected 'by the common interests of labour and trade, or by spiritual interests, or by both together. So that very often the men of one State were nearer and more essential to men of another State than their own countrymen, as is the case with workmen connected with employers of other nationalities, with commercial people, and above all with learned men and artists.'

In writing this Tolstoy underrated the inherent differences of temperament between nations, which indeed a true internationalism does not seek to reduce to a barren identity. But these differences need no longer be militant, unless they are inflamed by professional war-makers or by politicians who through arrogance or in obedience to financial interests have excited hostilities that they cannot appease.

And to-day, when our leading papers devote columns of appreciation and photographs to a display of tanks immediately after Armistice Day celebrations, we need no less than when he wrote it his indictment of those who build warships 'only for defence,' while vying with one another in the most solemn protestations of peaceful intentions, and who, like the French Academicians, in one breath deplore war and say that 'our soldiers and their arms, skilfully used, are perhaps the surest guarantee of the peace we all love'; of the intoxication too produced by such stimulants as parades, reviews, and religious solemnities, of the stupefied arrogance and stupefied servility of the military type, and of that imperial or financial greed which creates strife, and then demands with high-sounding appeals to national honour that the innocent shall quell it.

For not only does Tolstoy make our imagination revolt with his own before the spectacle of war, but he reveals its terrible stupidity. And above all he writes as one who has been himself guilty and who still is tormented with guilt in so far as personal, social, and national discord are the same in essence.

He could not, as we have said, appease this sense of guilt by constructive action, could not recognize that it is not so much the cunning of the oppressors as the ignorance of the oppressed which has kept the world uncivilized. He could only denounce the evil in the world like the evil of his own passions and bid the individual recover, if he could, the innocence and irresponsibility of the early Christians.

And to do this it was necessary to abandon all property and every physical tie, to prove practically the truth of his contention that 'a man cannot be placed against his will in a situation opposed to his conscience.'

For thirty years he endured such a situation and increasingly chafed against it. Two years before writing *The
Kingdom of God is Within You* he renounced his copy-
rights and divided his property among his family; six
years before he had renounced hunting, tobacco, and
animal food. Continually he worked with the peasants in
the fields, and more than once he determined to go away,
to abandon the comfortable family life which was bought
by the sufferings of the people and the wife whose love he
had described as 'an obstacle to the service of God.'

The struggle between the two loyalties became at last,
as we shall see, too painful to be borne. For it was not
only between his physical attachment to life and his negative idealism. His humanity also prevented him taking
what he considered to be the Kingdom of Heaven by force.
As his wife wrote of him amid all the pain and vexation of
their growing estrangement, 'There is something in you so
wise, kind, naïve, and obstinate, and it is all lit up by that
tender interest for everyone, natural to you alone.'

His foes might be those of his own household, but he
was too sensible of their feelings and at heart too apprecia-
tive of family life to offer them up on the altar of his own
ruthless self-disgust. Yet more and more he despised himself for continuing to live the lie which he had denounced
and inevitably he projected his bitterness and contempt
against those who aggravated it.

Tolstoy therefore by his study of Christ's teaching had
defined without resolving the conflict between his instincts and his conscience. And this is the final argument
against his interpretation. Even if it was a true one, it

was ineffective. 'To understand life,' he had written, 'we must know that the source of life is infinite good.' But such knowledge can scarcely be attributed to one who still feared death with as morbid an intensity and whose hatred of women had deepened into a fanatical horror.

It could not be otherwise for one who wrote in *The Spirit of Christ's Teaching* that 'life in the spirit is death in the body; in the spirit is life and good, in the body darkness and evil': or again, 'by subduing and quieting the flesh, men obtain the full satisfaction in the life of the spirit.'

For Tolstoy found, like other violent ascetics, that the flesh cannot be subdued, that if it is denounced as evil and denied as a medium of spirit, it remains evil, an active agent of death.

The knowledge of death rather than of infinite good underlies all the great religious autobiography which we have briefly considered. 'Death, death, death awaits you every second. Your life passes in the presence of death,' he wrote in *What I Believe*, and ten years later, at the end of *The Kingdom of God is Within You*, occurs the same grim reminder. 'Whatever we may do – found companies, build palaces and monuments, write songs and poems – it is all not for a long time. Soon it passes away, leaving no trace.'

It was essentially because he was obsessed by the thought of the nothingness of all material things that he rejected the possibility of a sane ordering of life. Despite his condemnation of those who accepted war as inevitable he too, so far as the war in his own being was concerned, was crushed under the weight of an immense discouragement.

But it was more than this: 'to live rationally,' he had written, 'you must live so that death cannot destroy life.' And death for him could only cease to destroy life if he continually denied the physical life over which it ruled. After all his ten years' search in the Scriptures for the secret of eternal life, he could still 'find nothing along the path of reasonable knowledge, except a denial of life.'

And so in all the great stories and dramas of his remaining years, with the possible exception of *Hadji Murad* in which he sought momentary relaxation from his religious obsession by renewing his memories of primitive Caucasian life, in *The Death of Ivan Ilyitch*, *The Power of Darkness*, *The Kreutzer Sonata*, and *Resurrection*, in his great criticism and interpretation of Art, which corresponded with as it succeeded his study of Christianity, and even in the *Popular Tales and Stories* in which he expressed positively the spirit of the Gospels and the simplicity and goodness of heart of the common people, he continued to deny, now with a transient moral satisfaction, now with an overpowering physical disgust, the flesh which, because he could not spiritualize it, he could not appease.

THE TRIUMPH OF DEATH

THE TRIUMPH OF DEATH

§ 1

*T*HE *Death of Ivan Ilyitch* and *The Kreutzer Sonata* were written in the years which followed Tolstoy's first protracted search for a religion which would enable him to live. He had enunciated such a religion and only by continuing to enunciate it until his death could he evade the fact that it did not resolve his discord. But after eight years wholly preoccupied by this search, he began again to express himself as an artist. And as an artist he unconsciously disproved the faith and the serenity which he claimed as a moralist.

The Death of Ivan Ilyitch and *The Kreutzer Sonata* are the two stories in which he betrayed most clearly that the extreme demands of his Christian ethic were dictated by an extreme horror of the flesh. No man could have written either who was not tortured by his appetites. Both are masterpieces by virtue of their intense physical reality, and although the horror of death predominates in the one, and of sexual passion in the other, the two are identical in essence. Ivan Ilyitch's married life, like Pozdnyshev's, contains islands of carnal love in an ocean of concealed hostility, and he dies with terror and nausea because, behind all his colourless decorum, he has lived grossly.

Once again in this story Tolstoy expressed the agony of a man who, like himself, had lost a natural relation to life and death, without achieving a spiritual. In telling the history of Ivan Ilyitch, which was 'the simplest, the most ordinary, the most awful,' he reconceived the intense physical revulsion from death which he first fully experienced at the death-bed of his brother Nicholas. 'He saw again that forehead, the nose that seemed squeezing the lip, and he felt frightened for himself.'

Ivan has no positive vices. He is the typical official, who worships correctness, makes a conventional marriage and derives his pleasures, apart from the satisfaction of his appetites, from petty professional pride and petty social vanity. And then he injures himself while arranging the furniture in the new house which signalizes his ascent in the scale of suburban respectability, and the fatal disease which is to destroy him at the age of forty-five after appalling suffering takes root.

And as the disease advances secretly within him, he becomes aware that he is a solitary, querulous individual in a household of mean souls, absorbed in their own trivial concerns. Even the doctors whom he consults are interested only in his medical aspect as he himself had been interested only in the legal aspect of his clients. He 'is left alone with the consciousness that his life is poisoned for him and poisons the life of others, and that this poison is not losing its force, but is continually penetrating more and more deeply into his whole existence. . . . And he had to live thus on the edge of the precipice alone, without one man who could understand and feel for him.'

And suddenly he realizes that it is death that has him, as it always has had him, in its grip. 'Death. Yes, Death. And they – all of them – don't understand, and don't want to understand, and feel no pity! . . . And the worst

of it was that It drew him to itself not for him to do anything in particular, but simply for him to look at It
straight in the face, to look at It and, doing nothing, suffer
unspeakably.'

He is, in short, like a rabbit paralysed by the approach of
a stoat, but, unlike the rabbit, he knows with a terrible
clearness the destructive force from which he cannot
escape and his knowledge intensifies his impotence. For
death has for him no meaning; he is enslaved by it as he
had been, behind a masque of decorum, by life. And
among all his household who flaunt their health in his face
he cannot find one who can feel for him. Instead they
lie to him, as they lie to themselves, to avoid unpleasant-
ness, pretending that death does not await him. Only the
peasant Gerasim does not lie. 'Everything showed clearly
that he alone understood what it meant, and saw no
necessity to disguise it, and simply felt sorry for his sick,
wasting master.'

And so the agony deepens. 'He cried at his own helplessness, at his awful loneliness, at the cruelty of people, at
the cruelty of God, at the absence of God.' And all the
time he is groping for a meaning, for some relation with
the universe which will deliver him from a loneliness 'than
which none more complete could be found anywhere –
not at the bottom of the sea, not deep down in the earth.'
And looking back on his life he finds it all, except his
childhood, unpleasant, disgusting, worthless, *deadly*, and
he suddenly knows that in spite of all his propriety he
has lived amiss, has perpetrated 'a horrible vast deception
that concealed both life and death.' He knows, but he

will not admit it fully. He will not accept the fact of death in his past life, and so he cannot accept it in the little life which remains to him.

Like Levin's brother and the lady in *Three Deaths*, he takes the sacrament and it merely renews his hope of physical recovery. And then follow three days of anguish mental and physical, through which he screams perpetually.

'He was struggling in that black sack into which he was being thrust by an unseen resistless force. He struggled as the man condemned to death struggles in the hands of the executioner and knows that he cannot save himself. . . . He felt that his agony was due both to his being thrust into the black hole and still more to his not being able to get right into it. What hindered him from getting into it was the claim that his life had been good. That justification of his life held him fast and would not let him get forward, and it caused him more agony than all.'

At last two hours before his death he really abandons the claim and finds peace. 'He looked for his old accustomed terror of death, and did not find it. "Where is it? What death?" There was no terror, because death was not either. . . . "Death is over," he said to himself, "It's no more."'

In no other story did Tolstoy express the physical reality of death so vividly, or so appallingly. Ivan's bodily sufferings are not realistically described; they are realized with imaginative as well as pathological exactitude. And his mental agony, if we strip it of Tolstoy's moral interpretation, resolves itself into a conflict between the will to

live and the assaults of pain. When Ivan ceased to claim
that his life had been good, he did not really comprehend
in what a good life consists. He merely ceased to desire
life for himself and so found death acceptable. Once again
Tolstoy expressed in this story the identity between a
mean, egotistic life and death, but once again, as in the
case of Prince Andrew or as later in the case of Vasili in
Master and Man whom the frost numbs into an acceptance
of death, he invested a mere abandonment of the will to
live with a moral value which it cannot possess.

More and more, however, he was compelled to adopt
such an attitude, to hate physical life in order to temper his
fear of death. And of this hatred woman became the
particular object.

In 1886 he was seriously ill and during his illness he
wrote *The Power of Darkness*, a play in which great tragedy
is wrung by sheer force of genius out of physical horror.
But of all the characters it is the women, Matryona and
Anisya, who are irreparably bad. What Gorki later
described as his 'implacable hostility' to women was indeed a necessary condition of his faith. For he felt that
women expressed with terrible seductiveness the physical
life which he must deny. He felt it so morbidly that he
could write in a letter, still unpublished, that 'in modern
times they appear to be possessed of devils, and career
round like cats on a roof.'

And the intensity of his fear and hatred, and the
physical enslavement to which it was due, he betrayed
with burning conviction in the cynical frenzy of *The
Kreutzer Sonata*. Certainly Pozdnyshev does not repre-

sent the whole of Tolstoy. But he represents the violent
sensualist in him, which dictated alike the qualities of
his art, the defects of his morality, and the discord of
his life.

The Kreutzer Sonata opens with a discussion in a rail-
way carriage in which an old man sneers, as Tolstoy himself had sneered, at women's claim to freedom and education. 'The first thing that should be required of a woman,'
he remarks, 'is fear,' and 'the female sex must be curbed
in time or else all is lost.' To which the lady, who personi-
fies modern and liberal ideas, answers, 'The chief thing
such people do not understand is that marriage without
love is not marriage; that love alone sanctifies marriage,
and that real marriage is only such as is sanctified by
love?' . . .

'Yes, but how is one to understand what is meant by
"true love"? said the gentleman with the glittering
eyes.' . . .

The question is never answered save by a demented
denial. Tolstoy had become convinced of the final and
fatal animalism of love between the sexes, of what he
called 'that enchanting, disgusting, frightful passion.' In
Resurrection occurs the sentence, 'He says that this love
arouses his energy, and is platonic, but I know that, even
if it is exceptional, still at the bottom of it lies the same
nastiness.' And Pozdnyshev expresses the same sentiment with cynical ferocity.

'Every man,' he says, 'experiences what you call love
for every pretty woman.' . . .

'But you are talking all the time about physical love.

Don't you acknowledge love based on an identity of ideals, on spiritual affinity?' asked the lady.

'Spiritual affinity! Identity of ideals!' he repeated. 'But in that case why go to bed together?'

And he continues, 'You know, what is vilest about it is that in theory love is something ideal and exalted, but in practice it is something abominable, swinish, which it is horrid and shameful to mention or remember.'

Here in fact the discord in Tolstoy's nature between instinct and intelligence finds its starkest expression. He was physically enslaved by passion, and so he denied that such passion could form the basis of a human and spiritual relationship. And because for him it could not do this, it was horrible and humiliating in itself.

This carnal conviction enabled him to attack with piercing insight through the medium of Pozdnyshev the sensualism which conceals itself behind a veil of false poetry and refinement, but it prevented him from offering any substitute for a false indulgence but a false asceticism.

Pozdnyshev describes how as a boy of sixteen, 'woman, not some particular woman, but woman as something to be desired, woman, every woman, woman's nudity tormented' him, how he lost his innocence, and his relationship with women was sullied and spoilt for ever.

'A libertine may restrain himself, may struggle, but he will never have those pure, simple, clean, brotherly relations with a woman. . . . And I had become, and I remained a libertine, and it was this that brought me to ruin. . . . So I lived till I was thirty, not abandoning for a moment the intention of marrying, and arranging for myself a most elevated and pure family life. . . . I remember how, when we were engaged, I showed her my Diary, from which she could learn something, if but a little of my past, especially about my last *liaison*. . . . I remember her horror, despair and confusion. . . .'

Up to this point Tolstoy was describing, if with some morbid exaggeration, his own early life. He too in actual life, as Gorki has testified, when discussing women could be 'unspeakably vulgar. It seemed as if he had once been hurt and could neither forget nor forgive.' And although the rest of the story ceases to be in any literal sense autobiographical, it expresses the dread of lust from which he found a temporary refuge in marriage but which more and more impelled him to seek escape from marriage itself.

To Pozdnyshev 'the most exalted poetic love, as we call it, depends not on moral qualities but on physical nearness . . . we are continually lying about high sentiments but only want her body . . . and all that presents it in the most deceptive light.'

And the art, the social habits and the education of the upper class are simply means to this end, veils behind which their one thought is: 'Take, take me!'

It is 'woman's vocation to afford pleasure to man, and the education given her corresponds with this view. . . . But you will perhaps say that this is true only of badly brought-up girls – those who among us are contemptuously called "young ladies" – you will say there is another, a serious education supplied in high schools – even classical ones – in midwifery, and in medical and university courses. That is not true. All female education of whatever kind has in view only the capture of men. Some girls captivate men by music and curls; others by political services. . . . No bringing up, no education can alter this as long as woman's highest ideal remains marriage, and not virginity and freedom from sensuality. Till then she will be a slave.'

Pozdnyshev only states here more extravagantly what Tolstoy expressed didactically elsewhere. And perhaps in no other passage in his writings is the false antagonism between the rational and the moral more apparent. It is not by fanatically denying their natural instincts that women will cease to be their slave, but through that education which Pozdnyshev dismissed as useless because among the Russian upper classes it reflected the general prostitution of their lives.

To a truly educated woman neither marriage nor virginity are ideals in themselves. In either state she may express her physical self, her intelligence and her desire for human service. Marriage indeed must satisfy best the expressive needs of many women, but the more educated in the true sense they are, the less restricted is the scope of their natural instincts.

In *The Kreutzer Sonata* Tolstoy drew upon his own tortured experience to expose the same animal rapacity underlying the proprieties of modern marriage and motherhood, as he had already shown to underlie the solemnities of modern government. But once again the solution which he offered was negative.

'The majority,' Pozdnyshev says, 'regard the going to church as only a spiritual condition for obtaining possession of a certain woman . . . an innocent girl is sold to a profligate.' And again of motherhood, 'You see, our women are unable to regard a child otherwise than as a pleasure. It is true that the birth is painful, but its little hands. . . . Ah! its little feet! Ah, it smiles! Ah, what a darling little body it has! Ah, and it smacks its lips and hiccups! In a word the animal maternal instinct is sensual. There is in it nothing at all of the mysterious meaning of the arrival of a new human being who will replace us.'

And such sensuality was inevitable so long as ignorance in a woman was confused with innocence, and timidity and a false delicacy was applauded because it stimulated the brutal aggressiveness of men. Woman can only cease to be the prey of the animal in man and in herself by becoming intelligently instinctive. To deny her physical being is to destroy the roots of her human genius. The animal maternal instinct, for example, far from being evil in itself, as Pozdnyshev suggests, is essential to a really creative experience of motherhood. For the art of love, as of parenthood, is, like every other art, a product of instinct and of intelligence, and Tolstoy's view of marriage was prejudiced by the same inability to reconcile the two as his view of Art.

When men and women understand their instincts and, while gladly accepting their physical compulsion, relate them to an intelligent creative purpose, the pleasure which they derive from them is no longer vicious but fertilizing. A mother's love for the body of her child is a beautiful impulse, provided it is not selfishly indulged. And it will not be so indulged if she has studied the science of the body and realizes how intimately the body is related to the mind and how the soul is born of the perfect fusion of the two. Similarly the sexual impulse is a lovely and enriching bond if it expresses a real identity of being between a man and a woman. And it can only express this if they are so intelligently sympathetic that neither could exploit the other sensually.

Admittedly such a harmony of body and mind in an art of life and of love presumes a capacity to which few have yet attained and which always will be an ideal hard to realize. It is too, of course, true that intelligence exclusively developed must lead, and in men has often led, to an aggravated, refined, or perverted sensualism. But such sensualism has been perpetuated by a morality based on fear of the instincts rather than on an informed delight in them and by the lack of sexual education in women, who by their more intimate loyalty to nature are far less liable than men to abuse intelligence in the process of developing it. Women, indeed, are generally wiser about life and more sensitive to its true values than men, and their thought, being more firmly rooted in the primitive, seldom leads them to sacrifice the primary realities of love and health and happiness to the pursuit of selfish and secondary advantages.

But Tolstoy did not believe that the instincts could be educated. And so instead of preaching a rational emancipation from the slavery and consequent horror of the senses, he urged that only by denying them could men and women live morally, although in fact such a denial was no less a confession of enslavement than the indulgence against which it was directed.

It was his own enslavement in marriage which he expressed in Pozdnyshev's words, 'For there to be morality between people in sexual relations, it is necessary that the aim they set themselves should be complete chastity. In striving towards chastity, man falls; he falls, and the result is a moral marriage; but if, as in our society, man aims directly at physical love, then, though it may clothe itself in the pseudo-moral form of marriage, that will merely be permitted debauchery with one woman – and will none the less be an immoral life.'

Tolstoy's own marriage was moral in this sense and yet it increasingly disgusted him. He was torn between a false ideal of celibacy and the physical demands of his nature, and his morality instead of bringing him inner freedom, only heightened his sense of servitude.

And the ultimate pessimism to which such an attitude logically led is expressed in Pozdnyshev's assertion, 'A pure girl only wants children. Children – yes, but not a husband.'

'How then,' I said with astonishment, 'how is the human race to be continued?'

'And why should it be continued?' was his rejoinder.

Tolstoy, like the interrogator in his story, may have been astonished that his morality should logically entail the cessation of the human race, but there can be no doubt that Pozdnyshev's attitude was his own. For all his moral and social philosophy reflects the same irrational negation and it drove him at last, a fugitive, from his own home.

Like Pozdnyshev he was convinced that 'of all the passions the strongest, cruellest, and most stubborn, is the sex-passion, physical love; and therefore if the passions are destroyed, including the strongest of them – physical love – the prophecies will be fulfilled, mankind will be brought into a unity.'

He would not admit that the unity would be one of death, that the passions were the necessary agents of life, and that the prophecies could only be fulfilled when they were creatively expressed. For him there could be no escape from the agony of sex, as from the agony of a death-bed, save in the death of the body. And his morality was but a preparation for and a prevision of that final surrender.

Only a man who had experienced himself the hatred, the stark alienation, inherent in animal passion could have created a Pozdnyshev. And so *The Kreutzer Sonata* is in essence a self-indictment and a confession. It was of himself that Tolstoy wrote – 'As soon as a man approaches a woman he succumbs to her stupefying influence and becomes intoxicated and crazy. I used formerly to feel uncomfortable and uneasy when I saw a lady dressed-up for a ball, but now I am simply frightened, and I plainly see her as something dangerous and illicit.' It was of his own relations with women and even with his wife that he wrote, if with some exaggeration, that 'love and animosity were one and the same animal feeling, only at opposite poles . . . animosity was nothing but the protest of our human nature against the animal nature that overpowered it. . . . She? But who is she? A mystery she was, and still is. I don't know her. I only know her as an animal.' And, again allowing for overstatement, it was of his own family that he wrote – 'Yes, my children are living and growing up just such savages as everybody around them . . . as they grew older and their characters became defined, it came about that they grew into allies whom each of us tried to draw to his or her side. . . . The girl was my ally, and the eldest boy, who resembled his mother and was her favourite, was often hateful to me.'

And it was because his own desires were so easily in-flamed that he could attack with such burning insight the sensual enslavement which underlay a false civilization, and was displayed in the shop-windows of any big town, in the luxuries of women's dress and jewellery, and in demoralizing art.

Once again he was right in his diagnosis and wrong in the remedy which he prescribed. Certainly so long as women are regarded by men as objects of sensuality, they will enslave. But it does not follow that a change will come 'only when woman regards virginity as the highest state.' Tolstoy was confusing here, as he always did, a physical with a spiritual state, the fact of virginity with the truth of chastity. Chastity, if it is more than physical timidity, survives the loss of virginity, and it is through the development of such chastity and not by a denial of her natural instincts that woman may be no longer 're-duced to the lowest stage of humiliation, while on the other hand she dominates.'

Woman ceases to be regarded as an instrument of en-joyment, when she ceases to regard herself as such. And she ceases to do so when she becomes an intelligent human being capable of living a full, individual life of her own. Tolstoy accused the girls of the upper classes with much justice of lacking such a capacity and of spending their days in physical idleness, playing with art and music, and abandoning themselves to false excitement and coquetry.

But such girls would be equally incapable of living a full life of their own, if they were taught to regard virginity as the highest state. To do so would be merely to substitute physical sterility for physical marriage.

Only in fact through the education at which Tolstoy sneered could woman be truly emancipated from men and men from women, and consequently truly related to each other whether in marriage or not. But he was too enslaved by the physical himself to visualize such a path to freedom. Women, he was convinced, lacked the 'capacity for spiritual development,' and if they did not exhaust their energies by mating and mothering as the peasants, or aspire to a self-destructive virginity, the world was inevitably at the mercy of their sensual power.

And closely associated with his hostility to women was his hostility to art. For 'everybody knows that it is by means of these very pursuits (e.g. the arts), especially of music, that the greater part of the adulteries in our society occur.'

Tolstoy's reaction to music and in a less degree to all art was, as we should expect, intensely physical. 'Music,' he wrote, 'is a sensual pleasure of hearing, just as taste is a sensual pleasure – there is no moral sense in it.' He was tormented by it because he was deaf to its metaphysical reality, while being morbidly sensitive to its physical appeal.

As his son has written of him – 'Never in my life have I met anyone who felt music so intensely as my father. He could not help listening to it; when he heard music that pleased him he became excited, there was a contraction in his throat, he sobbed and shed tears. The feelings aroused in him were unreasoning emotion and excitement. Some-times it excited him against his will and even tormented him, and he would say: "What does that music want of me?" '

Inevitably therefore he came to hate music as he hated women. 'Where you must have slaves,' he remarked, 'there you should have as much music as possible ' and we have described how, in listening to it, he would betray 'a slight pallor and a scarcely perceptible grimace, sugges-tive of something like terror.'

He was terrified of losing control, of being swept into an abyss of sensation in which he ceased to be human. He felt with Pozdnyshev that 'in general, music is a dreadful thing! What is it? I don't understand it. . . . They say music exalts the soul. Nonsense, it is not true! It has an effect, an awful effect – I am speaking of myself – but not of an exalting kind. It has neither an exalting nor a debas-ing effect, but it produces agitation. How can I put it? Music makes me forget myself. . . .'

And as such it allured and appalled. Music terrified him more than other arts because its appeal was most sensational. But champion as he was in so many ways of the natural, he always trembled before the nude. All

bodily beauty was terrible to him because it excited desire.
He even disliked a man in opera because he waved 'his
arm (which is of course bare) from under his mantle.'
The ballet, he wrote, 'in which half-naked women make
voluptuous movements, twisting themselves into various
sensual wreathings, is simply a lewd performance.' And
he described pictures by French artists representing
female nudeness in various forms as 'all the productions of
people suffering from erotic mania.'

But however just such criticism may have been in certain cases, it was prejudiced by the fact that he himself
suffered from the same disease. He projected his own
sensuality into all art which disturbed him physically.
And how morbid his response was, may be judged by his
interpretation of *The Kreutzer Sonata* itself, the finale of
which, he is reported by his son once to have said, 'simply
expresses sensuality.'

To the present writer at least it expresses a pure lyrical
frivolity, touched indeed with coquetry but innocent of
the slightest suggestion of grossness.

Tolstoy's moral conception then of art as of life was
distorted by his own inner conflict, and in criticizing his
writings on art it is essential to distinguish between his
moral truth and his sensual prejudice.

His revulsion from art had of course coincided with his
revulsion from family life. It was, as he had written in
A Confession, one of the two drops of honey which diverted
his eyes from the cruel truth longer than the rest. But it
was not until he was writing 'What then must we do?' that
he specifically attacked scientists and artists because they

did not make it their aim 'to serve the labourers, as they now make it their aim to serve the government and the capitalists.'

Already in writing this he was guilty of a fallacy, since to serve the labourers, as he suggested, would be no less 'an interested personal activity' than to serve the capitalists. All bad art is due to interested motives of this kind: all good art is a disinterested activity.

On the other hand, his attack on such art as was manufactured by those in privileged positions to relieve the dullness of the wealthy classes was wholly justified, as was his claim that art should be the whole reasonable activity of the whole of mankind without exception devoting its best strength to its service. The picture too which he drew of artists as men who are really called to serve others by mental labour and who always suffer in performing that service, was nobly and truly conceived. 'Plump self-satisfied thinkers and artists, enjoying themselves,' he wrote, 'do not exist. Mental activity and its expression, of a kind really needed by others, is the hardest and most painful calling for a man – his cross, as the Gospel expresses it. And the sole and indubitable indication of a man's vocation for it is self-denial, a sacrifice of himself for the manifestation of the power implanted in him for the benefit of others. . . .'

Here again the utilitarian fallacy crept in. Self-sacrifice and suffering will be the lot of a thinker and an artist not, primarily at least, 'because their aim is the welfare of man,' but because they are in travail with the truth. Their pangs are creative rather than purposefully humanitarian. To

realize and embody with absolute sincerity their experience is their proper aim and so far as the 'demands of men'
of whatever class trespass on this inner necessity, they are
untrue to their calling. Newton, for example, was no less
supreme as a scientist and as a benefactor to mankind
because he made his great discoveries wholly to satisfy
his own inquiring mind and without any feeling that he
was called upon to benefit humanity. During the next ten
years, however, Tolstoy gradually defined and elaborated
his views on art as a necessary sequel to his views on
Christianity. He defined them in incidental criticisms, in
an essay entitled 'On Art,' and in the profoundly chal-
lenging study of the subject which appeared in 1898
under the title of *What is Art?*

§ 2

'This investigation,' wrote Tolstoy, 'has brought me to
the conviction that almost all that our society considers to
be art, good art, and the whole of art, far from being real
and good art, is not even art at all, but only a counterfeit
of it.' In *What is Art?* he set himself to justify this conviction, to define the true nature of art and to show how
modern art had transgressed it.

The criterion, he argued, by which the modern world
distinguished between good and bad art, was a vague
conception of beauty. It might be a mystical conception,
deriving from Plato's, that beauty was something having
an independent existence, a manifestation of the absolutely
Perfect, of the Idea, of the Spirit, of Will or of God. Or it
might amount to no more than the view that 'beauty is a

kind of pleasure received by us, not having personal advantage for its object.'

But because the one conception was 'fantastic and founded on nothing,' while the other failed adequately to distinguish between one kind of pleasure and another, between for example the pleasure of touching a delicate skin and that of listening to great poetry, both, in his opinion, merely pandered to self-indulgence. 'The theory of art founded on beauty . . . is nothing but the setting up as good of that which has pleased and pleases us, that is, pleases a certain class of people . . . the object considered is the pleasure art may give and not the purpose it may serve in the life of man and of humanity. In order correctly to define art it is necessary first of all to cease to consider it as a means of pleasure, and to consider it as one of the conditions of human life.'

Tolstoy therefore began by rejecting a metaphysical conception of art. He did not merely reject the Platonic conception, because it was not grounded in human life and so, like the other-worldliness of the Church's Christianity, could be debased by the self-indulgent. He did not admit that the Idea of Beauty might be distinguished from a mere sensation of pleasure through being related to Truth, as Keats conceived it, the truth of human life disinterestedly experienced. Instead he substituted for a metaphysical, an imperfectly defined religious conception of art, and all that was arbitrary in his moral interpretation followed inevitably from this.

'Art,' he wrote, 'is a human activity consisting in this, that one man, consciously, by means of certain external signs, hands on to others feelings he has lived through, and that others are infected by these feelings and also experience them. . . . But by art, in the limited sense of the word, we do not mean all human activity transmitting feelings, but only that part which we for some reason select from it and to which we attach special importance. This special importance has always been given by all men to that part of their activity which transmits feelings flowing from their religious perception.'

The fundamental weakness in this definition, as we shall show in a moment, lies in the word 'feelings,' a word which he tried to define by the phrase 'flowing from their religious perception,' but which remained vague and adaptable to his own prejudiced religious perception because he disregarded the metaphysical nature of feeling, as expressed in art.

Against then a theory of art founded on beauty and conducing to self-gratification Tolstoy advanced one founded, not on truth disinterestedly conceived, but on the religious sense, common to a whole society, of what is good and what is bad.

Such a sense, he claimed, existed in every age and every human society. But from the time of the Middle Ages cultivated Europeans had lost it. 'Not in the depths of their hearts believing in the Church teaching – which had outlived its age and had no longer any true meaning for them – and not being strong enough to accept true Christianity, men of these rich, governing classes – popes, kings, dukes, and all the great ones of the earth – were left without any religion, with but the external forms of one, which they supported as being profitable and even necessary for themselves, since these forms supported a teaching which justified the privileges they made use of.' In reality these people believed in nothing. And having no religious view of life 'they could have no standard wherewith to estimate what was good and what was bad art, but that of personal enjoyment.'

Consequently 'since the upper classes of the Christian nations lost faith in Church-Christianity the art of those upper classes has separated itself from the art of the rest of the people and there have been two arts – the art of the people, and genteel art.' Genteel art has been affected, fabricated and cerebral: its aim has been to afford the greatest enjoyment to a certain class of society: it transmits 'feelings of people far removed from those conditions of laborious life which are natural to the great body of humanity. . . . Such feelings as form the chief subjects of present-day art – say, for instance, honour, patriotism, and amorousness – evoke in a working man only bewilderment and contempt and indignation.' And yet this art which is 'not produced by the masses, nor even chosen by them, is energetically thrust upon them.'

Such in brief was Tolstoy's view of the evolution of modern art as an expression of the privileged classes of society. Put even more summarily, he held that from the time of the Renaissance the educated classes abandoned Christianity for a godless pursuit of personal enjoyment, while the masses preserved it and purified it; that the art sense therefore of the masses was true and infallible because it was grounded in a religious perception, while that of the privileged was false and perverted for want of such a perception.

Such a view we hold to have been based upon an arbitrary interpretation of 'religious perception,' which blinded Tolstoy to the spiritual significance of the finest minds among the educated classes since the Renaissance and led him to attribute to the masses a higher comprehension of life than they actually possessed.

Tolstoy's theory of post-Renaissance development may be usefully compared with that of another Russian, with whom he would have had little sympathy. Trotsky in his *Literature and Revolution* argues, like Tolstoy, that post-Renaissance art has always been class-conscious. He too claims that it has increasingly reflected a vicious egotism and that man has grown farther and farther away from his roots in social life. His experience has become more and more exclusive and he has paid the penalty at last for his failure to relate himself to the broad principles of humanity and the simple realities of Nature in an idealism and an art which has little organic necessity, but is external, imitative or decorative, in mere subjective dreaming or in the cultivation of perverted, subtle and languid moods.

But Trotsky's solution, unlike Tolstoy's, is exclusively materialistic. In his view the removal of social inequalities will cure literature of the decadence which they have caused. No longer a leisured luxury, it will become a healthy and vital activity; the artist's individual consciousness will be saved from an over-subtle refinement by merging itself in a communal consciousness. He will no longer be found seeking comfort for himself in escape from a real world with which he cannot harmonize. He will not embellish life, but create it; and he will reject all vague mysticisms as the illusions of hysterical egotism.

Although expressed in different terms, Trotsky's diagnosis in many ways resembles Tolstoy's, and we may admit the truth of the parallel which he draws between the dualism in the cultivated consciousness by which the subjective became more and more unhealthily divorced from the objective, and the social cleavage that divided, in Russia at least, a narrow falsely refined aristocracy from the masses. To a less degree, in proportion as they have achieved a truer social equilibrium, it is applicable to other Western nations. The fact therefore upon which both are agreed is the morbid individualism of modern art, and this Tolstoy interpreted as a loss of Christian perception.

And this view we would oppose as being altogether too summary and as failing to express the true religious significance of the Renaissance as a new movement in the evolution of the human consciousness, having its roots indeed in the continuous tradition of culture inherited from the ancient world but seeking to adapt that culture and the impulses which it expressed to the needs of a finer and more informed humanity.

The finest minds since the Renaissance have rejected Church-Christianity, like Tolstoy himself, but they have not, in any true sense of the word, rejected religion. Religions, Tolstoy wrote, 'are the exponents of the highest comprehension of life accessible to the best and foremost men at a given time in a given society,' and one of the conditions which 'must be fulfilled to enable a man to produce a real work of art' is that he 'should stand on the level of the highest life-conception of his time.'

The greatest post-Renaissance artists, we contend, have fulfilled this condition. They have rejected orthodox Christianity, not self-indulgently, but because it no longer embodied for them the highest life-conception of which they were capable. And they have striven to realize such a conception by intrepid efforts after self-knowledge and self-enlargement instead of merely accepting, as Tolstoy bid men do, the primitive religious perception of the simple.

Tolstoy feared and hated himself too much to admit the significance of individualism in the evolution of a higher life-conception, or to distinguish between its true expression and its abuse. 'Our animal activity,' he wrote, 'is accomplished without ourselves,' and our spiritual activity, in his view, should be accomplished in the same way. Ultimately indeed the self is transcended in spiritual activity, but it is only transcended by being perfectly expressed, and the dynamic behind the greatest modern art from the time of Shakespeare has been the struggle to achieve this new synthesis between man's individual consciousness and the physical forces of life.

The struggle was the basic reality of Tolstoy's own life, but he could not achieve the synthesis. And it was because he was conscious only of a discord in himself which could not possibly be resolved, that he was blind to the religious significance of the harmony which the great modern artists had sought, and exaggerated the value of a

primitive religious perception, undisturbed and undis-
torted by self-development.

Individualism we hold to be an organic necessity of
growth in the human consciousness, and what Tolstoy
described as the 'malady of non-acceptance of Christ's
teaching' to be a necessary stage in man's advance towards
its truer realization. It is only through self-consciousness,
with all its attendant evils of self-indulgence, affectation,
and intellectual complexity, that there can be that 'movement forward of humanity, expressing itself in religious
consciousness' which Tolstoy demanded. Only by this
fall from primitive grace can man come eventually to discover 'a new relation to the world around him,' and the
finest modern minds have explored the paths which lead to
such a relation.

Humanity has not done, as Tolstoy asserted, 'with the
idea of life considered as an individual existence.' The
highest idea of life is at once the most individual and the
least self-limited. It is by developing personality and not
by renouncing it, by extending and deepening self-knowledge until nothing is alien or beyond the reach of
understanding, that man will realize the highest possibilities of his humanity.

The great post-Renaissance artists, who have been
faithful to such an impulse, have revealed a truer religious
perception than Tolstoy who tried to revert to a peasant
consciousness; they have not conformed to a primitive
Christianity, but they have come nearer, we believe, to the
reality of Christ's values.

Admittedly, however, the growth of individualism has

entailed abuses which go far to justify Tolstoy's contention that modern art and civilization have represented
nothing but a relapse 'into the worship of beauty and
egotism.' Yet he exaggerated when he wrote that the
range of feelings of the upper classes was confined to three
very insignificant and simple feelings, pride, sexual desire,
and weariness of life.

So far as pride and sexual desire were merely sensual
motives in modern art, his condemnation was justified.
But so far as they were passions which artists had struggled to translate into the purer terms of imagination and
humanity, they were necessary ingredients in a true life-
conception. But Tolstoy who tried to deny his passions
because he could not humanize them could not distinguish between their sensual and spiritual expression.

Again the discontent with life which he rightly described as typical of modern art was significant of more
than mere class ennui. It was a condition of man's revolt
against the Natural, temporarily indeed a disabling condition, but necessary to his ultimate liberation.

Tolstoy therefore failed to distinguish between the
imaginative originality of all great art and the merely
sensual or intellectual perversity of decadent art, and consequently, as we shall see, he dismissed as unintelligible
poetry, painting and music which reflected that very striving towards a new consciousness, in which both his own
and the world's salvation lay.

And his insensitiveness to the reality of the greatest
modern art and his assumption that all that is highest is
understood by simple, unperverted peasant labourers is

explained by his imperfect definition of the nature of the feeling which art expresses. His moral criterion, in fact, is prejudiced because it is based on a confused æsthetic; for the nature of true art and of true morality are indeed one, but the finality of a moral judgment depends on perfect æsthetic insight.

'The business of art,' Tolstoy wrote, 'lies just in this: to make that understood and felt which in the form of an argument might be incomprehensible and inaccessible.'

But surely the reality of great art consists in this, that it *cannot* be translated into 'the form of an argument,' that it is neither understood as logic is, nor felt as sensations are, but that it so inextricably blends feeling and thought, being and knowing, that the two cannot be dissociated. And to experience it we too have to renew in ourselves the intuition which the artist expressed. In this sense Tolstoy wrote truly enough – 'The chief peculiarity of this feeling (e.g. artistic) is that the recipient of a true artistic impression is so united to the artist that he feels as if the work were his own and not some one else's – as if what it expresses were just what he had long been wishing to express.'

But we cannot renew in ourselves an artist's intuition unless we can apprehend the thought as well as sympathize with the feeling of which it consists. And the fallacies in Tolstoy's argument are traceable to his inability to distinguish between infection by feeling and experience of intuitions.

Art, he argued, aims at infecting people with feeling experienced by the artist, and he added that in a real work of art such feeling is in accordance with the highest life-conception of the time. But to be in such accord it must be true to the highest intelligence of the time and indeed advance beyond it. For since art does not communicate simple feelings, but intuitions which, partaking of the nature both of feeling and thought, are of another nature than either, its evolution, as that of particular artists, consists in the deepening of intuition by a profounder reconciliation of thought and feeling.

Certainly, as Tolstoy wrote, 'art is differentiated from activity of the understanding, which demands preparation and a certain sequence of knowledge,' but only blindness to the part which understanding nevertheless plays in the process of intuition can explain his assumption that therefore 'it acts on people independently of their state of development and education, that the charm of a picture, of sounds, or of forms, infects any man, whatever his plane of development.'

Mental training may not increase a man's artistic perception and may even deaden it by starving his emotional nature. But the growth of thought as a factor in perception is essential for the appreciation of all but primitive art forms. A man cannot be 'so united to the artist that he feels as if the work were his own,' unless he stands on the level of the artist's life-conception. And the artist's life-conception is compact not only of inspired feeling but inspired thought.

Art in fact expresses, not feelings about life, good or bad, but a consciousness of life which will be deep or shallow, sensual or imaginative according to the intensity of thought and feeling of which it is the synthesis. And in the work of any great modern artist we may trace an advance from elementary to consciously informed perception, from a physical consciousness of life to a spiritual, from the unity of instinct to that of intuition. The higher unity may not be achieved or only in precarious moments, but in the very struggle for it, in the conflict of thought and instinct in a divided consciousness, we see the elements of which it consists.

The highest life-conception therefore of modern art, the intuition of the identity of knowing and being, beauty and truth, is not something which people possess independently of their state of development and education. For it is only to be achieved by an intellectual mastery of life as well as by emotional response to it.

Consequently the power to perceive great art is no less a matter of growth than the power to conceive it. But Tolstoy who considered the conscious mind as inevitably creating an unresolvable discord in man's physical nature, denied its significance in a true life-conception. And by a false simplification he reduced the nature of art to mere emotion, arbitrarily qualified as religious, and so put it on the level of the natural man.

There is indeed in all great art a fundamental naturalness. It originates in a deep instinctive impulse, but so far as it remains merely natural it lacks the very meaning which Tolstoy claimed that it should possess. To have real meaning life must be known as well as felt; the unconscious must be made conscious, a creature instinct transformed into creative understanding. And by this transformation a man ceases to be possessed by life and possesses it. He reconceives the world in himself and reconciles the natural with the human.

Certainly a man may cease to be natural by allowing his mind to become dominant and self-sufficient, or by living an artificial and luxurious life. And to this extent Tolstoy rightly claimed that 'the range of feelings experienced by the powerful and the rich, who have no experience of labour for the support of life, is far poorer, more limited, and more insignificant, than the range of feelings natural to working people.'

So far as 'the finest nurtured' have lost, rather than purified and transformed, a primitive relation to life, their feelings and their human value are certainly inferior to those of simple labourers who have preserved their natural integrity. But Tolstoy, disgusted by the worthlessness of the parasite, claimed for the natural integrity, and primitive sensibility of the peasant a value which it did not possess. 'An almost illiterate Russian peasant sectarian' does not 'see the meaning of life, without any mental effort, as it was seen by the greatest sages of the world,' because mental effort is a condition of spiritual consciousness apart from which life can have only the limited meaning of a necessary physical process.

Tolstoy, however, admitted no difference in kind between physical and spiritual perception. As in his discussion of marriage he betrayed his false naturalism by his use of physical analogies. He wrote, for example, 'To say that a work of art is good, but incomprehensible to the majority of men, is the same as saying of some kind of food that it is very good but that most people can't eat it.' Or again, 'For a country peasant of unperverted taste' the capacity to distinguish true from spurious art 'is as easy as it is for an animal of unspoilt scent to follow the trace he needs among a thousand others in wood or forest.'

He had come far nearer to the truth than this when he wrote in his Diary at the age of twenty-three, 'To be good, literary compositions must always be, as Gogol said of his *Farewell Tale*, "sung from my soul." . . . But how could anything likely to be accessible to the people be "sung from the soul" of authors who, for the most part, stand on a higher level of evolution? They would never be understood of the people.'

The aim of the modern artist who is loyal to the highest life-conception of which he is capable must be to 'school an Intelligence and make it a Soul,' and he can only be understood of those who are treading the same hard path. For a man is not endowed at birth with a soul as an animal is with an unspoilt scent. It exists potentially within him, but it can only be fully realized when its sensuous and rational elements have been brought into relation.

Great modern art is the expressive combination of these elements: certainly it does not transmit feelings 'accessible only to a man educated in a certain way, or only to an aristocrat or a merchant.' But the intuitions which it transmits are inaccessible to any man, be he aristocrat or labourer, who has not striven to know life, as well as to live it.

Tolstoy, however, was driven to deny the rational and evolutionary element in the life-conception of great art, because his own reason convinced him only of the fact of death. Yet it is this fact more than any other which such great modern artists as Shakespeare and Beethoven have striven to and have overcome, not by a surrender of reason and a renunciation of physical life, as with Tolstoy, but by the assimilation of both in a higher consciousness.

The manner in which Tolstoy justified his own and the peasant's insensibility to such art was characteristic. 'It cannot be said,' he wrote, 'that the majority of people lack the taste to esteem the highest works of art. The majority always have understood, and still understand what we also recognize as being the very best art: the epic of Genesis, the Gospel parables, folk-legends, fairy-tales, and folk-songs, are understood by all. How can it be that the majority has suddenly lost its capacity to understand what is high in our art?'

Or again – 'the *Iliad*, the *Odyssey*; the stories of Isaac, Jacob and Joseph; the Hebrew prophets, the psalms, the Gospel parables; the story of Sakya Murri, and the hymns of the Vedas: all transmit very exalted feelings, and are nevertheless quite comprehensible now to us, educated or uneducated, as they were comprehensible to the men of those times, long ago, who were even less educated than our labourers.'

In writing this Tolstoy was as exclusive as those whom he attacked. The examples of 'good, supreme art' which he cited, were almost all expressions of a primitive consciousness. They certainly satisfied his claim that a great artist must be preoccupied with the meaning of life and death. All great art is religious in this sense. But the purpose of the great artist is to discover new meaning and to advance and enrich the human consciousness by bringing a new tract of the unconscious within its comprehension.

Art, Tolstoy wrote, 'should be, and has actually always been, comprehensible to everybody, because every man's relation to God is one and the same.' But every man's relation to God is not one and the same, and the relation to God revealed in the works of Homer or the Hebrew prophets is to a modern perception imperfect.

The *Iliad* is great art because the religious and artistic impulses were at one in the primitive consciousness of its author. It is therefore organic and so moral according to Tolstoy's true definition. It has the 'completeness, oneness, the inseparable unity of form and content expressing the feeling the artist has experienced.' But it is moral only on an elementary plane. And it is strange that Tolstoy who attacked the motives of pride and sex in the upper classes and their exploitation of patriotism and war, should have interpreted them as exalted feelings in the *Iliad*.

He did so of course because in the *Iliad* they were the natural, unperverted expression of men who were still physically at one with life. But the modern consciousness is superior to Homer's in so far as its relation to God is of a higher order than the primitive. In aspiring to this higher order the modern artist may lose the physical integrity which Homer possessed and his art may reflect the disunity of his consciousness. But it is essential that he should strive for a new relation and a new unity, and when he achieves it his moral value is greater than Homer's because he is organic on a higher plane.

How entirely personal was Tolstoy's choice of 'good, supreme art' is shown by his indictment of critics, 'who in our times still praise rude, savage, and, for us, often meaningless works of the Ancient Greeks: Sophocles, Euripides, Aeschylus, and especially Aristophanes; or of modern writers Dante, Tasso, Milton, Shakespeare; in painting, all of Raphael, all of Michael Angelo, including his absurd "Last Judgment"; in music, the whole of Bach, and the whole of Beethoven.'

The savagery of Homer he could interpret as exalted feelings, but Sophocles or Euripides, who questioned the ways of God to men, who in fact sought far more than Homer for that meaning of life and death which must underlie great art, were 'rude, savage, and meaningless.'

Tolstoy, in fact, was himself guilty of that very sentimentalizing of certain forms of antiquity of which he complained in the worshippers of Hellenism. And his sentimentalism led him into obvious inconsistencies. While admitting, for example, that 'the feelings transmitted by the art of our time not only cannot coincide with the feelings transmitted by former art, but must run counter to it,' he denounced modern artists for arguing, as they must argue since new feelings demand new forms, that 'it is impossible for us now to write such stories as that of Joseph or the Odyssey, to produce such statues as the Venus of Milo, or to compose such music as the folk-songs.'

And in supporting his theory he could resort to such

special pleading as this — 'The artist of the future will understand that to compose a fairy-tale, a touching little song, a lullaby or an entertaining riddle, an amusing jest or to draw a sketch which will delight dozens of generations or millions of children and adults, is incomparably more important and more fruitful than to compose a novel or a symphony, or paint a picture, which will divert some members of the wealthy classes for a short time and then for ever be forgotten.'

To contrast good art of one kind with worthless art of another was mere casuistry. For a great symphony does not in fact divert only some members of the wealthy classes before being forgotten. It enriches the mature perception of generations, who discover in it more and more of meaning. And such a symphony has more artistic value than a folk-song or a proverbial jest, whatever its antiquity and recurrent appeal, judged by Tolstoy's own moral criterion. It excites not merely pleasure, but a profound awareness of 'the burden of the Mystery.' It is religious in the truest sense. It expresses implicitly an ideal of perfect human and spiritual harmony or the pursuit, baffled it may be, of such an ideal.

But Tolstoy's perception of what was unifying, or religious in the purest sense, was narrow and arbitrary. And this led him to denounce as bad art works which reminded him of his failure to apprehend positively the meaning of life, and to exaggerate the value of others which expressed his own ascetic and submissive interpretation of Christianity or reflected a primitive integrity. His taste in pictures, for example, his appreciation of the work of

Walter Langley or N. L. Gay, was dictated by his sympathy with their subject-matter, by the fact that they
painted peasant life, depicted incidents from the Gospels
or illustrated some abstract virtue such as 'Charity.' And
this blinded him to their lack of original vision and
second-rate technical capacity.

Art indeed has a 'fertilizing, improving influence,' but
it is not that of practical edification. It is innate in its
creativeness, its generous, ordered insight, its strength,
courage and truth. It is in these qualities that its moral
excellence resides.

Tolstoy confessed in his article 'On Shakespeare' that
by 'the religious essence of art,' he meant 'not an external
inculcation of any religious truths . . . but the expression
of a definite view of life corresponding to the highest
religious understanding of a given period.' This view he
defined in *What is Art?* as 'the consciousness that our
well-being, both material and spiritual, individual and
collective, temporal and eternal, lies in the growth of
brotherhood among men.'

An artist, however, who sets himself to express this
'definite view,' inevitably confuses 'an external inculcation
of religious truth' with 'the religious essence of art.'

The ideal of harmony to which a great modern artist
must subconsciously refer all his thought and feeling may
include a conscious desire for the growth of brotherhood
among men, but this does not prevent him from expressing his ideal in many other forms, or passions that may
conflict with this ideal and yet heighten its significance.
To confine the religious essence of art to the inculcation

of brotherhood is little less to restrict and stultify its
creative purpose than to demand that it should illustrate
Catholic or Protestant doctrine.

The great artist and the great thinker further the unity
of mankind in ways less obvious than this. The art of
Beethoven or of Shakespeare, the thought of Newton or of
Einstein, revolutionize our conception of the universe,
and so eventually our values and our conduct. The great
artist moulds the warring elements of the world and the
warring passions in himself into a new harmony; and in
the unified diversity of his art we feel the reality of
creative living.

To do this is to be more loyal to the religious essence of
art than to express a definite view of the necessity of
brotherhood among men, although such a definite view
may be intelligible to anyone independently of his level of
development. Certainly 'the perplexity produced in the
minds of children and plain folk' may be caused by worthless, perverted art, but it may be caused by their inability
to answer the demands which great original art makes
upon them. For such art is great and original in the
degree that it evokes and communicates a spiritual perception beyond the normal and the habitual.

Tolstoy, however, made the unintelligible an excuse for
denouncing every effort to extend man's perception of the
universe. 'Mark this above all,' he wrote: 'if only it be
admitted that art may be unintelligible to anyone of sound
mind and yet still be art, there is no reason why any circle
of perverted people should not compose works tickling
their own perverted feelings and comprehensible to no

one but themselves, and call it "art," as is actually being done by the so-called Decadents.'

This does in fact occur, and Tolstoy's analysis of specimens of such art, his contention that it lacked any inner necessity, transmitted no feeling, but at best only acted on the nerves, was imitation and as stupid as it was highly cultivated, was as cogent and convincing as Trotsky's.

But the perversities of 'Decadents' do not justify our submitting art to the censorship of the 'sound mind,' unless we distinguish it from the conventional or the primitive mind. And this Tolstoy failed to do. His narrow view therefore of the nature of religious perception, a view by which he interpreted, for example, Cervantes' magnanimously human 'Don Quixote' as merely fantastic and artificial, led him to the conclusion that since religious art had always been universally accepted and intelligible, nothing but that which was universally accepted and intelligible was art at all. And his standard of the universally accepted and intelligible was governed by his own prejudice.

To prove this we may instance his judgment of Beethoven and Shakespeare, both of whom express the modern religious consciousness to a superlative degree, and both of whom Tolstoy dismissed not only as worthless, but demoralizing, because they excited him without appeasing, and fought to victorious conclusion the battle in which he sought to justify his defeat.

§ 3

Beethoven expressed for Tolstoy 'feelings accessible only to people who have developed in themselves an unhealthy nervous irritation.' He contrasted the puzzling impression produced in particular by Beethoven's later works with that produced by Russian folk-songs, and of the Ninth Symphony he wrote – 'Beethoven's *Ninth Symphony* is considered a great work of art. To verify its claim to be such I must first ask myself whether this work transmits the highest religious feeling? I reply in the negative, for music in itself cannot transmit those feelings; and therefore I ask myself next, since this work does not belong to the highest kind of religious art, has it the other characteristic of the good art of our time – the quality of uniting all men in one common feeling. . . . And again I have no option but to reply in the negative. . . . For the music is exclusive and does not unite all men, but unites only a few, dividing them off from the rest of mankind.'

Tolstoy's insensibility to the religious essence of art and the fallacies into which it led him could not be better illustrated than in this passage. Unable to conceive of music as 'the art of thinking in sounds,' to quote Combarieu's definition, he could not realize that Beethoven's significance lay in the fact that, unlike his predecessors Mozart and Haydn, his chief aim was not to compose beautiful sounds in sequence but to transmit 'the highest religious feeling,' not to excite pleasure but to communicate an intensely spiritual and personal experience.

More perhaps than any other musician he satisfied Tolstoy's demand that an artist should be preoccupied with the meaning of life and death, should suffer in performing a service of intense mental labour, and should stand on the level of the highest life-conception of his time. His music

is a record of profound spiritual development, and therefore requires of those who would understand it, not only a
natural sensitiveness to sequences of sounds but a capacity
for spiritual experience.

And the Ninth Symphony, which Tolstoy described as
devoid of religious feeling, is, with the great Mass in D
and the later Quartets the peak of his spiritual progress.
In it he first clearly expressed that victory over life and
death, that ultimate acceptance of things, for which he
had been striving through most of his earlier symphonies.
His first two symphonies, which Tolstoy considered more
moral because more intelligible than his later works, were
in fact less moral judged by his own standards. They were
composed in the tradition of Haydn and Mozart and to
satisfy a purely musical instinct.

But from the third or Eroica Symphony Beethoven was
struggling to express the highest life-conception of which
he was capable. And the antagonisms which he sought
to reconcile were those which Tolstoy failed to reconcile,
the heroic will of the individual, his pride and strength on
the one hand, and fate or physical necessity on the other.
Beethoven, as the Coriolanus overture shows, realized
first, like Tolstoy, that blind pride inevitably leads to self-
destruction, and he experienced too the despair which
attends such a realization. This despair he expressed
most memorably in his fifth symphony, the despair consequent on a denial of life underlying the assertion of the
will over fate. In the fifth and the seventh symphony
there is a similar wistful or blindly ecstatic affirmation of
life, heroically conceived, over death.

But in the ninth the antagonism is resolved. Here Beethoven no longer challenged Fate heroically, or alternated between the expression of exultant energy and a majestic but self-pitying melancholy. He not only accepted the pain and death that is in life, but he understood the life that is in pain and death, and by this ultimate affirmation he came as near reconciling Freedom and Necessity, an ecstatic joy with the knowledge of all sorrow, as his fiery nature would allow. And in the final Chorus, which should surely have satisfied Tolstoy's demand that an artist should be conscious of the necessity of the growth of brotherhood among men, he poured forth through Schiller's somewhat paltry ode a summons to mankind to rebuild the world in the spirit of the ideal harmony which he had conceived.

Here in fact was a work which satisfied to an intense degree the religious requirements which Tolstoy demanded of art. And his insensibility to its significance can only be explained by his spiritual incapacity, an incapacity which he sought to defend by the assumption that religious art must be universally accepted and intelligible and that it communicated 'feelings' as distinct from intuitions.

Beethoven, too, expressed a divided consciousness. There are times indeed when the sickliness of his introspection, the strain of his nervous tension, oppress us, when his assertion of the will to live is like that of a captive giant beating defiant hands against his prison bars. And even in his last period the æthereal gaiety and tenderness of his acceptance is often poignant with pain and unsatisfied desire. A being of such vehement energy could not wholly subdue himself to life, and yet imperfect as the unity which he achieved may have been, he stood by virtue of his intrepid search for it on the level of the highest life-conception of his and our time.

But Tolstoy felt in him only the malady of the modern mind at war with life, the diseased yearning and despair, the proud egotism, the sense of baffled isolation, which had wrought such havoc in himself. And because he had sought refuge in a denial of life, Beethoven's final acceptance at once tempted, tantalized and disproved him, and in self-defence he denounced it as unintelligible.

The same necessity, we think, underlay his assertion that Shakespeare 'cannot be admitted to be either a great writer of genius, or even an average one.' For Shakespeare too strove with life for a meaning, loving and hating, asserting and denying it in turn, and finally won to that new consciousness in which hate and love are reconciled in understanding and the distracted self is unified and so reborn.

But Tolstoy criticized Shakespeare in far more detail than Beethoven, and his criticism confirms what we have said of his imperfect understanding of the nature of art. He based, for example, his condemnation of 'King Lear' on a detailed description of its plot. He had no difficulty in proving that from a realistic standpoint many of its situations were improbable or that their crude violence must evoke aversion in the man of to-day. Further, he argued that 'the struggle does not result from a natural course of events and from their own characters, but is quite arbitrarily arranged by the author, and therefore cannot produce on the reader that illusion which constitutes the chief condition of art.'

If 'King Lear' was only a melodrama it might be dismissed as worthless on the basis of a carelessly constructed and primitive plot. But it is a religious drama, expressing a conflict of ideas and passions in the mind of Shakespeare. It belongs to that order of Tragedy of which Mr. Cornford has written that it 'does not seek to ape the manners or portray the characters of everyday society; its function is to represent the destiny of man, the turning wheel of Time and Fate.'

And because it expresses an intuition of life, rather than represents life in merely physical or logical terms, its reality cannot be dissociated from the poetry through which it is expressed. It cannot in fact be paraphrased or translated into 'the form of an argument.' It may be that Tolstoy's insensitiveness to this reality was to some extent conditioned by the fact that his grasp of English was that of a foreigner, but essentially it was due to his lack of metaphysical insight.

Even if we admit that in 'Lear,' as in 'Hamlet,' Shakespeare imperfectly subdued the matter of an old play to his metaphysical purpose, he communicates so powerfully this purpose that the material discrepancies and crudities cannot seriously affect it. But how little Tolstoy could experience the spiritual through the physical may be judged from his comment that 'the extraordinary storm during which Lear roams about the heath, or the weeds which for some reason he puts on his head . . . far from

strengthening the impression, produce a contrary effect.'
The same literalism is revealed in his complaint that
kings, dukes, and courtiers did not exist in 800 B.C. or
that at the end of the play, when the stage is filled with
corpses, 'instead of feeling fear and pity one feels the
absurdity of the thing.'

Such criticism could come only from one who was
constitutionally incapable of rising to the height of
elemental conflict, or of apprehending the interfusion of
the timeless with the world in time, which the play expresses. And his criticism of Shakespeare's language and
characterization still further betrays this incapacity. He
complained that 'all his characters speak, not a language
of their own but always one and the same Shakespearean,
affected, unnatural language, which not only could they
not speak, but which no real people could ever have
spoken anywhere.'

Tolstoy is guilty here of Wordsworth's fallacy, so ably
exposed by Coleridge, concerning the language of real
life. We may admit that there are examples in Shakespeare of 'inflated, empty language' and even of 'pompous
verbosity.' But they are few, and for the most part his
language is only unnatural in the sense that it expresses
more than the natural. Here again Tolstoy erred because
he assumed that an artist expresses only natural *feelings*.
The language of imagination differs from that of good
sense or of 'real people' because it expresses a passionate
and unique realization of life, and commands that willing
suspension of unbelief by which we rise from fact to
reality. The poet recreates the world in harmony with his

idea of it and his language is necessarily of another order than the habitual. Shakespeare's characters may be said to lack a distinctive 'individuality of language' only in so far as they are all charged with the individuality of Shakespeare himself and are projections of the idea of life which he was striving to realize. They are, as Mr. Wyndham Lewis has recently written, 'immense shadows, rather than realities in a cheaply concrete sense.'

But Tolstoy, who was wholly insensitive to this idea, was equally insensitive to the variations in its expression. Of all Shakespeare's characters he would only admit that Falstaff possessed individuality, and he complained that he was a drunkard and a humbug.

Certainly Shakespeare by investing his characters with a language which only a great poet could compass sacrifices what Mr. Wyndham Lewis calls 'character-discrimination and a delicate adjustment and distribution of values.' The weakness of the grand style is that it 'transfigures everything at once, monotonously heightening it. . . . The most insignificant figures speak at a pitch of emotional tension and with a felicity of expression, that is as far beyond them as it is possible to be. Every king and chieftain speaks as only a great poet could make him . . . or as only a great poet would.'

But if character from a realistic standpoint is often lost in the reverberations of Shakespeare's liturgical line or its unearthly music, so that even a Caliban will suddenly break into angelic strains, it expresses with miraculous propriety his own intense perception of the reality which shapes all human forms and actions.

His grand style is in fact a ritual necessary to the expression of his religious perception. And it is a real as distinct from a conventional ritual, being informed beneath and through the 'monotony of an eternally repeated soliloquy' with infinite modulations of pitch and variations of meaning. Far from failing to 'produce on the reader that illusion which constitutes the chief condition of art,' such an elevation, combined with intense individuality, of style was essential to the creation of an illusion of a reality transcending that of the 'real' world of ordinary perception.

Shakespeare's choice of highly placed individuals as the victims of his tragedies was dictated by the same necessity, and not, as Tolstoy argued, by class bias. To quote Professor Bradley – 'the story of the prince, the triumvir, or the general, has a greatness and dignity of its own. His fate affects the welfare of a whole nation or empire; and when he falls suddenly from the height of earthly greatness to the dust, his fall produces a sense of contrast of the powerlessness of man, and of the omnipotence – perhaps the caprice – of Fortune or Fate, which no tale of private life can possibly rival.'

The divinity which hedged a king was, in Shakespeare's time, so real to the popular imagination that it heightened the tragic illusion, and may indeed do so to-day, if we can free our imaginations from democratic prejudice and regard kingship symbolically. For it was thus clearly that Shakespeare regarded it. Being an artist, he was essentially as detached from the political claims of kingship as from the vulgar demands of the rabble of the

Elizabethan pit, although as a hired entertainer he had in non-essentials to pay some consideration to the demands both of his aristocratic and his vulgar patrons.

But Tolstoy could not distinguish the essential in Shakespeare from the non-essential, the vital ritual of a great artist from the conventional ritual of priestcraft, and in his adverse criticism of Shakespeare's style and characters he betrayed the same physical limitations which governed him as an artist.

He preferred the older play to Shakespeare's 'King Lear' because it was naturalistic, and wholly free from the metaphysical reality, by virtue of which Shakespeare's perception was religious in the highest sense. 'Shakespeare,' he wrote, 'taking the characters already given in previous plays, stories, chronicles, or in Plutarch's *Lives*, not only fails to make them more true to life and more vivid, as his adulators assert, but on the contrary always weakens them.'

In fact Shakespeare transforms them from limited beings, no more than physically conceived, into ideal actors in the eternal mystery play of life. He subdued the material theatre, as he subdued the material universe, to his metaphysical purpose. And although the external action of his plays sometimes imperfectly expresses the drama of inward experience which became more and more their essence, it never destroyed, although at times it confused the coherence of this experience. To criticize him therefore because his plots are full of violence or to discuss whether he believed in democracy, is to divorce the letter from the spirit, and inevitably to find it meaningless.

Tolstoy could read only the letter of Shakespeare; he could only judge him on a practical and interested basis, and so his conclusion was that 'the content of Shakespeare's plays . . . is the lowest, most vulgar view of life, which regards the external elevation of the great ones of the earth as a genuine superiority; despises the crowd, that is to say the working classes; and repudiates . . . religious efforts directed towards the alteration of the existing order of society. . . . Sincerity is totally absent . . . one sees in all of his characters an intentional artificiality; it is obvious that he is not in earnest but is playing with words.'[1]

The restricted imagination which led Tolstoy to distort the moral implications of Christ's teaching, led him to deny to Shakespeare any moral value at all. And by this denial he betrayed more clearly perhaps than by any other the defects of his moral values.

Shakespeare is moral, as all great artists are, as Tolstoy himself was on a physical plane, by virtue of his disinterestedness. He expressed without prejudice the forces which impel men to create and to destroy, because he knew them in himself. His knowledge was not restricted, as was Tolstoy's, by terror and disgust. Disgust and

---

[1] Incidentally Tolstoy showed here a typical disregard of the conditions governing an Elizabethan dramatist. To quote Mr. Wyndham Lewis – 'As to the censorship (in the hands of the Master of the Revels, a subordinate to the Lord Chamberlain), Chambers says that Sir George Buck was on the look out especially for political criticism, and that in 1611 that would consist of criticism of the King and Court. Any passages speaking without sufficient respect of courtiers and court ladies, knights and so forth, were dropped on by him.'

terror he knew, as must any man who brings the passions to the bar of conscience and humanity, and behind the glamour of the senses sees the animal unmasked.

But his reason did not falter before the spectacle or his vision fail. He looked as searchingly into the animal nature of man as into the spiritual, and because he accepted both and the agony of their conflict in all its phases, as he knew it in himself, he conceived at last the reality in which they might be reconciled.

He conceived it without the aid of any revealed religion and it was a reality in which the passions were known and discriminated, but not denied. And by this conception he revealed, not indeed how the existing order of society might be altered, but how the very nature of man might and must be transformed, if the 'brave, new world,' which had been born in himself, was to be realized by mankind.

Such a new world was for Shakespeare no delicate and decorative conceit. It was won at the cost of a hard pilgrimage, with horrors and self-loathings by the way, hatred of physical life and the embitterment of shattered illusions. But it led at last to a true conversion, to the pure music of his last period, when he conceived a world no longer hostile, no longer torn between flesh and spirit; but one in which evil was at last appeased and knowledge ceased to sear with a sense of sin; in which men and women might regain the innocence that was before the fall with a difference, because though child-like they were not childish, being wise not only in nature but in humanity, and having the gaiety of those who have no need to forgive, because they have learnt to understand.

To this integrity of vision Tolstoy was wholly, and it might seem resentfully, blind. For it expressed a critical affirmation of life, and to him who interpreted Christianity as a religion of suffering, poverty and denial, the very splendour of Shakespeare's acceptance seemed only to reflect the pride and the egotism which he feared. All art which expressed the passions however sublimely had no value for him, because he could find no meaning in his own, could not see in the affluence of life its potential beauty. He had turned from art to a religion of abnegation that by denying life he might lighten the burden of death. But Shakespeare confronted death, where it ruled the physical plane of life, and defeated it in his art.

And because to achieve a passionate but disinterested relation to physical life is more moral than to deny it from interested motives, Shakespeare's morality is truer, is indeed of another order, than Tolstoy's. It is free from ethical bias and that hatred of pleasure which is inverted hedonism. It reconciles truth with what Wordsworth described as 'the grand elementary principle of pleasure, by which man knows, and feels, and lives, and moves.' Tolstoy perceived and splendidly exposed the disorganic worthlessness of such art as was merely sensual, brain-spun or egotistic, but he was too prejudiced to realize the essential morality of the art which embodied the conflict between man's reason and his senses, and the consequent struggle of the individual who had lost the organic unity of the creature, to achieve the perfected unity of the Creator.

At the end of *What is Art?* he wrote that 'Science and

art are as closely bound together as the lungs and the heart, so that if the one organ is vitiated the other cannot act rightly.' And his words might well be quoted against himself. For it was because he failed to admit the function of reason as a necessary principle of growth in an artist's life-conception that he could argue that art acts on people independently of their state of development or education.

Modern civilization and its art reflects indeed much of the rational viciousness, self-indulgence and false refinement with which Tolstoy charged it, but it can only rise to virtue by extending and deepening the reason which it has abused.

§ 4

Old age brought Tolstoy no cessation from conflict, but only an intenser desire to escape from it and from a way of life which he had denounced as corrupt. Excommunicated and proclaimed as anti-Christ, at once an accuser and a prisoner in his own household, haunted as ever by terror of lust and of death, he had succeeded only in substituting a personal, solitary wretchedness for the 'personal, solitary happiness,' from which he had fled thirty years before.

In *Resurrection*, the last of his great novels, as in *The Power of Darkness*, his greatest play, he strove to convince himself of the possibility of redemption from the stranglehold of the flesh. And yet the conviction was never his. For the nearer he drew to death, the more deadly seemed 'the whole abomination' of his past life.

'I am an old man,' he said to Gorki. 'It cuts me to the

heart when I remember something horrible.' And these recollections never left him. They could not leave him so long as he felt within himself that 'the flesh rages and riots, and the spirit follows it helpless and miserable.' The physical intensity of his description of Nekhlyudov's seduction of Katusha in *Resurrection*, culminating in the terrible insight of the phrase 'there was no smile in her soul, only fear,' and the primitive power of *Hadji Murad*, prove how little even seventy three years had reduced his sensual force. And his very morality by denying this force intensified it, and confirmed his subjection to the fact of death in life.

Sofya Stakhovich has described in a recent article how one evening Tolstoy came out of his study with a book in one hand. 'His face showed that he was agitated. He approached the table, waited till we stopped talking, and opening the book, *Pensées de Pascal*, began to read. At the first words his voice began to tremble. He handed the book to me to read out the following: "The last act was bloody, however beautiful the comedy was in every other way. Earth is thrown on one's head at last and that is all for ever." At the words "for ever" Tolstoy nodded affirmatively, and his look seemed to say "that is how it will be."' Again to Gorki he said, 'If a man has learned to think, no matter what he may think about, he is always thinking of his own death. . . . And what truths can there be, if there is death?'

Tolstoy could coquet with Death, as Gorki wrote, 'trying somehow to deceive her, saying: "I am not afraid of thee, I love thee, I long for thee"; but there was "no smile in his soul, only fear," because, even when he desired her, it was only in the hope of physical appease-ment. And like the conscious sensualist who hates the woman whom he desires, because he knows that by satisfying his desire he will destroy it, Tolstoy hated the death which he sometimes desired, because it meant for him a final dissolution.

And so it is rather in the description of Nekhlyudov's visit to the mortuary in *Resurrection* than in the moralized peace of Vasili's end, in *Master and Man*, that he expressed his real conviction of death.

'He came nearer and looked at the body. The small pointed beard turned upward, the firm, well-shaped nose, the high, white forehead, the thin curly hair – he recog-nized the familiar features, but could scarcely believe his eyes. Yesterday he had seen this face angry, excited, and full of suffering; now it was quiet, motionless and terribly beautiful. Yes, it was Kriltsov, or at any rate the trace of his material existence that remained. "Why has he suffered? Why had he lived? Has he now understood it?" Nekhlyudov thought, and there seemed to be no answer, seemed to be nothing but death, and he felt faint.'

Christianity, as he interpreted it, was powerless to save him from the awful realism of death. Still, with Prince Andrew, he stopped before that abyss and looked in. And as he shuddered upon its brink, he knew himself for ever alone, chained, as he put it, with all of his generation in whom the mind had become divorced from life, 'to a loneliness which dries up the soul.'

Certainly he had disciples, enthusiasts and fanatics who

came to consult him about his doctrine. But they were for the most part uneasy men like himself, and those of them who acted upon the doctrine which he expounded either put him to shame by their consistency or, by the failure of the colonies which they founded, troubled him with doubts.

But it was chiefly shame which he felt. Had he not taunted men for refusing to admit that Christ meant what he said, and had he not said that 'Whoso leaveth not house and lands and children for my sake is not worthy of Me'?

He might ease his sense of self-reproach by confessing his weakness, by admitting – 'I am not a saint: I have never professed to be one. I am a man who allows himself to be carried away, and who often does not say all that he thinks and feels; not because he does not want to, but because he cannot, because it often happens that he exaggerates or is mistaken. In my actions it is still worse. I am altogether a weak man with vicious habits, who wishes to serve the God of truth, but who is constantly stumbling. If I am considered as a man who cannot be mistaken, then each of my mistakes must appear as a lie or a hypocrisy. But if I am regarded as a weak man, I appear then what I am in reality: a pitiable creature, yet sincere; who has constantly and with all his soul, desired, and who still desires to become a good man, a good servant of God.'

Yet he had not enunciated his doctrine as a man who could be mistaken but as one who imposed on all men categorical commands. And so, even among devotees, he felt at heart that he was guilty and contemptible, and that his activity, however useful it might appear to certain people, lost the greater part of its importance by the fact that his life was not entirely in agreement with his professions.

More and more too the burden of family-life oppressed him as part of the burden of the flesh. For between his wife and himself there was and could be no community of spirit. 'I shall look for my friends,' he wrote, 'among the peasants. No woman can stand to me in the place of a friend. Why do we deceive our wives by pretending to consider them our best friends? For it is certainly not true.'

God was his desire and women were to him the enemies of God. And beyond this there was the contamination of property which he could not escape. As he wrote in *And Light shines in Darkness*, 'What can be done? One must not take part in this evil; one must not own land, nor devour their labours. But how to manage all this, I don't know.' Or again, in the same play, 'You, Lyuba, say that the Princess plays well. All of you here, seven, eight, healthy young men and women, have slept till ten o'clock; you drank, etc., are still eating and playing and talking about music; but there, where I have come from, they get up at three — some did not sleep at all, watching horses at grass, and the old and sick and weak, children, women nursing babies and pregnant women, work to the limit of their strength, in order that the product of their labours may be spent by us here. And as if this were not enough, at the present moment the only worker in the family is being dragged to prison because he cut down last spring in the forest, which is called *mine*, one out of the hundred thousand trees which grew there. And we here, washed, dressed, having left in the bedrooms to the care of servants what we have dirtied, eat, drink, argue about Schumann and Chopin, which moves us most and relieves our boredom.'

This of course was not a literal picture of Tolstoy's own household, but it was a real enough picture to him embittered by incessant 'conflict, accompanied by tears and mutual reproaches.' And when Marie Ivanovna says, in the same play, 'That's the chief thing – he destroys everything, and puts nothing in its place,' – she expresses what Tolstoy must have felt to be the spoken or unspoken criticisms of his wife or of those of his family who shared her views.

'This not being understood,' he wrote, 'is terrible,' but such criticism pained him the more because secretly he felt its justice. His aversion for them was an aversion for himself. And it was at times so intense that he could write, 'One refined life, led in moderation and within the bounds of decency, of what is commonly called a virtuous household, one family life absorbing as many working days as would suffice to maintain thousands of the poor that live in misery hard by, does more to corrupt people than thousands of wild orgies by coarse tradesmen, officers and artisans given to drunkenness and debauchery who smash mirrors and crockery for sheer fun.'

His wife on her part had done her best to satisfy the demand which he had made at the end of '*What then must we do?*' that 'a real mother, who knows the will of God

by experience, will prepare her children, also to fulfil it.'
But her God was not his God. She was content to express
Him in a life of practical physical activity and she could
not share, could not approach an understanding, of a faith
that was based on self-hatred and despair. As she wrote,
'I did not know how to live with such views; I was
ashamed, frightened, grieved. But with nine children I
could not, like a weather-cock, turn in the ever-changing
direction of my husband's spiritual going away.'

But in truth, for thirty years at least, there was little
change of direction. Through all those years Tolstoy
had been going away at heart, had laboured through
repeated revulsions and repeated returns, revulsions
more than once so extreme that he had even begun to go
away in fact.

It was only, however, towards the end of his life and
through his attachment to a disciple whom his wife suspected to be scheming against the interests of the family
that the physical knot which had held them together for
more than forty years broke beneath the strain of mental
alienation. For then, as Countess Tolstoy wrote, jealousy
woke up with terrible force and sapped the self-restraint
of her strong practical and courageous nature. She spied
upon all his movements, searched his papers, assailed him
with complaints and reproaches, until, exasperated beyond
endurance, the hostility which had always lurked in his
love for all women turned directly upon her. The last
barrier between him and the ultimate act of denial upon
which he staked all his hopes was removed.

And so early on an October morning in 1909, he

stumbled out into the darkness. He was strangely calm
and self-possessed, noting, for example, in his Diary, 'It
is night; pitch dark; I lose my way to the lodge; get
into the wood; I am pricked by the branches; knocked
against the trees; fall; lose my hat; cannot find it; get
out with difficulty.'

Even under the stress of a terrible excitement the artist
in him remained curious and observant. And the letter
which he left for his wife and that which he wrote to her
later, reveals the same strained detachment. He was
agitated, not by the thought of those whom he had left
behind, but by the fear of being overtaken. And so he
fled to Shamardino and thence to Astopovo where he
tottered from the train to die three days later in the room
which the station-master had offered him.

In the evening of his last day, his daughter tells us, 'as
some one was smoothing his bed, he said, "And think of the
peasants, the peasants, how they die," and he wept.' He
had longed to live as a peasant, and as a peasant he longed
to die, but for him, stricken with the egomania that makes
him one with our subtle, peevish age, there could be no
virtue in death's necessity.

For his last flight was not so much from his wife and
family as from himself. And the self with which he had
striven so frantically for a lifetime remained. To suggest,
as Gorki does, that his flight was dictated not so much by
an inner necessity as to force men by a last dramatic act
to accept his teaching, is to misread the impulse behind all
his actions. Certainly he had fled from the shame which
oppressed him, from those who taunted him as one who

left house and lands and children 'except in so far as he still clung to them.'

But his last act was essentially a last attempt to realize the innocency of childhood, to shuffle off not merely his property and his family, but his egotism. Forty years before he had written in *War and Peace* of Princess Mary that 'often listening to the pilgrims' tales, she was so stimulated by their simple speech . . . that several times she was on the point of abandoning everything and running away from home. In imagination she already pictured herself . . . dressed in coarse rags walking with a stick and a wallet at her back, along the dusty road, directing her wanderings, free from envy, human love, or desire, from one saint's shrine to another, and arriving at last at the place where there is no sorrow, or sighing, but eternal joy and bliss.

'I will come to a place, pray there, and before I have time to get used to it, or to get to love it, I will go farther. I will go on till my legs fail, and then I will lie down somewhere and die, and shall at last reach that eternal quiet haven where there is neither sorrow nor sighing.'

No longer, after the protracted warfare which had ensued since these words were written, could Tolstoy dream so sentimentally of escape. Yet beyond the need of consistency and the last throw of the desperate gambler, beyond the instinct, it might seem, of the animal who creeps away to die, lay the dream of an effortless sanctity.

But the dream was now involved in a creed of which the virtue was to be put to a final test. A year before he had written, 'I am eighty years old, and I am still searching for truth.' And could it be that he had **not** found it because he had always in practice compromised?

In going away, he was seeking an answer to that question, and so while he confessed himself very glad, he was also very much afraid, of what he had done, since to fail in this last venture would indeed be to receive a sentence of death from which there was no appeal, both as a man and a moralist.

It may be that he was spared the final disillusionment, that he died too soon to realize how the tortured egotism of his life logically culminated in the distracted isolation of his death at Astopovo, and that the peace which succeeded the long conflict was not the peace of victory, but of defeat.

EPILOGUE

Tolstoy was fated to bear the sins of a civilization which had outgrown the animal without achieving the human. Ruthless to himself, he was able as ruthlessly to expose the moral hypocrisy of a society which tolerated and even justified a state of sin kindred to his own. He tore the cloak of pomp and propriety from the sanctified brutalities of Church and State, and so far as the primary religious virtue is, as Professor Whitehead has written, 'sincerity, a penetrating sincerity,' he possessed it.

But if self-knowledge enabled him to expose the artificiality and animal greed characteristic of the Russian Society of his time, and to a less degree of all modern Western Civilization, the conflict of extremes in his own experience prevented him from rendering much immediate and practical help to the truly civilizing forces of his day or ours. He interpreted the world's needs according to his own needs. For him there existed only the alternatives of self-indulgence, with its tortures of remorse, and a complete self-denial, which in fact life disallowed. And if such self-denial were essential to Christianity it would indeed be a creed of despair at war with the best and most reasonable hopes of humanity.

But Christianity is itself an art of life in process of realization. We believe that it contains within itself the possibilities of a true synthesis, but men have interpreted it according to their level of development. To Tolstoy, as to all who have reached the point only of fearing the flesh and distrusting the intelligence, Christianity could not mean a positive disinterestedness, an extension of the

313

self giving full play to all the faculties in harmony. And yet such an affirmation of life, in which the natural and the intelligent man combine, is as essential to a true civilization as to a perfect humanity.

Tolstoy was never completely human because his animal instincts were opposed to his moral aspirations. The gulf between the animal and the human can only be bridged by intelligence, and self-consciousness and self-analysis are the scaffolding with which the bridge is built. Tolstoy constructed the scaffolding, but he could not build the bridge, and so he spurned the only means by which it could be built.

To write therefore, as Spengler does, that it was 'from the depth of his humanity' that he rejected the whole Western world idea, is unexact. It was rather from the depth of a naturalism which he could not humanize that he rejected it, and in so doing denied the possibility of making life into an art through science and love.

For the only valid substitute for the timorous religion of the Churches is the true religion of art informed by science. Tolstoy rejected both art and science because the one reflected an indulgent pursuit of beauty and the other a self-sufficient exercise of mind. But both were false only because they were divorced from each other, and Tolstoy, so far as he was blind to the necessity of combining them, propounded, like the Church which he attacked, a morality that tended to reinforce the destructive instincts and to stifle the creative ones.

His teaching concerning women and marriage, for example, could only perpetuate the ignorance and physical enslavement which the Church had consecrated, while his conviction of sin did not in essentials differ from the depressing dogma of original sin. Similarly his association of virtue with an utter lack of personal responsibility resembled the very mystical self-absorption which he denounced.

Certainly there are few signs even to-day of salvation coming to men through 'science wielded by love,' and the war which Tolstoy did not live to see, but which he foretold so accurately to deaf ears, proved how terrible science can be in the service of hate, greed and stupidity.

Nevertheless we believe that humanity has outgrown the uses of a negative morality, and that such a morality has always rather perpetuated the animal in man by falsely repressing or concealing it, than transformed it. If humanity is to survive the transition, through which it is still struggling from the brutal to the truly humane, it will be by an alliance of imagination and objective rationality, in which the life of instinct is rediscovered in the light of scientific knowledge, and transformed into a thing of beauty and understanding.

As Bertrand Russell has written, 'There is only one road to progress . . . and that is: Science wielded by love. Without Science, love is powerless; without love, science is destructive. . . . I think we should keep in our minds, as a guiding thread, the conception of gradual chequered progress, perpetually hampered by the savagery which we inherit from the brutes, and yet gradually leading on towards mastery of ourselves and our environment through knowledge. The conception is that of the human

race as a whole, fighting against chaos without and darkness within, the little tiny lamp of reason growing gradually, into a great light by which the night is dispelled.'

The religion therefore that is afraid of Science dis-
honours God by denying His intelligence, while that
which is afraid of instinct denies His vital force and com-
mits suicide. Certainly it was difficult not to distrust both
in a Russia in which the supposedly intelligent class
indulged its appetites in the name of art and refinement
and justified the most revolting barbarities in the name of
reasonable Government.

As Tolstoy wrote, a year before his death, in *I cannot
be Silent* – 'Everything now being done in Russia is done
in the name of the general welfare, in the name of the
protection and tranquillity of the inhabitants of Russia.
And if this be so, then it is also done for me, who live in
Russia. For me, therefore, exists the destitution of the
people, deprived of the first, most natural right of man –
the right to use the land on which he is born; for me the
half-million men torn away from wholesome peasant life
and dressed in uniforms and taught to kill; for me that
false so-called priesthood, whose chief duty it is to prevent
and conceal true Christianity; for me all these transpor-
tations of men from place to place; for me these hundreds
of thousands of hungry workmen wandering about Russia;
for me these hundreds of thousands of unfortunates dying
of typhus and scurvy in the fortresses and prisons which
do not suffice for such a multitude; for me the mothers,
wives and fathers of the exiles, the prisoners and those
who are hanged, are suffering; for me these dozens and

hundreds of men have been shot; for me the horrible work goes on of these hangmen, at first enlisted with difficulty, but who now no longer so loathe their work; for me exist these gallows, with well-soaped cords from which hang women, children and peasants; for me exists this terrible embitterment of man against his fellow-man.'

Well might it seem hopeless in a country where such things were done to work for practical reform. The temptation to escape the sense of responsibility which gnawed at the conscience by fleeing into the wilderness was overpowering. Yet to turn away from the diseased body of society and to bid others do likewise, rather than to risk contagion in an apparently hopeless effort of healing, was an act of egotism as well as of despair. To say that Tolstoy did no more than this is to exaggerate. Yet even the moral appeals which he addressed to the governing powers were primarily dictated by the need of relieving his tortured conscience.

That a loveless civilization must shortly destroy itself is certain, and Tolstoy lived and wrote in a country in which the process of self-destruction was terribly evident. But the only love which can save a civilization is an intelligent love, a love which will consider fearlessly the material conditions which have to be mastered, and also the forces and faculties in human nature which it seeks to transform.

And although full allowance must be made for the conditions amid which Tolstoy lived, fundamentally he despaired of civilization, because he despaired of himself. He did not believe in the gradual enlightenment of instinct by intelligence and their eventual fusion, because it failed in his own experience. He could not conceive of intellect as the faculty by which the physical man might grow into the spiritual. He saw it only as a pander to the flesh or the critical foe of the spirit. And because he could only achieve comparative harmony himself by doing violence to his nature, it seemed to him that the world could be saved only by doing similar violence to the faculties which had conspired together to beget so monstrous a civilization.

It may indeed be argued that such a nature as Tolstoy's refutes the possibility of evolutionary development which is the ground of our criticism; that his life and his teaching could not have been other than they were, and that since the growth of reason in man is bound to create discord, every civilization is doomed to be a perversion of the natural from which men in disgust relapse into barbarism, only to create a new perversion once again.

But men have alternated between savagery and degeneracy because their reason, whether in the form of a destructive morality or a selfish refinement, has warred upon the instincts which it should direct creatively. Although such a conflict, tragic because apparently insoluble, must to some extent have been inherent in Tolstoy's nature, it was inevitably aggravated by the circumstances of his upbringing which falsely excited his appetites and his egotism and provoked a moral revulsion that was itself inverted sensualism.

Certainly we have much to learn from his moral teaching. For our civilization is still morbid, and no man has exposed the conditions of its morbidity more powerfully than he. But his value is rather as the pathologist of a false civilization than the prophet of a true one.

The most influential prophets are those who have fought out their own spiritual battle in the wilderness before returning to instruct the world in the secret of their victory, those who, like George Fox, have no longer a conviction of sin or a cramping anxiety for their own salvation. Tolstoy, however, could only bid men retire to the wilderness to fight there a battle which he had not won himself. All his life he was fighting his own private, inconclusive battle, and as he hated and sought to suppress or exhaust the natural man in himself, so he hated and did violence to the material constitution of the world.

But in proportion as the modern world becomes reasonable, its conscience ceases to withdraw horror-stricken and self-obsessed from the brutalities it perceives. Its reason does not reject; it seeks to understand, reform, and construct, to realize the complete humanity latent in the natural man. And so the world of to-day has perhaps less need of a voice from the wilderness, charged however intensely with moral zeal, than of those who will work self-effacingly for social and individual betterment, who will increase the knowledge by which alone men may possess themselves and the forces at their command. For love cannot be disinterested without knowledge and a morality which spurns science is as often self-interested as a science which spurns morality.

Even the horrors of the Russian civilization which outraged Tolstoy were as much due to ignorance and stupidity as to want of love, and the Church that acquiesced in those horrors was an example of the fatal ease with which a religion preoccupied with personal salvation can be corrupted by selfishness. Tolstoy's private conscience was of course never divorced from his public conscience, but both were self-interested even in their denial of self-interest.

Nevertheless the imagination which made him a great artist invested his tortured personality with far more than a personal significance. He is, as Romain Rolland has said, our conscience. His personal problem is also the problem of our civilization in which both our salvation and our survival are involved. The science which he despised forces us to choose between moral relationships, in a sense which he imperfectly understood, and suicide. Without its help we cannot make a good life possible under the conditions which it has created. But unless it is put to the service of the love to which he so despairingly aspired, it will destroy us.